Aaron Bell

Donne's
SERMONS

Oxford University Press

London   Edinburgh   Glasgow   New York
     Toronto   Melbourne   Cape Town   Bombay

Humphrey Milford *Publisher to the University*

EFFIGIES REVERENDISS. VIRI IOHANNIS DONNE NUPER ECCLES PAULINÆ DECANI

Corporis hæc Animæ sit Syndon Syndon Jesu
Amen.

Mar in R. scup And are to be sould by R R and Ben: ffisher

Donne's
SERMONS

Selected Passages

WITH AN ESSAY

by

Logan Pearsall Smith

OXFORD
At the Clarendon Press
M DCCCC XIX

CONTENTS

Contents.

Contents.

Contents.

Frontispiece

Portrait of the Author in his Shroud:
the frontispiece to *Death's Duel* 1632

NOTE

I REFER in my notes to the three folios of Donne's Sermons as I, II, and III respectively. I is the first folio, *LXXX Sermons*, 1640; II is *Fifty Sermons*, 1649; III is *XXVI Sermons*, 1660. The text of each passage is taken from the first appearance of the sermon which contains it in print, whether in the folios, or in the earlier published quartos of separate sermons printed in Donne's lifetime, or shortly after his death. The original punctuation has been preserved; and also the original spelling, except in the use of 'i' for 'j', of 'u' for 'v' and vice versa, and of contractions for 'm' or 'n'. I refer to Professor Grierson's edition of Donne's Poems (*The Poems of John Donne*, edited by Herbert J. C. Grierson, M.A., Oxford, at the Clarendon Press, 1912) as *Poems*; to *The Life and Letters of John Donne*, by Edmund Gosse (London, William Heinemann, 1899), as *Gosse*; to *John Donne*, by Augustus Jessopp, D.D. (Methuen and Co., 1897), as *Jessopp*. *Spearing* refers to Miss Spearing's 'A Chronological Arrangement of Donne's Sermons' (*Modern Languages Review*, vol. viii, 1913); *Coleridge*, to Coleridge's 'Notes on Donne', published in *The Literary Remains of Samuel Taylor Coleridge*, collected and arranged by Henry Nelson Coleridge, 1838, vol. iii. *C. and T. Jas. I*, and *C. and T. Charles I*, refer to *The Court and Times of James the First* (1848), and *The Court and Times of Charles the First* (1848). The references to Donne's *Devotions* are to the first edition of 1624. *Ramsay* refers to Miss Ramsay's *Les Doctrines médiévales chez Donne, le Poète métaphysicien de l'Angleterre* (Oxford University Press, 1917). I must express my special thanks to Mr. Edmund Gosse, C.B., for his kindness in lending me a number of very rare first editions of Donne's sermons from his collection of Donne's works.

INTRODUCTION

THE remarkable and somewhat enigmatic figure of John Donne is one that has attracted a good deal of attention in recent years ; his life has been studied, his poems and letters carefully edited, his character analysed, and his position as a poet acutely debated. His harshness, his crabbed and often frigid way of writing, his forced conceits, his cynicism and sensuality, are extremely repellent to some readers ; while to others his sublety, his realism, and a certain modern and intimate quality in his poems, illuminated as they are with splendid flashes of imaginative fire, possess an extraordinary interest and fascination. There are people who hate Donne ; there are others who love him, but there are very few who have read his poems and remain quite indifferent to him. His character is still a puzzle, his reputation as a poet, eclipsed for a long time and only revived in our own day, is by no means yet the subject of final agreement.

In spite of this modern interest in Donne, and the study which has been devoted to his works, there is one aspect of them which, until recently, has received no very adequate attention. In addition to his poems, his letters, and a few minor prose pieces, Donne left behind him an immense body of theological writings. By birth and by the tradition of his family a Roman Catholic, and for that reason shut out in his youth from the paths of secular ambition which had so great an attraction for him, he was of necessity much preoccupied with theological considerations; and it was not till after much study of controversial divinity that he succeeded in convincing himself of the truth of the Anglican position, which he finally made his own, and which, even in his secular days, he emphatically defended. When at the age of forty-two, after long experience of poverty and many worldly disappointments, he found all other paths of preferment closed to him, and at last, after much hesitation, took religious orders, he then began that career as a great divine and preacher which, until the revival of interest in his poetry, remained his principal claim to remembrance. But his fame as a preacher has been this long time fame at second hand; it is due to Izaak Walton's descriptions of his sermons, rather than to any reading of the sermons themselves. The very quantity, indeed, of his sermons—and no Anglican divine of the period has left behind him such a number—has discouraged students from thorough study of them; and, indeed, to read these great folio volumes is a task not lightly to be undertaken. But it is not only the mere bulk and body of these folios, the great number and length of Donne's sermons, which daunts the reader; there is much in the writing itself which renders it difficult and distasteful to the modern mind. In the first place sermons themselves, and especially old sermons, have fallen somewhat out of fashion; they are not often read now, and the collected and republished editions of the great seventeenth century divines rest for the most part unopened on our shelves. People read novels, biographies, books of travel, social and political treatises instead of the sermons in which their grandfathers and grandmothers delighted: Hooker, Barrow, South, Tillotson are names indeed, but little more than names to most of us; and even so great a writer of English prose, so exquisite an artist as Jeremy Taylor, is familiar to us only in extracts and selected passages. For modern theologians this old divinity, with its obsolete learning and forgotten controversies, has little more than an archaeological interest; while to the more secular-minded, the old divines, whose severe brows and square faces meet our eyes when we open their great folios, seem, with their imposed dogmas, their heavy and obsolete methods of exposition and controversy, almost as if they belonged to some remote geological era of human thought. We are reminded of Taine's image of them as giant mastodons or megatheria, slowly winding their scaly backs through the primeval slime, and meeting each other, armed with syllogisms and bristling with texts, in theological battle, to tear the flesh from one another's flanks with their great talons, and cover their opponents with filth in their efforts to destroy them.

And yet these old divines were great men and great writers, their voices enthralled the best and wisest of their own generation, and it is a misfortune for their fame, and a misfortune for our literature, that they put their wisdom and observation and deep feeling, their great gifts of imagination, and their often exquisite mastery of the art of expression into the hortatory and controversial form of the sermon which time has rendered obsolete.

It must be admitted that all the reasons, good or bad, which keep us from reading writers like Jeremy Taylor and South, face us at once, and seem even more valid, when we open a volume of Donne's sermons. All that has ceased to interest, all that actually repels us in the old theology, the scholastic divinity, the patristic learning, the torturing of texts, the interpretation of old prophesies, the obsolete controversies and refutation of forgotten heresies, the insistence on moral commonplaces, the intolerance of human frailty, and the menaces of fearful judgement on it—with all these stock subjects, Donne, like his contemporaries, filled his sermons. But his case is even worse than theirs; not only as a theologian was he of an older breed, more remote and medieval than Jeremy Taylor or South, he had also, personal to himself, the unhappy faculty of developing to their utmost the faults of any form of literary expression he adopted; and when he abandoned verse for sermon-writing, every defect of this kind of composition, everything that most offends us in the old preachers and sound expositors, was carried by him to a pitch which gives him a bad eminence over the most unreadable of them all.

That sermons like Donne's should have held great congregations spellbound seems astonishing, not only to the secular mind, but to theologians themselves. One of Donne's most distinguished successors at the Deanery of St. Paul's, Dean Milman, has written of them:

'It is difficult for a Dean of our rapid and restless days to imagine, when he surveys the massy folios of Donne's

sermons—each sermon spreads out over many pages—
a vast congregation in the Cathedral or at Paul's Cross,
listening not only with patience but with absorbed
interest, with unflagging attention, even with delight
and rapture, to these interminable disquisitions, to us
teeming with laboured obscurity, false and misplaced wit,
fatiguing antitheses. However set off, as by all accounts
they were, by a most graceful and impressive delivery,
it is astonishing to us that he should hold a London
congregation enthralled, unwearied, unsatiated. Yet
there can be no doubt that this was the case. And this
congregation consisted, both of the people down to the
lowest, and of the most noble, wise, accomplished of that
highly intellectual age. They sat, even stood, undisturbed,
except by their own murmurs of admiration, sometimes
by hardly suppressed tears.' [1]

It is only necessary to open a volume of Donne's sermons
to find a justification for his successor's criticism. For
instance, in preaching to Charles I at Whitehall on the
text ' In my Father's house are many mansions, if it were
not so, I would have told you ', he begins :

' There are occasions of Controversies of all kinds in this
one Verse ; And one is, whether this be one Verse or
no ; For as there are Doctrinall Controversies, out of
the sense and interpretation of the words, so are there
Grammaticall differences about the Distinction, and
Interpunction of them : some Translations differing
thereinn from the Originall (as the Originall Copies are
distinguished, and interpuncted now) and some differing
from one another. The first Translation that was, that
into Syriaque, as it is expressed by *Tremellius*, renders
these words absolutely, precisely as our two Translations
doe ; And, as our two Translations doe, applies the

[1] *Annals of S. Paul's Cathedral*, Henry Hart Milman, D.D., 2nd ed.,
1869, p. 328.

second clause and proposition, *Si quo minus, if it were not so, I would have told you*, as in affirmation, and confirmation of the former, *In domo Patris, In my Fathers house there are many Mansions*, For, *if it were not so I would have told you*. But then, as both our Translations doe, the Syriaque also admits into this Verse a third clause and proposition, *Vade parare, I goe to prepare you a place*. Now *Beza* doth not so ; *Piscator* doth not so ; They determine this Verse in those two propositions which constitute our Text, *In my Fathers house, etc.* And then they let fall the third proposition, as an inducement, and inchoation of the next Verse.' [1]

So the sermon goes inexorably on, immense paragraph after paragraph filled with quotations from the Fathers and quibbling controversies with Roman Catholic theologians, till suddenly the page lights up with a description of the unending day of eternity unsurpassed in our literature, how ' all the foure Monarchies, with all their thousands of yeares, And all the powerfull Kings, and all the beautifull Queenes of this world, were but as a bed of flowers, some gathered at six, some at seaven, some at eight, All in one Morning, in respect of this Day ', and how, during all the time that had passed since the Creation, in this timeless mansion of Eternity, ' there was never heard quarter clock to strike, never seen minute glasse to turne '.[2]

Contrasts almost as surprising as this meet us in the sermons of other seventeenth century preachers, and here and there we come on passages of poignant expression and lyrical or sombre beauty clothed in the noblest language. For while the sermon, regarded merely as

[1] I, p. 737.   [2] See No. 153.

a form of literary expression, has undoubted disadvantages which render the sermons of one age difficult for the next age to appreciate, yet on the other hand this form of expression is one—since its subject matter is nothing less than the whole of life—which gives the widest possible scope to a great preacher. He can pour his whole soul into his sermon, his hopes, fears, and self-accusations, the furthest flights of his imagination, the ripest results of his philosophic meditations, all the wisdom of mellow experience, and even the most amusing details of satiric observation. The very circumstances of his delivery, the ceremonious solemnity of the church and pulpit, the great responsibility of the occasion, give a nobility to his utterance; and the presence of the congregation, the need to speak directly to the hearts and minds of men and women, lends a certain dramatic intensity to all he says. Such circumstances, while they are full of danger for an insincere and rhetorical preacher, provide the most splendid opportunities for one endowed with earnest purpose and a sincere imagination. The exhortations of such a preacher can hardly help being noble in expression; and it is in the sermon therefore that we find some of the highest achievements of English prose—in the sermon, or in prophetic or didactic or even political eloquence written with the same high impulse and inspiration. For great prose needs a great subject matter, needs great themes and a high spectacular point of vision, and solemn and clear and steadfast conception of life and its meaning. It must handle with deep earnestness the most profound themes, Good and Evil, Desire and Disillusion, the briefness of Life and the mystery of

Death—the universal material and the great common-places of human thought in all ages. Such a mood is the mood of religion, in whatever dogmas it may be clothed ; and it is the religious writer who can most impressively touch those great organ stops of grave emotion which move us in the highest achievements of prose literature.

The seventeenth century divines, moreover, with all the lumber which they inherited from the past, inherited much also that gives an enduring splendour to their works. In the doctrines of their faith they found a complete conception of existence, a scheme elaborated in all its details, and rich in memories and associations accumulated from the dawn of history. The Creation of the world, the Fall of Man, all the vicissitudes of the Chosen People, the sins and punishments of their Kings, the vehemence of their Prophets and their supernatural foresight, and the great central tragedy and hope of the Redemption—these were themes that came to their hands elaborated by the Fathers of the Church and by a whole succession of medieval writers ; and now, just at this time, the Sacred Books which were the original sources of this deposit of Christian history and doctrine had been re-translated and clothed afresh in an unsurpassable beauty of language.

This noble diction, this intensity, and what we might almost call inspiration of language, which gives so poetic a colouring to the English version of the Scriptures, was not the achievement of one man, but almost the universal birthright of the time : with the Elizabethan dramatists and translators, the preachers and theological writers had their share in this great utterance, which, whether

due to linguistic causes which ceased to operate, or to
an intensity of poetic vision which afterwards vanished,
certainly grows fainter and thinner and gradually dies
away as the seventeenth century advances, and the age
of theology is superseded by the age of Reason and
common sense.

If Donne's sermons are full, as we have said, of all that
in the old divinity which has become distasteful to us,
if he surpasses the preachers of that period in their faults
and drawbacks, he shares also in their achievements,
and indeed in many ways he overtops them all. Lost
in the great crabbed, unread, unreadable folios of his
sermons, these ' volumes of religion and mountains of
piety ', there are pages and passages of great and surprising
beauty, which are nevertheless entirely unknown to
English readers. It is indeed somewhat curious that with
the growing recognition of Donne's merits as a poet,
so little attention has been paid to the excellence of his
prose. Equal in power and beauty to that of Sir Thomas
Browne or Jeremy Taylor, and in passionate intensity
surpassing even these great writers, it is almost un-
represented in our prose anthologies ; and indeed, the
best of these, Basil Montagu's *Selections*, includes no
specimen of his writing. But the explanation of this is
after all a simple one ; unlike Jeremy Taylor or Sir Thomas
Browne, Donne was famous first of all as a poet, and save
for his little-known *Devotions*, he wrote no small book,
no *Holy Dying* or *Urn Burial* in which he gave evidence
of his powers as a prose writer. His shorter prose pieces,
his *Paradoxes* and *Biathanatos*, and his elaborate letters
do not represent him at his best ; it is only here and there

in isolated passages of his sermons that he put forth his full strength; and his best prose, not being therefore easily accessible, has almost entirely escaped notice, and few even of the most enthusiastic readers of Donne's verse are aware that however highly they estimate his merits as a poet, he is equally worthy of fame as a prose writer—that, indeed, his mastery of the means of expression was perhaps even greater in prose than in poetry; was less impeded by those defects of technique and temperament which kept him from reaching the highest level of poetic achievement.

The object of this volume is to remedy if possible this neglect. After reading Donne's sermons more than once, I have chosen for reprinting those passages which especially impressed me, and which I think will be of interest to modern and secular-minded readers like myself. Any volume of selections from a voluminous author must be always unsatisfactory, for there are many canons of choice, many sieves for the sifting, by means of which such a selection can be made. Donne preached his sermons of course for the purpose of exhortation and religious edification; while there is much in his theology and controversial preaching which is now out of date, he nevertheless stated the main doctrines of the English Church with such moderation and such learning, that a selection of passages from his sermons might make a useful volume of Anglican apologetics; and it was indeed with this object in view that they were reprinted eighty years ago by an Anglican divine, Henry Alford (afterwards Dean of Canterbury), in whose opinion they were ' one of the earliest and best expositions of the divinity of our English Church '—' a genuine body of orthodox divinity (in the best sense of the words) not to be found, perhaps, in any other English theologian '.[1] Then, too, as a preacher Donne was a moralist, and from his denunciations of evil and his exhortations to repentance might be made a handbook of edification which could have its use and value.[2] Or again, taking Donne as a representative mind of his period, one might use his sermons for illustrating the history of human thought, and by selecting typical pages from them give a picture, not only of the theological conceptions of the time, but of the philosophy then current, and the main ideas that were accepted by the cultivated men of that period. The recent and learned volume of Miss Ramsay, *Les Doctrines médiévales chez Donne, le Poète métaphysicien de l'Angleterre*,[3] with its copious citations from Donne's sermons, has shown how great would be the historical interest of such a selection, and what a treasure-house can be found in Donne's writings of passages illustrating the thought and speculation of the early seventeenth century in England.

The purpose underlying this selection is not, however, theological, didactic, nor even historical. It is concerned with Donne as a man, as an artist and writer, with his personal accent and speaking voice; first of all with the man himself, and only in the second place with the doctrines he expounded and the age he lived in. When

[1] *The Works of John Donne, D.D.* With a Memoir of his Life, by Henry Alford, M.A., 1839, vol. i, pp. v, xxi.

[2] Such a selection of edifying passages, *Selections from the Works of John Donne, D.D.*, was published, with no editor's name, by D. A. Talboys, at Oxford, 1840.

[3] Oxford University Press, 1917.

Donne took orders in the English Church the doctrines
and apologetics and controversial positions of that Church
were so to speak imposed upon him; he accepted them
without demur, and as Professor Grierson says,

' In Donne's scholastic, ultra-logical treatment, the rigid
skeleton of seventeenth century theology is, at times,
presented in all its sternness and unattractiveness. From
the extremest deductions, he is saved by the moderation
which was the key-note of his church, and by his own
good sense and deep sympathy with human nature.
But Donne is most eloquent when, escaping from
dogmatic minutiae and controversial " points ", he
appeals directly to the heart and conscience. A reader
may care little for the details of seventeenth century
theology and yet enjoy without qualification Donne's
fervid and original thinking, and the figurative richness,
and splendid harmonies of his prose in passages of argument, of exhortation and of exalted meditation. It is
Donne the poet who transcends every disadvantage of
theme and method, and an outworn fashion in wit and
learning. There are sentences in the sermons which,
in beauty of imagery and cadence, are not surpassed by
anything he wrote in verse, or by any prose of the century
from Hooker's to Sir Thomas Browne's.' [1]

It is these passages which Professor Grierson so well
describes, passages which illustrate what he calls ' the
unique quality, the weight, fervour and wealth, of
Donne's eloquence ', that I have first of all chosen, and
any one who may be inclined to think this praise of Donne's
prose exaggerated he should read—and above all, read
aloud—some of the following pages, the description for
instance of God's bounty,[2] which Professor Saintsbury has

[1] *Cambridge History of Literature*, iv. 220-1.
[2] p. 139.

called unsurpassed, perhaps never equalled for the beauty of its rhythm and the Shakespearean magnificence of its diction ; or the great peroration on ' falling out of the hands of God ', in which Donne sums up in a sombre and terrible sentence—one of the longest and most splendid sentences in the English language—the horror of the deprivation of God's love, and of eternal banishment from His presence.[1]

The great preachers of this, as of other periods, inherited certain set subjects and splendid commonplaces which it was their practice to repeat and elaborate and adorn. The Mercy of God, the Sinfulness of Man, the vanity of this world and the sorrows of the wicked, the sinner's death-bed, the Day of Judgement, the eternal torments of Hell, and the glory and blessedness of the saints in Heaven—these great themes formed the culminating points in their sermons, and were subjects which called for all their powers. Donne's own temperament and experience, his melancholy cast of thought and his mystical sense of another world, enabled him to treat many of these great themes and religious pieces with a vividness of feeling which removes them far from the region of the conventional and commonplace.

The great subject of Sin especially preoccupied him ; his poet's sensibility and sensuous nature—and Donne is the most sensual of all the great English poets—made the allurements of the flesh very real to him ; he knew all about temptation and the weakness of man's moral nature ; like St. Augustine, with whom he has been more than once compared, the memory of his own transgres-

[1] pp. 208–10.

sions and of the excesses of his youth was always with him; and his treatment of the psychology of sin, his descriptions of the 'various and vagabond heart of the sinner', are written with a modern subtlety of analysis, a frankness of self-confession, a curious mingling of asceticism and regret, which we find nowhere else except perhaps in the writings of St. Augustine, and which must hold the attention of the least theological reader; while his denunciations of judgements on sin, and his accounts of the sinner's death-bed, 'the clangour of the angels' trumpets and the horrour of the ringing bell', are inspired by the feelings of one to whom these judgements and these terrors are very real and very dreadful.

Another of his special themes is the great theme of Death. Donne's mind was in many ways essentially medieval, and in no way more so than in his medieval sense of death's horror. Even in his profane and secular poetry we note a preoccupation with this thought; and when as a preacher it was his duty to treat of Death in his sermons he spared his hearers none of the most *macabre* of his imaginations about it. There was an almost morbid love of ugliness in his curious temperament, a delight like that of Swift in what is repulsive and even loathsome, and in his sermons on death he could freely indulge his taste for the grotesque and the disgusting, for dreadful details of the grave's horrors, for decay and putrefaction, and—what was almost an hallucination with him—the activities of the loathsome worm. Unpleasant in their details as are most of these great passages, there is a kind of splendid horror about them which has made me include many—I hope not too many

Introduction.

—of them in this selection ; they are very characteristic of Donne, and indeed his last great sermon, ' Death's Duell ', preached in his final illness not long before he died, is one great and unrelieved threnody on the horror and majesty of Death and the universal dominion of the worm.

Donne's third great theme was God, his omnipotence, his mercy, his wrath, and his terrible justice ; and so real and vivid was his sense of God and the glory of the beatific vision, that unlike other preachers of the time he felt no need to terrify his congregations with the flames and physical horrors of Hell—to his religious mind the deprivation of God's love was in itself Hell, and no fires and tortures could add to that punishment. Save, therefore, as an eternal banishment from God's presence, Donne does not speak of Hell ; but the description of Heaven, the glory of Heaven, was a theme that called forth his highest powers of eloquence and impassioned imagination.

Although Donne had studied the ' new philosophy ', and was aware of the discoveries of Copernicus, and could, for the purposes of metaphor and fancy, make a literary use of these conceptions, his mind still had its habitation in the smaller, earth-centred Ptolemaic creation ; the full realization of these new discoveries, the sense of the immensity of space and the unimportance of this earth in its unmeasured vastness, was a more modern way of feeling in which Donne had no share—which belongs later on in the seventeenth century to the time of Pascal. But contrasted with his imperfect realization of the infinity of space, his sense of the infinity of time was extremely vivid ;

the contrast between eternity and the briefness of human life he felt and described with sombre and ecstatic impressiveness. Eternity, the eternity of God and Heaven, is a theme to which he continually recurs, and which sheds a strange, still atmosphere over his descriptions of the timeless existence of the Blessed in their heavenly abodes.

The circumstances of Donne's early life, the strong Roman Catholic traditions of his family, and the atmosphere of Roman Catholic devotion in which he was educated, were no hindrance, but rather a help to him as an Anglican preacher; and although, as duty and perhaps conviction compelled him, he denounced what he considered the corruptions of Roman Catholicism as vigorously as his fellow divines, yet in his heart there lingered a certain love of the older faith, of stately ceremonial and ancient rites and personal cults and devotions, which gives a warmth, an unction, an unprotestant glow of eloquence to his preaching.

As a poet Donne seems to have adopted a certain harsh and crabbed way of writing, in revolt against the mellifluence of the Elizabethan taste; his poems show here and there that he could, if he wished, touch those harpstrings of sweet music; but they also show, only too abundantly, that in this soft harmony he could not find the medium for the personal expression he desired. This crabbedness shows itself, too, in his letters and his earlier prose writing, and also in the uninspired portions of his sermons. But when he was most in earnest, when he came to treat with passionate seriousness some great theme of faith or morals, his wilfulness of language fell from him; and in his attempt to bring his message home to the hearts of his congregation he availed himself without stint of his own gifts as a poet, and all the music and splendour of the great contemporary speech.

Donne, indeed, often makes use of musical metaphors when he speaks of preaching; the preacher, he says, is a watchman, placed on a high tower to sound a trumpet; his preaching was the trumpet's voice, it was thunder, it was the beating of a drum, the tolling of a bell of warning, it was 'a lovely song, sung to an instrument'; the preacher should not speak with 'uncircumcised lips or an extemporal or irreverent or over-homely and vulgar language'; his style should be modelled on that of the Holy Ghost, whose style was 'a dilligent, and an artificial style', and who in penning the Scriptures 'delights himself, not only with a propriety, but with a delicacy, and harmony, and melody of language; with height of Metaphors, and other figures, which may work greater impressions upon the Readers'.[1] In addition to this august model, the style of the Church Fathers formed Donne's other model in his preaching, and he more than once calls attention to their 'elegant phrases', their 'cadences and allusions and assimilations', to Jerome's epistles 'full of heavenly meditation and curious expressions', to Augustine's study to 'make his language sweet and harmonious', and St. Bernard's effort to exalt 'devotion from the melodious fall of words'.

Coleridge, in his curious notes on Donne's sermons, remarks on the patristic leaven, the rhetorical extravagance, the taste for forced and fantastic analogies, which Donne derived from his study of the early Fathers;

[1] No. 22.

and, indeed, the influence of these models, falling in as it did with his natural taste for 'wit' and extravagant conceits, resulted often in far-fetched and fantastic passages; and there are whole sermons built up on one metaphor, on blood or water or tears or kisses, and even on vomit and circumcision, in which one image is turned and twisted and elaborated and swollen out with figurative, moral, and mystical meanings, grotesquely adorned with medical analogies and legal jargon and scholastic quibbles and rabbinical speculations, until we share to the full Dean Milman's amazement at the taste of those immense and attentive congregations, and are not surprised to hear that noblemen and gentlemen were taken up for dead, after listening to one of these hour-long conceits and overwhelming metaphors.

But then again this cumbrous style takes fire, this vast edifice of elaborate adornments blazes up into a splendid illumination; and remote as we are in time and taste from the audiences which stood for hours in the open air at Paul's Cross, or filled the choir of old St. Paul's, we share, if but for a moment, the delight which drew those ancient crowds to hear these products of what one contemporary called his 'Giant phancie',[1] to witness the gleams of what another described as that 'awfull fire'[2] which burned in the clear brain of the great preacher.

But what compels our attention most in these discourses is when Donne 'preaches himself' in them, speaks of his past life, his sins and his remorse for them, of his present temptations, of his fears for his future fate, or his hopes of Heaven. 'When I consider what I was in my parents

---

[1] *Poems,* i. 379.   [2] *Ibid.,* p. 371.

loynes', he begins, 'when I consider what I am now, . . . an aged childe, a gray-headed Infant, and but the ghost of mine own youth, When I consider what I shall be at last, by the hand of death, in my grave' [1]—it is in passages like this, or in his forecasts of his own death-bed, 'when everlasting darknesse shall have an inchoation in the present dimnesse of mine eyes, and the everlasting gnashing in the present chattering of my teeth,' [2] that Donne becomes most impressive, and we are best able to understand the sombre fascination of his preaching.

These personal passages have often for us another interest : we find in them a curious modern note or quality which we find almost nowhere else in the literature of that age. For in spite of his medieval cast of thought Donne was in some ways the most modern writer of his period ; in his poems and in his strange, feverish *Meditations* there is a subtlety of self-analysis, an awareness of the workings of his own mind, which seems to belong to the nineteenth rather than to the seventeenth century. We hear him confessing, for instance, in one of his sermons, the wanderings of his mind in his strongest devotions, and how in the midst of prayer he is distracted by the noise of a fly, the rattling of a coach [3]; or how, while he is preaching, he is partly in the pulpit, partly in his library at home ; partly expounding his text, and partly thinking what his congregation will say to each other of his sermon when it is finished. [4]

Donne was in the habit of drawing a distinction, in his letters, between the Jack Donne of his earlier life

---

[1] No. 2.   [2] No. 126.
[3] No. 4.   [4] No. 3.

and Dr. Donne, the Dean and grave divine and preacher. But, as he himself said, men do not change their passions, but only the objects of them; God does not take men from their calling, but mends them in it; He loves renovations, not innovations. Just as each of the authors of the books of Scripture, whether they were courtiers or shepherds or fishermen, kept the idiom and the interests of their profession in their sacred writings, so the regenerate soul, whether amorous, ambitious, or covetous, could find in God ' a fit subject, and just occasion to exercise the same affection piously, and religiously, which had before so sinfully transported, and possesst it '.[1] So Donne retained his old passions and ways of thought; but whereas he had formerly, as he himself says of St. Augustine, made sonnets of his sins, he now made sermons of them. Dr. Donne was still Jack Donne, though sanctified and transformed, and those who have learned to know the secular poet will find in the writer of religious prose the same character-istics, the subtle, modern self-analytic mind moving in a world of medieval thought, the abstract, frigid scholastic intellect and the quickest senses, the forced conceits and passionate sincerity, the harsh utterance and the snatches of angel's music—in fact all that has attracted or perhaps repelled them in the author of the ' love-songs and satiric weeds', the sensual elegies and rugged verse-letters of his earlier period. They will also often find the man of the world beneath the surplice, with his appreciation of worldly values, rank and circumstance and office, and that 'inward joy and outward reverence and dignity that

[1] No. 21.

accompanies riches ' [1]; the courtier who had the courtier's desire for the favour of great persons, and who pictured Heaven as a royal court, and God as a king in his palace; who described earthly kings as metaphorical gods, and pious courts as copies of the Communion of the Saints.

In the sermons also they will find that broad humanity, that sympathy with all kinds of people, that good common sense, which made Donne a reasonable human being, and moved him often to declare that religion was a serious but not a sullen thing, and a merry heart and a cheerful countenance a better way to God than dejection of spirit, and all the ' sad remorses of the world '.[2]

A preacher or moralist often betrays himself indirectly, for he is apt to see his own faults in others, and to dwell, in his exhortations, on the temptations and weaknesses to which he is especially exposed. It is characteristic of Donne that he should so frequently inveigh against the sins of the senses, and especially of the eye, which he said was ' the devil's doore, before the ear '[3]; and characteristic also his frequent recurrence to the danger of remembering past sins—' the sinfull remembrance of former sins, which is a dangerous rumination, and an unwholesome chawing of the cud '. [4] Another sin to which Donne frequently recurs is the sin of curiosity, the sin of the curious and subtle intellect, which, dissatisfied with the ' solid and fundamentall ' doctrines necessary to salvation, longed for ' birds of Paradise, unrevealed mysteries out of Gods own bosom '.[5] His reprobation

[1] ii, p. 416.   [2] iii, p. 318.   [3] i, p. 228.
[4] ii, p. 159.   [5] i, p. 308.

of this unchastened curiosity, this presumption of men who ' being but worms will look into Heaven ',[1] was partly, no doubt, an attack on the rising tide of Puritan and schismatic speculation ; but it was also an indirect confession of the attraction, for his boundless intellectual curiosity, of the high and inexplicable problems of Christian metaphysics. Donne echoes Luther's denunciation of the ' hatefull, damnable Monosyllable, How '[2]; again and again he warns his congregation against inquiries which were ' forc'd dishes of hot brains, and not sound meat ', ' spirituall *wantonnesses*, and unlawful and dangerous dallyings with mysteries of Divinity '[3]; and yet again and again we find his own thoughts losing their way among mysteries above the reach of reason, the nature of the Trinity, Predestination, Election, Original Sin, many strange scholastic questions about the Angels, the Devil, and the possibility of his ultimate salvation, and such high, insoluble problems as for instance whether the Serpent, as many of the Fathers believed, had feet and walked upright before the Fall.

Such was Donne as he reveals himself in his sermons, essentially in mind and temperament the same person as the poet, but turning his native gifts, and even his acquired stock of conceits and images, to new and sanctified uses. The mood resulting from this transformation has been well described by Professor Saintsbury as ' a mood in which the memory of bygone earthly delights blends inextricably with the present fervour of devotion, and which to a fancy resembling his own might suggest a temple of Aphrodite or Dionysus turned into a Christian

---

[1] iii, p. 77.   [2] i, p. 301.   [3] ii, p. 36.

church, and served by the same priest as of old, with complete loyalty to his new faith, but with undying consciousness of the past '.[1]

Thus one tries to explain Donne's sermons and account for them in a satisfactory manner. And yet in these, as in his poems, there remains something baffling and enigmatic which still eludes our last analysis. Reading these old hortatory and dogmatic pages, the thought suggests itself that Donne is often saying something else, something poignant and personal, and yet, in the end, incommunicable to us. It sometimes seems as if he were using the time-honoured phrases of the accepted faith, its hope of heaven, and its terror of the grave, to express a vision of his own—a vision of life and death, of evil and horror and ecstasy—very different from that of other preachers; and we are troubled as well as fascinated by the strange music which he blows through the sacred trumpets.

From the sermons themselves we can gather some impression of the effect in his own age of Donne's preaching, either at court, where he often preached before James I or Charles I,[2] or at Lincoln's Inn, or at his parish church of St. Dunstan's, or in the open air at Paul's Cross, and above all before his 'great and curious auditories' at St. Paul's, when the choir was so crowded that

[1] Professor Saintsbury in *English Prose Selections*, edited by Henry Craik, 1894, ii, p. 85.

[2] It would appear that the court sermons, preached 'to the Nobility' and the king, were sometimes open-air sermons. See *C. and T. Jas. I*, ii. 386: 'the king came hither the 5th of this present, and the next day, being Palm Sunday, the lord archbishop preached at court, in the open-preaching place'.

many of the poorer sort could not have seats, but must
'stand and thrust', and where long murmurs of approval
sometimes, he said, swallowed up one-quarter of his
hour's sermon.[1]

We have other and outside evidence, too, of his influence
as a preacher, and his manner and appearance in the pulpit.
A member of the Dutch embassy in England, Constantine
Huyghens, writes of the 'wealth of his unequalled wit,
and yet more incomparable eloquence in the pulpit'[2];
we read of the great concourse of noblemen and gentlemen at one of his sermons at Lincoln's Inn 'whereof two
or three were endangered and taken up dead for the time,
with the extreme press and thronging',[3] of another sermon
preached in the open air at Paul's Cross, which was listened
to by 'the Lords of the Council and other honourable
persons' including the Archbishop of Canterbury, Bacon,
the Lord Keeper, Sir Julius Caesar, the Master of the Rolls,
Lord Arundel, Lord Southampton, and 'divers other great
men'.[4]

Izaak Walton has described for us his manner in the
pulpit,

'preaching the Word so, as shewed his own heart was
possest with those very thoughts, and joyes that he
labored to distill into others: A Preacher in earnest,
weeping sometimes for his Auditory, sometimes with
them: always preaching to himself, like an Angel from
a cloud, but in none; carrying some, as St. *Paul* was,
to Heaven in holy raptures, and inticing others by
a sacred Art and Courtship to amend their lives; here
picturing a vice so as to make it ugly to those that

[1] No. 17.   [2] Quoted in *Poems*, ii, p. lxxvii.
[3] See note to No. 70.   [4] See note to No. 29.

practised it; and a vertue so, as to make it beloved even by those that lov'd it not; and, all this with a most particular grace and an unexpressible addition of comeliness.' [1]

There are other evidences of the manner and effect of his preaching in the commendatory verses written at his death, in which mention is made of his ' speaking action ', ' pale looks, faint breath, and melting phrases'.

Mee thinkes I see him in the pulpit standing,
Not eares, or eyes, but all mens hearts commanding,
Where wee that heard him, to our selves did faine
Golden Chrysostome was alive againe;
And never were we weari'd, till we saw
His houre (and but an houre) to end did draw.
How did he shame the doctrine-men,[2]

one poet writes, and another :

thy one houre did treate
The thousand mazes of the hearts deceipt;
Thou didst pursue our lov'd and subtill sinne,
Through all the foldings wee had wrapt it in.[3]

While another poet gives in Latin verses an even more vivid picture of his preaching :

' Whenever the orator stood in St. Paul's I have seen and heard with amazement the wonderful power with which he held men, as they lifted up their hearts and eyes, whilst he poured forth the wise eloquence of a Nestor, sweeter than honey. Now he holds them thunderstruck whilst he preaches the mystery of holy things never before granted to the people and not yet understood; they ponder his words with admiration, and

[1] Walton's *Lives*, 1670; *Donne*, p. 38.
[2] *Poems*, i, p. 386.   [3] *Ibid.*, i, p. 393.

stand with outstretched ears. Presently his manner
and form of speaking are changed, and he treats of sad
things—fate and the mournful hour of death, and the
body returning to its primal ashes : then you might
have seen all groan and grieve, and one here and there
unable to restrain his tears.'[1]

From these contemporary glimpses, and from the sermons themselves we can form some notion of the power,
the grace, the eloquence which made Donne the most
famous preacher of the time, and one of his great sermons
an important event for his contemporaries. As we read
these sermons, amid much that is remote and meaning-
less to us, we seem now and then to hear the timbre of
a living voice, and then for a moment the past returns ;
and in the vast, dim-lit cathedral of old St. Paul's we
seem to see that awe-struck congregation as they gaze up
at the courtly, spectral figure standing with his hour-
glass in the pulpit, and pouring forth in impassioned
eloquence his inmost thoughts of remorse and ecstasy,
his poignant sense of the grave's unspeakable horror, and

[1]   Vidi,
   Audivi & stupui quoties orator in Æde
   Paulina stetit, & mira gravitate levantes
   Corda, oculosᐢviros tenuit : dum Nestoris ille
   Fudit verba (omni quanto mage dulcia melle ?)
   Nunc habet attonitos, pandit mysteria plebi
   Non concessa prius nondum intellecta : revolvunt
   Mirantes, taciticque arrectis auribus astant.
   Mutatis mox ille modo, formaᐢ loquendi
   Tristia pertractat : fatumᐢ & flebile mortis
   Tempus, & in cineres redeunt quod corpora primos.
   Tunc gemitum cunctos dare, tunc lugere videres,
   Forsitan à lachrymis aliquis non temperat.—*Ibid.* i, p. 391.

Heaven's unutterable glory; and this image is added to those many deeply coloured pictures which, hung in the chamber of the historic imagination, form for us our vision of that illustrious and varied period of English history.

We look back at this early period of the seventeenth century in England, not only through the windows which history opens for us; we see it even more clearly, though diversely tinctured, through the minds and imaginations of certain writers of the time; fresh in the morning light of Milton's early poems, calm in the sabbath sunshine of George Herbert's *Temple*, or dusky with the twilight of Sir Thomas Browne's meditations. It is the purpose of the present book to draw aside at least one corner of the heavy curtain which hides from us another casement of that age's imagination, a sombre, deep-emblazoned gothic window, through which nevertheless the sunlight of to-day sometimes seems to strike, as it lights up the ascetic, enigmatic figure which it frames.

Donne's ecclesiastic career has been so adequately recounted by his biographers, Dr. Jessopp and Mr. Gosse, that only the briefest recapitulation is necessary here. John Donne was born in 1573; he was the elder son of a rich London ironmonger, who died in 1576 leaving him a considerable fortune. His mother, who was descended from a sister of Sir Thomas More, came of a famous Roman Catholic family; she had two brothers who were Jesuits, and numbered among her relatives many prisoners and exiles for the sake of the Roman faith. She remained a devout Roman Catholic till the end of her life, and her son's earliest years were spent in an atmosphere of Roman Catholic devotion. At the early age of eleven Donne went to Oxford, and afterwards to Cambridge ; in 1590 we find him in London again, and in 1592 he was admitted to Lincoln's Inn. A young man of brilliant intellect, the master of a considerable fortune, he now found himself, as a Roman Catholic, shut out from the usual paths of honourable ambition, and faced with the problem whether he should remain in the old faith, and so sacrifice his worldly prospects, or should join the English Church and take his share in the life and interests of his country. Before coming to any conclusion he first surveyed and digested, he tells us, ' the whole body of divinity, controverted between ours and the Roman Church ' ; and if his final decision coincided with his interests, and if ten years later we find Donne a convinced opponent of Romanism, though we can hardly regard his change of faith as due to a genuine conversion to Anglicanism, or to any belief that it was alone the true church, it does not appear on the other hand to have been a mere apostasy prompted by political considerations. Donne was genuinely convinced that there was truth in each form of Christian religion, and that it was wisest and best for each man to accept the faith of his own country.

When after his somewhat stormy and spendthrift youth Donne made his rash marriage in 1601, and found himself desperately poor in consequence, half in disgrace, and with small prospects of worldly advancement, he resumed his theological studies ; and in 1605 we find him assisting Dr. Thomas Morton, afterwards Bishop of

Durham, in his controversies with the Roman Catholic writers. During the next few years he wrote three books, the *Pseudo-Martyr, Ignatius his Conclave*, and the *Biathanatos*, all of which were, as Mr. Gosse says, written more as a lawyer than a divine, though each was on the borderland of theology. In spite of his theological occupations, Donne, as his letters show, was still ambitious of worldly preferment, and when his patron, Dr. Morton, became Dean of Gloucester in 1607, and offered to resign a living to him if he would take orders, Donne refused the offer. Walton tells us that this refusal was due to a sense of his own unworthiness, and the fear that the irregularities of his past life might bring dishonour on the sacred calling, but it is more likely, as his letters of the time suggest, that he had not yet abandoned the hope of some court advancement. But this hope was repeatedly disappointed: Donne was poor, burdened with a large family, and forced to live in humiliating dependence on the bounty of rich friends; and in 1612 we find him writing to the new court favourite, Rochester, that he had resolved to take orders. Rochester, however, seems to have discouraged this resolution, and it was not till three years later, and after further disappointments, that Donne, yielding to the persuasions of King James himself, finally determined to enter the Church. In January 1615 he was ordained, and in the same year he became one of the king's chaplains and was made a Doctor of Divinity by the University of Cambridge.

Donne's earliest court sermon which has come down to us, and perhaps the first sermon which he preached as chaplain to the king, is dated April 21, 1616. Though

much was expected of him, Izaak Walton tells us, his
preaching exceeded all expectation; and indeed, if we
recall the circumstances of the time, when the Overbury murder, one of the greatest scandals of English
history, had just been made public in all its dreadful
details; when the once omnipotent favourite of the king,
the Earl of Somerset, stood publicly accused of com-
plicity in this crime, and his guilty wife was imprisoned in
the Tower, Donne's analysis of the beginning and growth
of evil in the sinner's heart, and his sombre and terrible
denunciations of God's judgements on the wicked,
must have produced an astonishing effect on his auditory.
'God is *the Lord of Hosts*', he proclaimed to them, 'and
he can proceed by Martial Law : he can hang thee upon
the next tree ; . . . he can sink down the Stage and the
Player, the bed of wantonness, and the wanton actor,
into the jaws of the earth, into the mouth of hell.' 'Thou
canst not lack Examples, that he hath done so upon others,'
he continues, with a reference that must have been
obvious to all, ' and will no proof serve thee, but a speedy
judgement upon thyself ? ' [1]

In this year, 1616, Donne was presented to two
country livings, and appointed Divinity Reader to
the Benchers of Lincoln's Inn. This important and
lucrative post, which involved, it has been calculated,
the preparation of not fewer than fifty sermons a year, he
held till he became Dean of St. Paul's, about six years
later.

In March 1617 Donne was appointed to preach in
the famous open-air pulpit of London at Paul's Cross,

[1] See Nos. 87, 105, 108.

before the Lords of the Council and the City Magistrates.
These sermons at Paul's Cross, which were preached by
the most distinguished divines of England, had an official
character of high importance, and were one of the great
events of contemporary London. Donne on his first
appearance in this open-air pulpit preached a sermon
of enormous length, which, if delivered as printed, must
have kept his audience standing for at least two hours.
It was, however, in contemporary opinion 'a dainty
sermon', and was 'exceedingly well liked' especially
for the praise he gave to Queen Elizabeth.[1]

In this year Donne lost the dearly-loved wife whom he
had married in such romantic circumstances, and in his
grief at this irreparable loss he seems to have taken his
final 'step to the altar', and to have undergone a real
conversion; his mind was now more wholly set on
heavenly things; and to his intellectual interest in
theology and dogma was added a passionate devotion
which increased as the years went by, till he became
almost absorbed in that life of asceticism and spiritual
exaltation which is reflected in his religious poetry, his
meditations, and his great sermons. The chief events of
his remaining years can be briefly recounted.

In 1619 he was appointed to go as King's Chaplain
with his friend, Lord Doncaster, on a mission to Germany.
His farewell sermon to the Benchers of Lincoln's Inn has
been preserved,[2] also one of the two sermons he preached
before the Electress Palatine, afterwards the Queen of
Bohemia, at Heidelberg,[3] and a sermon he preached at
The Hague. This last he afterwards enlarged into two

[1] See No. 29 and note. [2] No. 26. [3] No. 124.

sermons of considerable length, which are chiefly remarkable for the wealth of sustained nautical metaphors
which pervade them. Donne, who in his youth had
sailed with Essex on two long voyages, is remarkable as
a poet, among the somewhat inland English writers
of his time, for his frequent use of nautical terms
and his references to seafaring life and the ways of
ships. He carried this breath of the sea with him
into the pulpit; his sermons abound in nautical terms
and images, and now he preached to this seafaring nation
on the Apostles as fishers of men, taken from their nets
' weather-beaten with North and South winds, and
rough-cast with foame, and mud ' [1]; and elaborated
a giant simile of the world as a sea, in which all the
inhabitants are fishes to be caught in the net of the
Gospel and served up at the great marriage feast in
Heaven, where, he added characteristically—and we must
think surprisingly to the Dutch—whoever is a dish is
a guest also, and whoever is served at the table sits at it. [2]

After his return to England he was appointed, towards
the end of 1621, to the Deanery of St. Paul's. His first
sermon preached in that cathedral was on Christmas
Day, 1621. This sermon is a closely reasoned one, less
adorned with those elaborate allusions and quotations and
conceits of which he was so fond, but containing a clear
statement of the relation between reason and faith
which was the basis of his religious philosophy. [3] Donne's
Christmas sermons preached at St. Paul's for all the

[1] i, p. 720.
[2] No. 44. For other extracts from this sermon, see Nos. 86 and 112.
[3] No. 58.

subsequent years of his life except the last have been
preserved, also the great sermons he was accustomed to
preach there on Easter Day and Whitsunday, and
a number of the sermons which he also preached as
Prebend of the Cathedral, besides others delivered
at various dates in the same pulpit. Next to these in
number are the sermons preached at court, sometimes
at St. James's, but for the most part at Whitehall. In
1624 he was presented to the living of St. Dunstan's in
the West, then a fashionable church, in which as parish
vicar he was able to come into closer personal relations
with his congregation than he could with his great
audiences at St. Paul's; and in his first sermon there he
described in the elaborate metaphor of a marriage
between the Minister and his Congregation what he felt
should be his relation to his parishioners.[1] A number
of other sermons preached in this pulpit have been preserved.

Before this date, however, he preached two sermons
of some importance. The first of these was to the
Virginia Company, which was then trying to collect sub-
scriptions for the earliest English colony in America, and
to renew popular interest in this settlement. Donne took
the point of view, which has become since so popular, that
English conquest and colonization was, or should be, carried
on for the purpose of religious propaganda, to furnish
salvation to the benighted heathen; and he preached, on
this occasion, what has been called the first English missionary sermon.[2] Later in this year, 1622, a more
unpleasant task was imposed on him, and he was ordered

[1] No. 27.   [2] No. 31.

by James I, who was then engaged in his negotiations
for the Spanish Match, to preach at Paul's Cross in
defence of the instructions the king had issued forbidding
the polemical preaching of Protestant doctrines. There
was an immense crowd at the sermon; but a contemporary tells us that he gave no satisfaction, speaking
indeed, some thought, as if he were by no means satisfied
himself.[1] In the autumn of the next year he was struck
down by that severe illness which he so vividly describes
in his *Devotions*, published in 1624.

His next sermon of public importance was preached
in St. James's Palace a few days after the death of his
old master James I. James died on March 27, 1625,
at Theobald's; the new king, Charles I, had shut
himself up in St. James's Palace, but on Sunday the 3rd
of April he sent for Donne to preach to him in the palace
chapel. From a few scraps of old paper preserved by
chance, we are able to make for ourselves a more than
usually vivid picture of this Sunday afternoon nearly
three hundred years ago. Donne, who had been seriously
ill, was plainly thrown into great agitation by the royal
command to preach before the inscrutable prince who was
now beginning his fateful reign. He writes to a friend
at court begging that on his arrival at the palace he may
hide himself in an out-chamber or closet till the time for
the sermon. He must preach fasting, he says, refusing
an invitation to dinner, and after the sermon would steal

---

[1] See note to No. 37. This sermon, preached on the text about the
stars fighting against Sisera, was printed in 1622 with a dedication to the
new favourite, the Marquis of Buckingham. It was not included in the
three folios, but was reprinted by Alford, vi, pp. 191–222.

into his coach and return home. Another letter of a contemporary witness describes the very pale face and deep mourning of the young king as he went to the chapel, draped in a plain black cloak that fell to his ankles. Donne began his sermon with a discreet reference to the death of the old king, and then proceeded to preach a controversial sermon against the Roman Catholic and Puritan controversialists of the time [1]; but three weeks later, preaching at Denmark House, where the embalmed body of James I lay in state, his references to his departed master are more explicit; and in one splendid passage about the king's dead hand, he keeps repeating, at the end of his intricate clauses, the word ' dead ' in a way that makes it ring out like the tolling of a bell, and which in his accomplished delivery must have produced a strange effect of musical and sombre rhetoric. [2]

In 1625 he was driven out of London by the plague and took refuge with his friend Magdalen Herbert, George Herbert's mother, who was now married to Sir John Danvers, and lived in Danvers House in what was then the village of Chelsea. In 1627 Lady Danvers died and was buried in the parish church of Chelsea, where Donne preached the funeral sermon. In his unregenerate days Donne had written poems to Mrs. Herbert, almost as a lover; he had immortalized her in those famous lines,

No *Spring*, nor *Summer* Beauty hath such grace,
As I have seen in one Autumnall face,

and now, after an invocation to this loved ghost to arise from the consecrated dust in which she slept, he

---

[1] For this sermon see No. 75 and note.   [2] No. 34.

proceeds, in a long and noble panegyric to paint a portrait of her as she lived and as he and her family and friends knew her—a portrait [1] which is one of the most vivid and beautiful we possess of those Elizabethan great ladies who befriended the poets of the time and still live for us immortalized in their poems.

Izaak Walton tells us that he was present in the church, and saw and heard Donne weep and preach this funeral sermon; and he repeats Donne's characteristic wish that 'all his Body were turn'd unto tongues, that he might declare her just praises to posterity'.

The time was approaching when Donne must preach his own funeral sermon; his strength gradually declined, twice he was afflicted with severe illness, and in 1630 his health finally gave way, and he retired to the country. But early in the next year he dragged himself up to London to preach his usual Lent sermon to the court— to sing, as one of his panegyrists wrote, like a swan, his mournful dirge—the great sermon which was published after his death as 'Death's Duell', and in which his sombre imagination and his morbid and fantastic genius shone forth with unearthly splendour. Walton gives a vivid description of this last dramatic appearance, how when to the amazement of the beholders he appeared in the pulpit 'many of them thought he presented himself not to preach mortification by a living voice: but, mortality by a decayed body, and dying face ',[2] and how as they saw his tears and heard his faint and hollow voice, as he preached on his text, 'To God the Lord belong the issues from death,' they felt that the text had been prophetically

[1] No. 28.   [2] Walton's *Lives*, 1670, *Donne*, p. 71.

chosen and that he had preached his own funeral sermon. Donne then retired to the Deanery and began that spectacular preparation for death, that ' elaborate public decease ', as Mr. Gosse describes it, ' so long-drawn, so solemn, so boldly picturesque ' which so greatly impressed his contemporaries, and which, in the monument designed after the picture he had had painted of himself dressed in a winding sheet, has left in St. Paul's so strange and so beautiful a memorial for the admiration of posterity.

Six of Donne's sermons had been published in his life-time, and he left at his death a large number prepared for the press. His last sermon was printed after his death in 1632, and in 1634 six more sermons were published by the Cambridge University Press. In 1640 Donne's son, John Donne, published the first folio of eighty sermons, all hitherto unpublished, and in 1649 he printed the second folio, *Fifty Sermons*, containing ' Death's Duell ' and the six published in 1634 and forty-three new ones. In 1660 he published the third folio, entitled *XXVI Sermons*, although it only contains twenty-four, as two of them were printed twice. In 1839, Henry Alford, afterwards Dean of Canterbury, published the 154 sermons from the three folios, and three of the six printed in Donne's lifetime, in an edition which was intended to be a complete edition of Donne's writings, though this plan was afterwards abandoned, and only the sermons, the *Devotions*, the poems, and the letters were included in it. Alford so expurgated the poems, and was so careless in his printing of the letters, that this edition of his has been much abused by scholars. He admits that he bowdlerized a few of the earlier sermons;

but save for this and for the modernization of the spelling, the text of the sermons is accurate, and as the old folios are now rare (the third is almost unprocurable) Alford's edition is the one which is most accessible to modern readers.[1]

We possess, therefore, 160 of Donne's sermons, of which all but three were reprinted by Alford, where they fill about three thousand pages. Some of these sermons are of enormous length, and if preached as written must have taken two or three hours to deliver, instead of the hour marked by the running sands in the conspicuous hour-glass, to which Donne was accustomed to confine himself. But there is plenty of evidence to show that we do not now possess the sermons as he preached them. Donne, like other divines of the period, took no fully written manuscript with him into the pulpit; he preached from notes; and although when preaching at court or at St. Paul's on great occasions he would no doubt commit much of his sermon to memory, the whole text would be written out from memory afterwards, and subject to many additions and changes in the process of writing.[2]

[1] In 1840 Pickering published a beautifully printed volume, *Devotions by John Donne, D.D.*, which contains two of Donne's sermons, 'Death's Duell' and the Chelsea sermon on the death of Lady Danvers.

[2] In a letter of 1621 Donne promises to write out one of his sermons for a friend 'though in good faith I have half forgot it' (*Gosse*, ii, p. 151). In 1625, when he had taken refuge at Chelsea from the plague in London, he says, in explaining how he has spent his time there, ' I have revised as many of my sermons as I had kept any note of, and I have written out a great many, and hope to do more. I have already come to the number of eighty, of which my son . . . may hereafter make some use ' (*ibid.*, p. 225). Donne's sermon preached at The Hague is introduced in

It only remains to say a few words about the plan
of this small volume of extracts from Donne's sermons.
The arrangement is not chronological, and indeed, since
many of the sermons are undated, such an arrangement
would be at the best highly uncertain and conjectural.
They are placed in a certain sequence according to their
subjects, first the more autobiographical passages, the
pages or paragraphs where Donne speaks most directly
and intimately of himself, his own feelings and moods,
his own conception of the preacher's office, his literary
tastes, and the references, though these are not many, to
his own life and travels. Next follow the scanty allusions
he makes to events of contemporary history, the death
of Queen Elizabeth, the accession of James I, the Gunpowder Plot, the new settlements in America, the
great plague of 1625, and the death of King James ; after
these come passages illustrating the more secular aspects
of his thought, his remarks on life and men and women,
on poverty and riches, a portrait he gives in a funeral
sermon of a rich London merchant of the time, and his
reflections on the 'new philosophy' of Copernicus,
and on human knowledge in general. Then following
the process of his thought, we come to religious faith, as
founded on, and yet contrasted with, mere human reason,
and the revelation of that faith through the Scriptures
and the teaching of the Church. Next follow those
passages in which he attains the greatest heights of
the first folio, with this note, ' At the *Haghe* Decemb. 19. 1619. I Preached
upon this Text. Since my sicknesse at *Abney-hatche* in Essex, 1630.
revising my short notes of that Sermon, I digested them into these two.'
Two sermons follow on the same text, and there are other sermons which
seem to have been expanded and divided in the same way.

eloquence—passages in which the body of that revelation is expressed, our knowledge of God and of man's fall, the inheritance of Original Sin, the corrupt nature of man, the sinful state of the world, the penalty of death with all its horrors, the terrors of the Day of Judgement, the misery of the damned, and the everlasting joy and glory of the blessed souls in Heaven. The book ends with extracts from the sombre and impressive last sermon, in which he made his farewell to the world.

DONNE'S SERMONS

1. *The Preacher.*

IN the great Ant-hill of the whole world, I am an Ant; I have my part in the Creation, I am a Creature; But there are ignoble Creatures. God comes nearer; In the great field of clay, of red earth, that man was made of, & mankind, I am a clod; I am a man, I have my part in the Humanity; But Man was worse then annihilated again. When satan in that serpent was come, as *Hercules* with his club into a potters shop, and had broke all the vessels, destroyed all mankind, And the gracious promise of a Messias to redeeme all mankind, was shed and spread upon all, I had my drop of that dew of Heaven, my sparke of that fire of heaven, in the universall promise, in which I was involved; But this promise was appropriated after, in a particular Covenant, to one people, to the Jewes, to the seed of *Abraham*. But for all that I have my portion there; for all that professe Christ Jesus are by a spirituall engrafting, and transmigration, and transplantation, in and of that stock, and that seed of *Abraham*; and I am one of those. But then, of those who doe professe Christ Jesus, some grovell still in the superstitions they were fallen into, and some are raised, by Gods good grace, out of them ; and I am one of those ; God hath afforded me my station, in that Church, which is departed from Babylon.

Now, all this while, my soule is in a cheerefull progresse ; when I consider what God did for Goshen in Egypt, for a little parke in the midst of a forest ; what he did for Jury, in the midst of enemies, as a shire that should stand out against a Kingdome round about it : How many Sancerraes he hath delivered from famins, how many Genevaes from plots, and machinations against her ; all this while my soule is in a progresse : But I am at home, when I consider Buls of excommunications, and solicitations of Rebellions, and pistols, and poysons, and the discoveries of those ; There is our *Nos*, *We*, testimonies that we are in the favour, and care of God ; We, our Nation, we, our Church ; There I am at home ; but I am in my Cabinet at home, when I consider, what God hath done for me, and my soule ; There is the *Ego*, the particular, the individuall, I.

2. *When I consider.*

AMOROUS soule, ambitious soule, covetous soule, voluptuous soule, what wouldest thou have in heaven ? What doth thy holy amorousnesse, thy holy covetousnesse, thy holy ambition, and voluptuousnesse most carry thy desire upon ? Call it what thou wilt ; think it what thou canst ; think it something that thou canst not think ; and all this thou shalt have, if thou have any Resurrection unto life ; and yet there is a *Better Resurrection.* When I consider what I was in my parents loynes (a substance unworthy of a word, unworthy of a thought) when I consider what I am now, (a Volume of diseases bound up together, a dry cynder, if I look for naturall, for radicall moisture, and yet a Spunge, a bottle of overflowing Rheumes, if I consider accidentall ; an aged childe, a gray-headed Infant, and but the ghost of mine own youth) When I consider what I shall be at last, by the hand of death, in my grave, (first, but Putrifaction, and then, not so much as Putri-faction, I shall not be able to send forth so much as an ill ayre, not any ayre at all, but shall be all insipid, tastlesse, savourlesse dust ; for a while, all wormes, and after a while, not so much as wormes, sordid, senslesse, namelesse dust) When I consider the past, and present, and future state of this body, in this world, I am able to conceive, able to expresse the worst that can befall it in nature, and the worst that can be inflicted upon it by man, or fortune ; But the least degree of glory that God hath prepared for that body in heaven, I am not able to expresse, not able to conceive.

3. *I am Not all Here.*

I AM not all here, I am here now preaching upon this text, and I am at home in my Library considering whether *S. Gregory,* or *S. Hierome,* have said best of this text, before. I am here speaking to you, and yet I consider by the way, in the same instant, what it is likely you will say to one another, when I have done, you are not all here neither ; you are here now,

hearing me, and yet you are thinking that you have
heard a better Sermon somewhere else, of this text
before ; you are here, and yet you think you could have
heard some other doctrine of down-right *Predestination*,
and *Reprobation* roundly delivered somewhere else with
more edification to you ; you are here, and you remember
your selves that now yee think of it : This had been the
fittest time, now, when every body else is at Church,
to have made such and such a private visit ; and because
you would bee there, you are there.

4. *Imperfect Prayers.*

BUT when we consider with a religious serious-
nesse the manifold weaknesses of the strongest
devotions in time of Prayer, it is a sad consideration.
I throw my selfe downe in my Chamber, and I call in,
and invite God, and his Angels thither, and when they
are there, I neglect God and his Angels, for the noise of
a Flie, for the ratling of a Coach, for the whining of a
doore ; I talke on, in the same posture of praying ;
Eyes lifted up ; knees bowed downe ; as though I prayed
to God ; and, if God, or his Angels should aske me,
when I thought last of God in that prayer, I cannot tell :
Sometimes I finde that I had forgot what I was about,
but when I began to forget it, I cannot tell. A memory
of yesterdays pleasures, a feare of to morrows dangers,
a straw under my knee, a noise in mine eare, a light in
mine eye, an any thing, a nothing, a fancy, a Chimera
in my braine, troubles me in my prayer. So certainely
is there nothing, nothing in spirituall things, perfect in
this world.

5. *Powers and Principalities.*

I PASSE my time sociably and merrily in cheerful conversation, in musique, in feasting, in Comedies, in wantonnesse; and I never heare all this while of any power or principality, my Conscience spies no such enemy in all this. And then alone, between God and me at midnight, some beam of his grace shines out upon me, and by that light I see this Prince of darknesse, and then I finde that I have been the subject, the slave of these powers and principalities, when I thought not of them. Well, I see them, and I try then to dispossesse my selfe of them, and I make my recourse to the powerfullest exorcisme that is, I turne to hearty and earnest prayer to God, and I fix my thoughts strongly (as I thinke) upon him, and before I have perfected one petition, one period of my prayer, a power and principality is got into me againe. *Spiritus soporis*, The spirit of slumber Esay 29.10. closes mine eyes, and I pray drousily; Or *spiritus* Esa. 19. 14. *vertiginis*, the spirit of deviation, and vaine repetition, and I pray giddily, and circularly, and returne againe and againe to that I have said before, and perceive not that I do so; and *nescio cujus spiritus sim*, (as our Saviour Luk. 9. 55. said, rebuking his Disciples, who were so vehement for the burning of the Samaritans, *you know not of what spirit you are*) I pray, and know not of what spirit I am, I consider not mine own purpose in prayer; And by this advantage, this doore of inconsideration, enters *spiritus erroris*, The seducing spirit, the spirit of error, 1 Tim. 4. 1. and I pray not onely negligently, but erroniously, dangerously, for such things as disconduce to the glory of God, and my true happinesse, if they were granted.

Hosea 4.12. Nay, even the Prophet *Hosea's spiritus fornicationum*,
5. 4. enters into me, *The spirit of fornication*, that is, some
remembrance of the wantonnesse of my youth, some
mis-interpretation of a word in my prayer, that may
beare an ill sense, some unclean spirit, some power or
principality hath depraved my prayer, and slackned my
zeale.

6. *Infecting God.*

AS S. *Chrysostome* sayes, every man is *Spontaneus
Satan*, a Satan to himselfe, as Satan is a
Tempter, every man can tempt himselfe ; so I will be
Spontaneus Satan, as Satan is an Accuser, an Adversary,
I will accuse my selfe. I consider often that passionate
Luk. 5. 8. humiliation of S. *Peter, Exi à me Domine, He fell at Iesus
knees, saying, Depart from me, for I am a sinfull man,
O Lord* ; And I am often ready to say so, and more ;
Depart from me, O Lord, for I am sinfull inough to
infect thee ; As I may persecute thee in thy Children,
so I may infect thee in thine Ordinances ; Depart, in
withdrawing thy word from me, for I am corrupt inough
to make even thy saving Gospel, the savor of death
unto death ; Depart, in withholding thy Sacrament,
for I am leprous inough to taint thy flesh, and to make
the balme of thy blood, poyson to my soule ; Depart,
in withdrawing the protection of thine Angels from me,
for I am vicious inough to imprint corruption and
rebellion into their nature. And if I be too foule for
God himselfe to come neare me, for his Ordinances to
worke upon me, I am no companion for my selfe, I must

not be alone with my selfe; for I am as apt to take, as to give infection; I am a reciprocall plague; passively and actively contagious; I breath corruption, and breath it upon my selfe; and I am the Babylon that I must goe out of, or I perish.

7. *Forgiveness of Sins.*

SO the Spirit of God moves upon the face of these waters, the Spirit of life upon the danger of death. Consider the love, more then love, the study, more then study, the diligence of God, he devises meanes, that his banished, those whom sins, or death had banished, be not expelled from him. I sinned upon the strength of my youth, and God devised a meanes to reclaime me, an enfeebling sicknesse. I relapsed after my recovery, and God devised a meanes, an irrecoverable, a helpless Consumption to reclaime me; That affliction grew heavy upon me, and weighed me down even to a diffidence in Gods mercy, and God devised a meanes, the comfort of the Angel of his Church, his Minister, The comfort of the Angel of the great Counsell, the body and blood of his Son Christ Jesus, at my transmigration. Yet he lets his correction proceed to death; I doe dye of that sicknesse, and God devises a meanes, that I, though banished, banished into the grave, shall not be expelled from him, a glorious Resurrection.

8. *Forgive my Sins.*

FORGIVE me O *Lord*, O *Lord* forgive me my sinnes, the sinnes of my youth, and my present sinnes, the sinne that my Parents cast upon me, Originall sinne, and the sinnes that I cast upon my children, in an ill example ; Actuall sinnes, sinnes which are manifest to all the world, and sinnes which I have so laboured to hide from the world, as that now they are hid from mine own conscience, and mine own memory ; Forgive me my crying sins, and my whispering sins, sins of uncharitable hate, and sinnes of unchaste love, sinnes against *Thee* and *Thee*, against thy Power O Almighty Father, against thy Wisedome, O glorious Sonne, against thy Goodnesse, O blessed Spirit of God ; and sinnes against *Him* and *Him*, against Superiours and Equals, and Inferiours ; and sinnes against *Me* and *Me*, against mine own soul, and against my body, which I have loved better than my soul ; Forgive me *O Lord, O Lord* in the merits of thy *Christ* and my *Jesus*, thine Anointed, and my Saviour ; Forgive me my sinnes, all my sinnes, and I will put *Christ* to no more cost, nor thee to more trouble, for any reprobation or malediction that lay upon me, otherwise then as a sinner. I ask but an application, not an extention of that Benediction, *Blessed are they whose sinnes are forgiven* ; Let me be but so blessed, and I shall envy no mans Blessednesse : say thou to my sad soul, *Sonne be of good comfort, thy sinnes are forgiven thee*, and I shall never trouble thee with Petitions, to take any other Bill off of the fyle, or to reverse any other Decree, by which I should be accurst, before I was created, or condemned by thee, before thou saw'st me as a sinner.

9. *Let Me Wither.*

LET me wither and weare out mine age in a dis-
comfortable, in an unwholesome, in a penurious
prison, and so pay my debts with my bones, and
recompence the wastfulnesse of my youth, with the
beggery of mine age; Let me wither in a spittle under
sharpe, and foule, and infamous diseases, and so recompence the wantonnesse of my youth, with that loathsomnesse in mine age; yet, if God with-draw not his
spirituall blessings, his Grace, his Patience, If I can call
my suffering his Doing, my passion his Action, All this
that is temporall, is but a caterpiller got into one corner
of my garden, but a mill-dew fallen upon one acre of
my Corne; The body of all, the substance of all is safe,
as long as the soule is safe. But when I shall trust
to that, which wee call a good spirit, and God shall
deject, and empoverish, and evacuate that spirit, when I
shall rely upon a morall constancy, and God shall shake,
and enfeeble, and enervate, destroy and demolish that
constancy; when I shall think to refresh my selfe in
the serenity and sweet ayre of a good conscience, and
God shall call up the damps and vapours of hell itselfe,
and spread a cloud of diffidence, and an impenetrable
crust of desperation upon my conscience; when health
shall flie from me, and I shall lay hold upon riches to
succour me, and comfort me in my sicknesse, and riches
shall flie from me, and I shall snatch after favour, and
good opinion, to comfort me in my poverty; when
even this good opinion shall leave me, and calumnies
and misinformations shall prevaile against me; when

I shall need peace, because there is none but thou, O Lord, that should stand for me, and then shall finde, that all the wounds that I have, come from thy hand, all the arrowes that stick in me, from thy quiver ; when I shall see, that because I have given my selfe to my corrupt nature, thou hast changed thine ; and because I am all evill towards thee, therefore thou hast given over being good towards me ; When it comes to this height, that the fever is not in the humors, but in the spirits, that mine enemy is not an imaginary enemy, fortune, nor a transitory enemy, malice in great persons, but a reall, and an irresistible, and an inexorable, and an everlasting enemy, The Lord of Hosts himselfe, The Almighty God himselfe, the Almighty God himselfe onely knowes the waight of this affliction, and except hee put in that *pondus gloriæ*, that exceeding waight of an eternall glory, with his owne hand, into the other scale, we are waighed downe, we are swallowed up, irreparably, irrevocably, irrecoverably, irremediably.

10. *Donne and the Worm.*

IF my soule could aske one of those *Wormes* which my dead body shall produce, Will you change with me ? that worme would say, No ; for you are like to live eternally in torment ; for my part, I can live no longer, then the putrid moisture of your body will give me leave, and therefore I will not change ; nay, would the *Devill* himselfe change with a damned soule ? I cannot tell.

11. *Preaching Consolation.*

WHO but my selfe can conceive the sweetnesse
of that salutation, when the Spirit of God
sayes to me in a morning, Go forth to day and preach,
and preach consolation, preach peace, preach mercy,
And spare my people, spare that people whom I have
redeemed with my precious Blood, and be not angry
with them for ever; Do not wound them, doe not
grinde them, do not astonish them with the bitternesse,
with the heavinesse, with the sharpnesse, with the
consternation of my judgements. *David* proposes to
himselfe, that he would *Sing of mercy, and of judgement* ; Psal. 101.1.
but it is of mercy first ; and not of judgement at all,
otherwise then it will come into a song, as joy and
consolation is compatible with it. It hath falne into
disputation, and admitted argument, whether ever God
inflicted punishments by his good Angels ; But that
the good Angels, the ministeriall Angels of the Church,
are properly his instruments, for conveying mercy,
peace, consolation, never fell into question, never
admitted opposition. . . .

What a Coronation is our taking of Orders, by which
God makes us a Royall Priesthood ? And what an
inthronization is the comming up into a Pulpit, where
God invests his servants with his Ordinance, as with
a Cloud, and then presses that Cloud with a *Væ si non*,
woe be unto thee, if thou doe not preach, and then
enables him to preach peace, mercy, consolation, to the
whole Congregation. That God should appeare in
a Cloud, upon the Mercy Seat, as he promises *Moses* Levit. 16.2.

he will doe, That from so poore a man as stands here,
wrapped up in clouds of infirmity, and in clouds of
iniquity, God should drop, raine, poure downe his dew,
and sweeten that dew with his honey, and crust that
honied dew into Manna, and multiply that Manna into
Gomers, and fill those Gomers every day, and give every
particular man his Gomer, give every soule in the Congregation, consolation by me; That when I call to God
for grace here, God should give me grace for grace,
Grace in a power to derive grace upon others, and that
this Oyle, this Balsamum should flow to the hem of
the garment, even upon them that stand under me;
That when mine eyes looke up to Heaven, the eyes of
all should looke up upon me, and God should open my
mouth, to give them meat in due season; That I should
not onely be able to say, as Christ said to that poore
soule, *Confide fili*, My son be of good comfort, but
Fratres & Patres mei, My Brethren, and my Fathers,
nay *Domini mei*, and *Rex meus*, My Lords, and my King
be of good comfort, your sins are forgiven you; That
God should seale to me that Patent, *Ite prædicate omni
Creaturæ*, *Goe and preach the Gospell to every Creature*,
be that creature what he will, That if God lead me into
a Congregation, as into his Arke, where there are but
eight soules, but a few disposed to a sense of his mercies,
and all the rest (as in the Arke) ignobler creatures, and of
brutall natures and affections, That if I finde a licentious
Goat, a supplanting Fox, an usurious Wolfe, an ambitious
Lion, yet to that creature, to every creature I should
preach the Gospel of peace and consolation, and offer
these creatures a Metamorphosis, a transformation,

a new Creation in Christ Jesus, and thereby make my
Goat, and my Fox, and my Wolfe, and my Lion, to
become *Semen Dei*, The seed of God, and *Filium Dei*,
The child of God, and *Participem Divinæ Naturæ*,
Partaker of the Divine Nature it selfe; This is that which
Christ is essentially in himselfe, This is that which
ministerially and instrumentally he hath committed to
me, to shed his consolation upon you, upon you all;
Not as his Almoner to drop his consolation upon one
soule, nor as his Treasurer to issue his consolation to
a whole Congregation, but as his Ophir, as his Indies,
to derive his gold, his precious consolation upon the King
himselfe.

12. *The Beauty of the Soul.*

*I*NSANIEBAT *amatoriam insaniam Paulus*, S. *Paul* Theophil.
was mad for love; S. *Paul* did, and we doe take
into our contemplation, the beauty of a Christian soul;
Through the ragged apparell of the afflictions of this
life; through the scarres, and wounds, and palenesse,
and morphews of sin, and corruption, we can look upon
the soul it self, and there see that incorruptible beauty,
that *white* and *red*, which the *innocency* and the *blood*
of Christ hath given it, and we are mad for love of this
soul, and ready to doe any act of danger, in the ways of
persecution, any act of diminution of our selves in the
ways of humiliation, to *stand at her doore*, and *pray*, and
begge, that *she would be reconciled to God.*

13. *Spiritual Liberality.*

AS an *Hezekias,* a *Iosias* is a Type of Christ, but yet but a Type of Christ; so this civill Liberality, which we have hitherto spoken of, is a Type, but yet but a Type of our spirituall Liberality. For, here we doe not onely change termes, the temporall, to spirituall, and to call that, which we called Liberality in the former part, Charity in this part; nor do we onely make the difference in the proportion & measure, that that which was a Benefit in the other part, should be an Almes in this. But we invest the whole consideration in a meere spirituall nature; and so that Liberality, which was, in the former acceptation, but a relieving, but a refreshing, but a repairing of defects, and dilapidations in the body or fortune, is now, in this second part, in this spirituall acceptation, the raising of a dejected spirit, the redintegration of a broken heart, the resuscitation of a buried soule, the re-consolidation of a scattered conscience, not with the glues, and cements of this world, mirth, and musique, and comedies, and conversation, and wine, and women, (miserable comforters are they all) nor with that Meteor, that hangs betweene two worlds, that is, Philosophy, and morall constancy, (which is somewhat above the carnall man, but yet far below the man truly Christian and religious) But this is the Liberality, of which the Holy Ghost himselfe is content to be the Steward, of the holy, blessed, and glorious Trinity, and to be notified, and qualified by that distinctive notion, and specification, *The Comforter.*

To finde a languishing wretch in a sordid corner, not

onely in a penurious fortune, but in an oppressed conscience, His eyes under a diverse suffocation, smothered
with smoake, and smothered with teares, His eares
estranged from all salutations, and visits, and all sounds, but
his owne sighes, and the stormes and thunders and earth-
quakes of his owne despaire, To enable this man to open
his eyes, and see that Christ Jesus stands before him,
and sayes, *Behold and see, if ever there were any sorrow, like
my sorrow*, and my sorrow is overcome, why is not thine ?
To open this mans eares, and make him heare that voyce
that sayes, *I was dead, and am alive, and behold, I live* Revel.1.18.
for evermore, Amen ; and so mayest thou ; To bow downe
those Heavens, and bring them into his sad Chamber,
To set Christ Jesus before him, to out-sigh him, out-weepe
him, out-bleed him, out-dye him, To transferre all the
fasts, all the scornes, all the scourges, all the nailes, all
the speares of Christ Jesus upon him, and so, making him
the Crucified man in the sight of the Father, because
all the actions, and passions of the Son, are appropriated
to him, and made his so intirely, as if there were never
a soule created but his, To enrich this poore soule, to
comfort this sad soule so, as that he shall beleeve, and by
beleeving finde all Christ to be his, this is that Liberality
which we speake of now, in dispensing whereof, *The
liberall man deviseth liberall things, and by liberall things
shall stand.*

14. *Eagle's Wings.*

FOR as those words are well understood by many of
the Ancients, *To the Woman were given two wings* Revel. 12.
of an Eagle, that is, to the Church were given able and 14.

sufficient Ministers, to carry and convey her over the Nations : So are those words which are spoken of God Deut. 32. 11. himself, appliable to his Ministers, that first, *The Eagle stirreth up her nest,* The Preacher stirres and moves, and agitates the holy affections of the Congregation, that they slumber not in a senselesnesse of that which is said, *The Eagle stirreth up her nest,* and then as it is added there, *She fluttereth over her young* ; The Preacher makes a holy noise in the conscience of the Congregation, and when hee hath awakened them, by stirring the nest, hee casts some claps of thunder, some intimidations, in denouncing the judgements of God, and he flings open the gates of Heaven, that they may heare, and look up, and see a man sent by God, with power to infuse his feare upon them ; *So she fluttereth over her young* ; but then, as it followes there, *She spreadeth abroad her wings* ; she over-shadowes them, she enwraps them, she armes them with her wings, so as that no other terror, no other fluttering but that which comes from her, can come upon them ; The Preacher doth so infuse the feare of God into his Auditory, that first, they shall feare nothing but God, and then they shall feare God, but so, as he is God ; And God is Mercy ; God is Love ; and his Minister shall so spread his wings over his people, as to defend them from all inordinate feare, from all suspition and jealousie, from all diffidence and distrust in the mercie of God ; which is farther exprest in that clause, which followes in the same place, *She taketh them and beareth them upon her wings* ; when the Minister hath awakened his flocke by the stirring of the nest, and put them in this holy feare, by this which the Holy Ghost cals a

Fluttering ; and then provided, by spreading his wings, that upon this feare there follow not a desperation ; then he sets them upon the top of his best wings, and shewes them the best treasure that is committed to his Steward-ship, hee shewes them Heaven, and God in Heaven, sanctifying all their crosses in this World, inanimating all their worldly blessings, rayning downe his blood into their emptinesse, and his balme into their wounds, making their bed in all their sicknesse, and preparing their seate, where he stands soliciting their cause, at the right hand of his Father. And so the Minister hath the wings of an Eagle, that every soule in the Congregation may see as much as hee sees, that is, a particular interest in all the mercies of God, and the merits of Christ.

15. *The Hour-Glass.*

I HAVE seen Minute-glasses ; Glasses so short-liv'd. If I were to preach upon this Text, to such a glass, it were enough for half the Sermon ; enough to show the worldly man his Treasure, and the Object of his heart (*for, where your Treasure is, there will your Heart be also*) to call his eye to that Minute-glass, and to tell him, There flows, there flies your Treasure, and your Heart with it. But if I had a Secular Glass, a Glass that would run an age ; if the two Hemispheres of the World were composed in the form of such a Glass, and all the World calcin'd and burnt to ashes, and all the ashes, and sands, and atoms of the World put into that Glass, it would not be enough to tell the godly man what his Treasure, and the Object of his Heart is. A Parrot, or a Stare, docile Birds, and of pregnant imitation, will sooner be brought to relate to us the wisdom of a Council Table, then any *Ambrose*, or any *Chrysostome* men that have Gold and Honey in their Names, shall tell us what the Sweetness, what the Treasure of Heaven is, and what that mans peace, that hath set his Heart upon that Treasure.

16. *Preaching.*

*In concl-
onibus.
1 Cor. 1. 21.*

BECAUSE God cals *Preaching foolishnesse*, you take God at his word, and you thinke Preaching a thing under you. Hence is it, that you take so much liberty in censuring and comparing Preacher and Preacher, nay Sermon and Sermon from the same Preacher ; as though we preached for wagers, and as though coine were to be valued from the inscription meerely, and the image, and the person, and not for the metall. You measure all by persons ; and yet, *Non erubescitis faciem Sacerdotis,* *You respect not the person of the Priest*, you give not so much reverence to Gods Ordinance, as he does. In no Church of Christendome but ours, doth the Preacher preach uncovered. And for all this good, and humble, and reverend example, (fit to be continued by us) cannot we keepe you uncovered till the Text be read. All the Sermon is not Gods word, but all the Sermon is Gods Ordinance, and the Text is certainely his word. There is no salvation but by faith, nor faith but by hearing, nor hearing but by preaching ; and they that thinke meanliest of the Keyes of the Church, and speake faintliest of the Absolution of the Church, will yet allow, That those Keyes lock, and unlock in Preaching ; That Absolution is conferred, or withheld in Preaching, That the proposing

Lam. 4 16.

of the promises of the Gospel in preaching, is that binding
and loosing on earth, which bindes and looses in heaven.
And then, though Christ have bid us, *Preach the Gospel* Mar. 16. 15.
to every creature, yet, in his own great Sermon in the
Mount, he hath forbidden us, *to give holy things to dogs,* Mat. 7. 6.
*or to cast pearle before swine, lest they trample them, and
turne and rend us.* So that if all those manifold and fearfull
judgements, which swell in every Chapter, and blow
in every verse, and thunder in every line of every Booke
of the Bible, fall upon all them that come hither, as well,
if they turne, and rend, that is, Calumniate us, the person
of the Preacher, as if they trample upon the pearles,
that is, undervalue the Doctrine, and the Ordinance it
selfe; If his terrible Judgements fall upon every uncharitable mis-interpretation of that which is said here, and
upon every irreverence in this place, and in this action;
Confesse, that though he be *the God of your salvation,* and
doe *answer you,* yet, *by terrible things doth the God of your
salvation answer you.* And confesse it also, as in manners,
and in prayers, and in preaching, so in the holy and blessed
Sacrament.

17. *Applause.*

*S*IDONIUS APOLLINARIS, (a Bishop himselfe,
but whether *then* or no, I know not) saith of another
Bishop, that hearing even *prædicationes repentinas,* his
extemporall Sermons, *raucus plausor audivi,* I poured
my selfe out in loud acclamations, till I was hoarse :
And, to contract this consideration, wee see evidently,
that this fashion continued in the Church, even to Saint
Bernards time. Neither is it left yet in some places,

beyond the Seas, where the people doe yet answer the Preacher, if his questions be applyable to them, and may induce an answer, with these vocall acclamations, *Sir, we will, Sir, we will not.* And truely wee come too neare re-inducing this vain glorious fashion, in those often periodicall murmurings, and noises, which you make, when the Preacher concludeth any point ; for those impertinent Interjections swallow up one quarter of his houre, and many that were not within distance of hearing the Sermon, will give a censure upon it, according to the frequencie, or paucitie of these acclamations.

18. *The Bellman.*

HE that will dy with Christ upon Good-Friday, must hear his own bell toll all Lent ; he that will be partaker of his passion at last, must conform himself to his discipline of prayer & fasting before. Is there any man, that in his chamber hears a bell toll for another man, and does not kneel down to pray for that dying man ? and then when his charity breaths out upon another man, does he not also reflect upon himself, and dispose himself as if he were in the state of that dying man ? We begin to hear Christs bell toll now, and is not our bell in the chime ? We must be in his grave, before we come to his resurrection, and we must be in his death-bed before we come to his grave : we must do as he did, fast and pray, before we can say as he said, that *In manus tuas*, Into thy hands O Lord I commend my Spirit. You would not go into a Medicinal Bath without some pre-paratives ; presume not upon that Bath, the blood of Christ Jesus, in the Sacrament then, without preparatives neither. Neither say to your selves, we shall have preparatives enough, warnings enough, many more Sermons before it come to that, and so it is too soon yet ; you are not sure you shall have more ; not sure you shall have all this ; not sure you shall be affected with any. If you be, when you are, remember that as in that good Custome in these Cities, you hear cheerful street musick in the winter mornings, but yet there was a sad and doleful bel-man, that wak'd you, and call'd upon you two or three hours before that musick came ; so for all that blessed musick which the servants of God shall present to you in this place, it may be of use, that a poor bell-man waked you before, and though but by his noise, prepared you for their musick.

19. *Favourite Scriptures.*

ALMOST every man hath his *Appetite*, and his *tast* disposed to some kind of *meates* rather then others ; He knows what dish he would choose, for his first, and for his second course. We have often the same disposition in our *spirituall Diet* ; a man may have a particular love towards such or such a book of Scripture, and in such an affection, I acknowledge, that my spirituall appetite carries me still, upon the *Psalms of David*, for a first course, for the Scriptures of the Old Testament : and upon the *Epistles of Saint Paul*, for a second course, for the New, and my meditations even for these *publike exercises* to Gods Church, returne oftnest to these two. For, as a hearty entertainer offers to others, the meat which he loves best himself, so doe I oftnest present to Gods people, in these Congregations, the meditations

which I feed upon at home, in those two Scriptures.
If a man be asked a reason why he loves one meat better
then another, where all are equally good, (as the books
of Scripture are) he will at least, finde a reason in some
good example, that he sees some man of good tast, and
temperate withall, so do : And for my Diet, I have Saint
Augustines protestation, that he loved the *Book of Psalms*,
and Saint *Chrysostomes*, that he loved Saint *Pauls Epistles*,
with a particular devotion. I may have another more
particular reason, because they are Scriptures, written
in such forms, as I have been most accustomed to ;
Saint *Pauls* being Letters, and *Davids* being Poems : for,
God gives us, not onely that which is meerly necessary, but that which is convenient too ; He does not
onely feed us, but *feed us with marrow, and with fatnesse* ;
he gives us our instruction in cheerfull forms, not in
a sowre, and sullen, and angry, and unacceptable way,
but cheerfully, in *Psalms*, which is also a limited, and
a restrained form ; Not in an *Oration*, not in *Prose*, but in
Psalms ; which is such a form as is both curious, and
requires diligence in the making, and then when it is
made, can have nothing, no syllable taken from it, nor
added to it : Therefore is Gods will delivered to us in
Psalms, that we might have it the more cheerfully, and
that we might have it the more certainly, because where
all the words are numbred, and measured, and weighed,
the whole work is the lesse subject to falsification, either
by substraction or addition. God speaks to us *in oratione
strictâ,* in a limited, in a diligent form ; Let us ⟨not⟩ speak
to him *in oratione solutâ* ; not *pray*, not *preach*, not *hear*,
slackly, suddenly, unadvisedly, extemporally, occasionally,

indiligently ; but let all our speech to him, be weighed, and measured in the weights of the *Sanctuary*, let us be content to preach, and to hear within the compasse of our Articles, and content to pray in those *formes* which the Church hath meditated for us, and recommended to us.

20. *The Psalms.*

THE Psalmes are the Manna of the Church.   As Manna tasted to every man like that that he liked best, so doe the Psalmes minister Instruction, and satisfaction, to every man, in every emergency and occasion. *David* was not onely a cleare Prophet of Christ himselfe, but a Prophet of every particular Christian ; He foretels what I, what any shall doe, and suffer, and say.   And as the whole booke of Psalmes is *Oleum effusum*, (as the Spouse speaks of the name of Christ) an Oyntment powred out upon all sorts of sores, A Searcloth that souples all bruises, A Balme that searches all wounds ; so are there some certaine Psalmes, that are Imperiall Psalmes, that command over all affections, and spread themselves over all occasions, Catholique, universall Psalmes, that apply themselves to all necessities.   This is one of those ; for, of those Constitutions which are called Apostolicall, one is, That the Church should meet every day, to sing this Psalme.   And accordingly, S. *Chrysostome* testifies, That it was decreed, and ordained by the Primitive Fathers, that no day should passe without the publique singing of this Psalme.   Under both these obligations, (those ancient Constitutions, called the Apostles, and those ancient Decrees made by

Marginal notes: Wisd. 16. 20. — Cant. 1. 3. — Constitut. Apostol. — Chrysost.

the primitive Fathers) belongs to me, who have my part
in the service of Gods Church, the especiall meditation,
and recommendation of this Psalme. And under a third
obligation too, That it is one of those five psalmes, the
daily rehearsing whereof, is injoyned to me, by the
Constitutions of this Church, as five other are to every
other person of our body. As the whole booke is Manna,
so these five Psalmes are my Gomer, which I am to fill
and empty every day of this Manna.

21. *Sanctified Passions.*

AS the Prophets, and the other Secretaries of the
holy Ghost in penning the books of Scriptures,
do for the most part retain, and express in their writings
some impressions, and some air of their former professions ;
those that had been bred in Courts and Cities, those
that had been Shepheards and Heardsmen, those that
had been Fishers, and so of the rest ; ever inserting
into their writings some phrases, some metaphors, some
allusions, taken from that profession which they had
exercised before ; so that soul, that hath been transported
upon any particular worldly pleasure, when it is entirely
turn'd upon God, and the contemplation of his all-
sufficiency and abundance, doth find in God fit subject,
and just occasion to exercise the same affection piously,
and religiously, which had before so sinfully transported,
and possesst it.

A covetous person, who is now truly converted to God,
he will exercise a spiritual covetousness still, he will
desire to have him all, he will have good security, the
seal and assurance of the holy Ghost ; and he will have

his security often renewed by new testimonies, and
increases of those graces in him ; he will have witnesses
enough ; he will have the testimonie of all the world,
by his good life and conversation ; he will gain every
way at Gods hand, he will have wages of God, for he will
be his servant ; he will have a portion from God, for he
will be his Son ; he will have a reversion, he will be sure
that his name is in the book of life ; he will have pawns,
the seals of the Sacraments, nay, he will have a present
possession ; all that God hath promised, all that Christ
hath purchased, all that the Holy Ghost hath the steward-
ship and dispensation of, he will have all in present, by
the appropriation and investiture of an actual and
applying faith ; a covetous person converted will be
spiritually covetous still.

So will a voluptuous man, who is turned to God,
find plenty and deliciousnes enough in him, to feed his
soul, as with marrow, and with fatness, as *David* expresses
it ; and so an angry and passionate man, will find zeal
enough in the house of God to eat him up.

All affections which are common to all men, and those
to which in particular, particular men have been addicted
to, shall not only be justly employed upon God, but also
securely employed, because we cannot exceed, nor go
too far in imploying them upon him. According to this
Rule, St. *Paul*, who had been so vehement a persecutor,
had ever his thoughts exercised upon that ; and thereupon
after his conversion, he fulfils the rest of the sufferings
of Christ in his flesh, he suffers most, he makes most Col. 1. 24.
mention of his suffering of any of the Apostles.

And according to this Rule too, *Solomon*, whose

disposition was amorous, and excessive in the love of women, when he turn'd to God, he departed not utterly from his old phrase and language, but having put a new, and a spiritual tincture, and form and habit in all his thoughts, and words, he conveys all his loving approaches and applications to God, and all Gods gracious answers to his amorous soul, into songs, and Epithalamians, and meditations upon contracts, and marriages between God and his Church, and between God and his soul; as we see so evidently in all his other writings, and particularly in this text, *I love them,* &c.

In which words is expressed all that belongs to love, all which, is to desire, and to enjoy; for to desire without fruition, is a rage, and to enjoy without desire is a stupidity: In the first alone we think of nothing, but that which we then would have; and in the second alone, we are not for that, when we have it; in the first, we are without it; in the second, we were as good as we were, for we have no pleasure in it; nothing then can give us satisfaction, but when those two concurr, *amare* and *frui,* to love and to enjoy.

22. *Style and Language.*

THE Holy Ghost in penning the Scriptures delights himself, not only with a propriety, but with a delicacy, and harmony, and melody of language; with height of Metaphors, and other figures, which may work greater impressions upon the Readers, and not with barbarous, or triviall, or market, or homely language: It is true, that when the Grecians, and the Romanes, and S. *Augustine* himselfe, undervalued and despised the

Scriptures, because of the poore and beggerly phrase, that they seemed to be written in, the Christians could say little against it, but turned still upon the other safer way, wee consider the matter, and not the phrase, because for the most part, they had read the Scriptures only in Translations, which could not maintaine the Majesty, nor preserve the elegancies of the Originall.

Their case was somewhat like ours, at the beginning of the Reformation ; when, because most of those men who laboured in that Reformation, came out of the Romane Church, and there had never read the body of the Fathers at large ; but only such ragges and fragments of those Fathers, as were patcht together in their Decretat's, and Decretals, and other such Common placers, for their purpose, and to serve their turne, therefore they were loath at first to come to that issue, to try controversies by the Fathers. But as soon as our men that imbraced the Reformation, had had time to reade the Fathers, they were ready enough to joyne with the Adversary in that issue : and still we protest, that we accept that evidence, the testimony of the Fathers, and refuse nothing, which the Fathers unanimly delivered, for matter of faith ; and howsoever at the beginning some men were a little ombrageous, and startling at the name of the Fathers, yet since the Fathers have been well studied, for more then threescore yeares, we have behaved our selves with more reverence towards the Fathers, and more confidence in the Fathers, then they of the Romane perswasion have done, and been lesse apt to suspect or quarrell their Books, or to reprove their Doctrines, then our Adversaries have been. So, howsoever the Christians at first were fain to sink a little under that imputation, that their Scriptures have no Majesty, no eloquence, because these embellishments could not appeare in Translations, nor they then read Originalls, yet now, that a perfect knowledge of those languages hath brought us to see the beauty and the glory of those Books, we are able to reply to them, that there are not in all the world so eloquent Books as the Scriptures; and that nothing is more demonstrable, then that if we would take all those Figures, and Tropes, which are collected out of secular Poets, and Orators, we may give higher, and livelier examples, of every one of those Figures, out of the Scriptures, then out of all the Greek and Latine Poets, and Orators; and they mistake it much, that thinke, that the Holy Ghost hath rather chosen a low, and barbarous, and homely style, then an eloquent, and powerfull manner of expressing himselfe.

23. *Style of the Holy Ghost.*

Exultatio.   THE Holy Ghost is an eloquent Author, a vehement, and an abundant Author, but yet not luxuriant; he is far from a penurious, but as far from a superfluous style too.

24. *Compliments.*

WE have a word now denizened, and brought into familiar use amongst us, Complement; and for the most part, in an ill sense; so it is, when the heart of the speaker doth not answer his tongue; but God forbid but a true heart, and a faire tongue might very well consist together: As vertue it self receives an addition, by being in a faire body, so do good intentions of the heart, by being expressed in faire language. That man aggravates his condemnation, that gives me good words, and meanes ill ; but he gives me a rich Jewell, and in a faire Cabinet, he gives me precious wine, and in a clean glasse, that intends well, and expresses his good intentions well too. If I beleeve a faire speaker, I have comfort a little while, though he deceive me, but a froward and peremptory refuser, unsaddles me at first. I remember a vulgar Spanish Author, who writes, the *Iosephina*, the life of *Ioseph*, the husband of the blessed Virgin *Mary*, who moving that question, why that Virgin is never called by any style of Majesty, or Honour in the Scriptures, he sayes, That if after the declaring of her to be the Mother of God, he had added any other Title, the Holy Ghost had not been a good Courtier, (as his very word is) nor exercised in good language, and he thinks that had been a defect in the Holy Ghost in himself. He meanes surely the same that *Epiphanius* doth, That in naming the Saints of God, and especially the blessed Virgin, we should alwayes give them the best Titles that are applyable to them ; *Quis unquam ausus,* Epiphan. (saies he) *proferre nomen Mariæ, & non statim addidit* Hæres. 78: *virgo ?* Who ever durst utter the name of that *Mary*, without that addition of incomparable honour, *The Virgin Mary ?*

That Spanish Author need not be suspitious of the Holy Ghost in that kinde, that he is no good Courtier so ; for in all the books of the world, you shall never reade so civill language, nor so faire expressions of themselves to one another, as in the Bible : When *Abraham* shall call himself *dust, and ashes,* (and indeed if the Son of

God were *a worme and no man*, what was *Abraham?*)
If God shall call this *Abraham*, this Dust, this Worme
of the dust, *The friend of God*, (and all friendship implyes
a parity, an equality in something;) when *David* shall
call himself *a flea, and a dead dog*, even in respect of *Saul*,
and God shall call *David, A man according to his own
heart*, when God shall call us, *The Apple of his own eye,
The Seale upon his own right hand*, who would go farther
for an Example, or farther then that example for a Rule,
of faire accesses, of civill approaches, of sweet and
honourable entrances into the affections of them with
whom they were to deale?

25. *Lying at Aix.*

LYING at *Aix*, at *Aquisgrane*, a well known Town
in *Germany*, and fixing there some time, for the
benefit of those *Baths*, I found my self in a house, which
was divided into many families, & indeed so large as it
might have been a little Parish, or, at least, a great lim
of a great one; But it was of no Parish: for when
I ask'd who lay over my head, they told me a family of
Anabaptists; And who over theirs? Another family
of *Anabaptists*; and another family of *Anabaptists* over
theirs, and the whole house, was a nest of these boxes;
several artificers; all *Anabaptists*; I ask'd in what room
they met, for the exercise of their Religion; I was told
they never met: for, though they were all *Anabaptists*,
yet for some collaterall differences, they detested one
another, and, though many of them, were near in bloud,
& alliance to one another, yet the son would excommunicate the father, in the room above him, and the Nephew

the Uncle. As S. *John* is said to have quitted that *Bath*, into which *Cerinthus* the Heretique came, so did I this house; I remembred that *Hezekiah* in his sicknesse, turn'd himself in his bed, to pray *towards that wall*, that look'd to *Ierusalem*; And that *Daniel* in *Babylon*, when he pray'd in his chamber, opened those windows that look'd *towards Ierusalem*; for, in the first dedication of the Temple, at *Ierusalem*, there is a promise annext to the prayers made *towards the Temple*: And I began to think, how many roofs, how many floores of separation, were made between God and my prayers in that house. And such is this multiplicity of sins, which we consider to be got over us, as a roof, as an arch, many arches, many roofs: for, though these habituall sins, be so of kin, as that they grow from one another, and yet for all this kindred excommunicate one another, (for covetousnesse will not be in the same roome with prodigality) yet it is but going up another stair, and there's the tother *Anabaptist*; it is but living a few years, and then the prodigall becomes covetous. All the way, they separate us from God, as a roof, as an arch; & then, an arch will bear any weight; An habituall sin got over our head as an arch will stand under any sicknesse, any dishonour, any judgement of God, and never sink towards any humiliation.

26. *Farewell on Going to Germany.*

NOW to make up a circle, by returning to our first word, remember: As we remember God, so for his sake, let us remember one another. In my long absence, and far distance from hence, remember me, as I shall do you in the ears of that God, to whom the farthest East, and the farthest West are but as the right and left ear in one of us; we hear with both at once, and he hears in both at once; remember me, not my abilities; for when I consider my Apostleship that I was sent to you, 1 Cor. 15. 9. I am in St. *Pauls quorum, quorum ego sum minimus,* the least of them that have been sent; and when I consider my infirmities, I am in his *quorum,* in another commission, 1 Tim. 1. 15. another way, *Quorum ego maximus;* the greatest of them; but remember my labors, and endeavors, at least my desire, to make sure your salvation. And I shall remember your religious cheerfulness in hearing the word, and your christianly respect towards all them that bring that word unto you, and towards my self in particular far bove my merit. And so as your eyes that stay here, and mine that must be far of, for all that distance shall meet every morning, in looking upon that same Sun, and meet every night, in looking upon the same Moon; so our hearts may meet morning and evening in that God, which sees and hears every where; that you may come thither to him with your prayers, that I, (if I may be of use for his glory, and your edification in this place) may be restored to you again; and may come to him with my prayer, that what *Paul* soever plant amongst you, or what *Apollos* soever water, God himself will give the increase: That if I never meet you again till we have all passed the gate of death, yet in the gates of heaven, I may meet you all, and there say to my Saviour and your Saviour, that which he said to his Father and our Father, *Of those whom thou hast given me, have I not lost one.* Remember me thus, you that stay in this Kingdome

of peace, where no sword is drawn, but the sword of
Justice, as I shal remember you in those Kingdomes,
where ambition on one side, and a necessary defence
from unjust persecution on the other side hath drawn
many swords ; and Christ Jesus remember us all in his
Kingdome, to which, though we must sail through
a sea, it is the sea of his blood, where no soul suffers
shipwrack ; though we must be blown with strange
winds, with sighs and groans for our sins, yet it is the
Spirit of God that blows all this wind, and shall blow
away all contrary winds of diffidence or distrust in Gods
mercy ; where we shall be all Souldiers of one Army,
the Lord of Hostes, and children of one Quire, the God
of Harmony and consent : where all Clients shall retain
but one Counsellor, our Advocate Christ Jesus, not
present him any other fee but his own blood, and yet
every Client have a Judgment on his side, not only in
a not guilty, in the remission of his sins, but in a *Venite
benedicti*, in being called to the participation of an
immortal Crown of glory : where there shall be no
difference in affection, nor in mind, but we shall agree
as fully & perfectly in our *Allelujah*, and *gloria in
excelcis*, as God the Father, Son, and Holy Ghost agreed
in the *faciamus hominem* at first ; where we shall end,
and yet begin but then ; where we shall have continual
rest, and yet never grow lazie ; where we shall be stronger
to resist, and yet have no enemy ; where we shall live
and never die, where we shall meet & never part.

27. *The Vicar of St. Dunstan's.*

NOW in a Matrimoniall state, there is *Onus* and *Honos*, a burden to be born, an *Honour* to be received. The burden of the sinnes of the *whole world*, was a burden onely for *Christs* shoulders ; but the sinnes of *this Parish*, will ly upon my shoulders, if I be *silent*, or if I be *indulgent*, and denounce not Gods Judgement upon those sinnes. It will be a burden to us, if we doe not, and God knowes it is a burden to us, when we do denounce those Judgements. *Esay* felt, and groned under this burden, when he cried *Onus Babylonis, Onus Moab,* and *Onus Damasci, O the burden of Babylon,* and the *burden of Damascus,* and so the other Prophets grone often under this burden, in contemplation of other places : It burdened, it troubled, it grieved the holy Prophets of God, that they must denounce Gods judgements, though upon Gods enemies. We reade of a compassionate *Generall,* that looking upon his great Army, from a hill, fell into a bitter weeping, upon this consideration, that in fiftie or sixtie yeares hence, there will not be a man of these that fight now, alive upon the earth. What Sea could furnish mine eyes with teares enough, to poure out, if I should think, that of all this Congregation, which lookes me in the face now, I should not meet one, at the Resurrection, at the right hand of God ! And for so much as concerns me, it is all one, if none of you be saved, as if none of you be saved by *my help,* my means, my assistance, my preaching. If I put you upon miraculous wayes, to be saved without hearing, or upon extraordinary wayes to be saved by *hearing others,* this

shall aggravate my condemnation, though you be saved :
How much more heavy must my burden be, if by my
negligence both I and you perish too ? So then this
calling, this marriage, is a burden every way. When at
any midnight I heare a bell toll from this steeple, must
not I say to my selfe, what have I done at any time for
the instructing or rectifying of that mans Conscience,
who lieth there now ready to deliver up his own account,
and my account to Almighty God ? If he be not able
to make a good account, he and I are in danger, because
I have not enabled him ; and though he be for himself
able, that delivers not me, if I have been no instrument
for the doing of it. Many, many burdens lie upon this
calling, upon this marriage ; but our *recompense* is, that
marriage is as well an honourable as a painefull calling.

28. *Funeral Sermon on Magdalen Herbert,*
Lady Danvers, 1627.

I PROPOSE to my selfe, and to this Congregation,
two Workes for this day ; That wee may walke
together two miles, in this Sabbath daies journey ; First,
To instruct the Living, and then *To commemorate the Dead.*
Which office, as I ought, so I should have performed
sooner, but that this sad occasion surprized me under
other *Pre-obligations* and *Pre-contracts,* in the services
of mine own Profession, which could not be excused,
nor avoided. And being come now to this double worke,
whether I looke up to the *Throne of Heaven,* and that
Firmament, for my first worke, *The Instruction of the
Living,* or downe to the *stones* of the *Grave,* and that

pavement, for my second worke, *The commemoration of the Dead,* I need no other words than these which I have read to you, for both purposes ; For, to assist the Resurrection of your soules, I say, And to assure the Resurrection of your bodies, she saies, *Neverthelesse, we according to his promise looke for new Heavens, and new Earth, wherein dwelleth Righteousnesse. . . .*

Close we here this *Booke of life,* from which we have had our *first Text,* And, *Surge, quæ dormis in pulvere,* Arise, thou *Booke of Death* ; thou, that sleepest in this *consecrated dust,* and hast beene going into *dust,* now, almost a *Moneth* of *dayes,* almost a Lunarie *yeere,* and dost deserve such *Anniversaries,* such quick returnes of *Periods,* and a *Commemoration,* in every *such yeere,* in every *Moneth* ; Arise thou, and bee another *Commentary* to us ; and tell us, what this *new Heaven,* and *new Earth* is, in which, now, thou *dwel'st,* with that *Righteousnesse.* But wee doe not invoke thee, as thou art a *Saint in Heaven* ; Appeare to us, as thou didst appeare to us a moneth agoe ; At least, appeare in thy *history* ; appeare in our *memory* ; that when every one of us have lookt upon thee, by his owne *glasse,* and seene thee in his owne *Interest,* such, as thou wast to him, That when *one* shall have seene thee, the *best wife,* And a larger number, the *best mother,* And more then they, a whole *Towne,* the best *Neighbour,* and more then a *Towne,* a large body of noble friends, the *best Friend,* And more than all they, *all the world,* the *best example,* when thou hast receiv'd this Testimony from the *Militant Church,* as thou hast the recompence of all this, in thy Blessed Soule, in the *Triumphant,* yet, because thy *body* is still within these Walls, bee still content, to bee one of this Congregation, and to heare some parts of this *Text* re-applied unto thee.

Our first word, *Neverthelesse,* puts us first upon this consideration, That she liv'd in a time, wherein this *Prophecie* of Saint *Peter,* in this *Chapter,* was over-abundantly perform'd, That there should bee *scoffers, jesters* in divine things, and matters appertaining to *God,* and his *Religion.* For, now, in these our dayes, excellency of *Wit,* lies in *prophanenesse ;* he is the *good Spirit,* that dares abuse *God ;* And hee *good company,* that makes his company the worse, or keepes them from goodnesse. This being the Aire, and the Complexion of the *Wit* of her Times, and her inclination, and conversation, naturally, cheerfull, and merry, and loving facetiousnesse, and sharpnesse of wit, *Neverthelesse,* who ever saw her, who ever heard her countenance a *prophane speech,* how sharpe soever, or take part with *wit,* to the prejudice of *Godlinesse ?* From this I testify her *holy cheerfulnesse,* and *Religious alacrity,* (one of the best *evidences* of a *good conscience*) That as shee came to this place, *God's house of Prayer,* duly, not onely every *Sabbath,* when it is the house of other exercises, as well as of *Prayer,* but even in those *weeke-dayes,* when it was onely a house of *Prayer,* as often as these doores were open for a *holy Convocation,* And, as she ever hastned her *family* and her *company* hither, with that cheerfull provocation : *For God's sake let's go, for God's sake let's bee there at the Confession* : So her selfe, with her whole family, (as a *Church* in that *elect* Ladie's house, to whom *John* writ the second *Epistle*) did, every Sabbath, shut up the day, at night, with a generall, with a cheerfull *singing of Psalmes ;* This *Act of cheerful-*

nesse, was still the last *Act* of that family, united in it selfe, and with *God*. *God loves a cheerfull* giver; Much more, a cheerfull giver of himselfe. Truly, he that can close his eyes, in a holy cheerfulnesse, every night, shall meet no distemper'd, no inordinate, no irregular sadnesse, then, when *God*, by the hand of *Death*, shall close his eyes, at last.

But, returne we againe to our *Neverthelesse*; You may remember, that this word in our former part, put us first upon the consideration of *Scoffers* at the *day of judgement*, and then, upon the consideration of *Terrours*, and sad *Apprehensions* at that *day*. And for her, some sicknesses, in the declination of her yeeres, had opened her to an overflowing of *Melancholie*; Not that she ever lay under that *water*, but yet, had sometimes, some high Tides of it; and, though this distemper would sometimes cast a cloud, and some halfe damps upon her naturall cheerfulnesse, and sociablenesse, and sometimes induce darke and sad apprehensions, *Neverthelesse*, who ever heard, or saw in her, any such effect of *Melancholy* as to murmure, or repine, or dispute upon any of *Gods* proceedings, or to lodge a Jealousie, or Suspition of his mercy, and goodnesse towards her, and all hers? The *Wit* of our time is *Prophanenesse*; *Neverthelesse*, shee, that lov'd *that*, hated *this*; Occasionall *Melancholy* had taken some hold in her, *Neverthelesse*, that never Ecclipst, never interrupted her cheerfull confidence, & assurance in *God*.

Our second word denotes the *person* : *We*, *Neverthelesse We*; And, here in this consideration, *Neverthelesse shee*. This may seeme to promise some picture, some

Character of her *person*. But shee was no stranger to
them that heare me now; nor scarce to any that may
heare of this hereafter, which you heare now, and therefore, much needes not, to that purpose. Yet, to that
purpose, of her *person*, and *personall circumstances*, thus
much I may *remember* some, and *informe* others, That
from that *Worthy family*, whence shee had her originall
extraction, and birth, she suckt that love of *hospitality*, *
(*hospitality*, which hath celebrated that *family*, in many
Generations, successively) which dwelt in her, to her
end. But in that *ground*, her Fathers family, shee grew
not many yeeres. Transplanted young from thence,
by mariage, into another *family* of *Honour*, as a flower †
that doubles and multiplies by transplantation, she
multiplied into *ten Children*, *Job's* number; and *Job's*
distribution, (as shee, her selfe would very often remember) *seven sonnes*, and *three daughters*. And, in this
ground, shee grew not many yeeres more, then were
necessary, for the producing of so many plants. And
being then left to chuse her own ground in her *Widow-
hood*, having at home establisht, and increast the estate,
with a faire, & noble Addition, proposing to her selfe,
as her principall care, the education of her *children*, to
advance that, shee came with them, and dwelt with
them in the *Universitie*; and recompenc't to them, the
losse of a *Father*, in giving them *two mothers*; her owne

* Daughter of Sir Rich., sister of Sir Fran., Aunt of Sir Richard
Neuport, of Arcol.

† Rich. Herbert, *of Blachehall*, *in* Montgomery *Esqu. lineally
descended from that great Sir* Rich. Herbert in Ed. 4. *time, and father
of* Ed. Lord Herbert *Baron of* Castle-Island, *late Embassador in* France,
and now of his majesties Councel of Warre.

personall care, and the advantage of that place ; where shee contracted a friendship, with divers reverend persons, of eminency, and estimation there ; which continued to their ends. And as this was her greatest *businesse*, so she made this state, a large *Period* ; for in this state of *widowhood*, shee continued twelve yeeres. And then, returning to a *second marriage*, that *second marriage* turnes us to the consideration of another *personall circumstance* ; that is, the *naturall endowments of her person* ; Which were such, as that, (though her *virtues* were his principall *object*) yet, even these, her *personall*, and *naturall*, endowments, had their part, in drawing, and fixing the affections of such a person, as by his *birth*, and *youth*, and *interest in great favours in Court*, and *legall proximity* to great possessions in the world, might justly have promist him acceptance, in what *family* soever, or upon what *person* soever, hee had directed, and plac't his Affections. He plac't them here ; neither *diverted* then, nor *repented* since. For, as the well tuning of an *Instrument*, makes *higher* and *lower strings*, of one sound, so the inequality of their yeeres, was thus reduc't to an evennesse, that shee had a *cheerfulnesse*, agreeable to his *youth*, and he had a *sober staidnesse*, conformable to her *more yeeres*. So that, I would not consider her, at so much more then *forty*, nor him, at so much lesse than *thirty*, at that time, but, as their *persons* were made *one*, and their *fortunes* made one, by *mariage*, so I would put their *yeeres* into *one number*, and finding a *sixty* betweene them, thinke them *thirty* a peece ; for, as twins of one houre, they liv'd. *God*, who join'd them, then, having also separated them now, may make their *yeres* even, this other way

Sir Iohn
Danvers
onely
brother to
the Earle
of Danby.

too; by giving him, as many yeeres after her going out of this World, as he had given her, before his comming into it; and then, as many more, as *God* may receive *Glory*, and the World, *Benefit*, by that Addition; That so, as at their first meeting, she was, at their last meeting, he may bee the *elder person*.

To this consideration of her *person* then, belongs this, that *God* gave her such a *comelinesse*, as, though shee were not *proud* of it, yet she was so content with it, as not to goe about to mend it, by any *Art*. And for her *Attire*, (which is another *personall circumstance*), it was never *sumptuous*, never *sordid*; But always agreeable to her *quality*, and agreeable to her *company*; Such as shee might, and such, as others, such as shee was, did weare. For in such things of *indifferency* in themselves, many times, a *singularity* may be a little worse, then a fellowship in that, which is not altogether so good. It may be *worse*, nay, it may be a *worse pride*, to weare worse things, than others doe. Her *rule* was *mediocrity*.

And, as to the consideration of the *house*, belongs the consideration of the *furniture* too, so in these *personall circumstances*, we consider her *fortune*, her *estate*. Which was in a faire, and noble proportion, deriv'd from her *first husband*, and fairely, and nobly dispenc'd, by herselfe, with the allowance of her *second*. In which shee was one of God's true *Stewards*, and *Almoners* too. There are dispositions, which had rather *give presents*, than *pay debts*; and rather doe good to *strangers*, than to those, that are *neerer* to them. But *shee* alwayes thought the care of her family, a *debt*, and upon that, for the *provision*, for the order, for the *proportions*, in a good largenesse, shee plac't her first thoughts, of that kinde. For, for our *families*, we are *Gods Stewards* ; For those without, we are his *Almoners*. In which office, shee gave not at some *great dayes*, or some solemne.goings abroad, but, as *Gods true Almoners*, the *Sunne*, and *Moone*, that passe on, in a continuall doing of good, as shee receiv'd her *daily bread* from God, so, *daily*, she distributed, and imparted it to others. In which office, though she never turn'd her face from those, who in a strict inquisition, might be call'd idle, and vagrant Beggers, yet shee ever look't first, upon them, who *labour'd*, and whose *labours* could not overcome the *difficulties*, nor bring in the *necessities* of this life ; and to the *sweat of their browes*, shee contributed, even her *wine*, and her *oyle*, and any thing that was, and any thing, that might be, if it were not, prepar'd for her owne table. And as her house was a *Court*, in the conversation of the best, and an *Almeshouse*, in feeding the *poore* ; so was it also an *Hospitall*, in ministring releefe to the *sicke*. And truly, the love of doing good in this kind, of *ministring to the sicke*, was the *hony*, that was spread over all her bread ; the *Aire*, the *Perfume*, that breath'd over all her house ; The disposition that dwelt in those her children, and those her kindred, which dwelt with her, so bending this way, that the *studies* and *knowledge* of one, the *hand* of another, and *purse* of all, and a *joynt-facility*, and *opennesse*, and *accessiblenesse* to persons of the meanest quality, concur'd in this blessed *Act* of *Charity*, to *minister releefe to the sicke*. Of which, my selfe, who, at that time, had the favour to bee admitted into that *family*, can, and must testifie this, that when the late heavy *visitation* fell hotly upon this Towne, when every doore was shut up, and, lest *Death* should enter into the house, every house was made a *Sepulchre* of them that were in it, then, then, in that time of *infection*, divers persons visited with that *infection*, had their releefe, and releefe *applicable to that very infection*, from this house.

Now when I have said thus much, (rather thus little) of her *person*, as of a *house*, That the *ground* upon which it was built, was the *family* where she was *borne*, and then, where she was *married*, and then, the time of her *widow-hood*, and lastly, her *last marriage*, And that the *house* it selfe, was those fair *bodily endowments*, which *God* had bestow'd upon her, And the *furniture* of that *house*, the *fortune*, and the *use* of that *fortune*, of which *God* had made her *Steward* and *Almoner*, when I shall also have said, that the *Inhabitants* of this *house*, (rather the *servants*, for they did but wait upon *Religion* in her) were those married couples, of *morall virtues*, *Conversation* married with a *Retirednesse*, *Facility* married with a *Reservednesse*, *Alacrity* married with a *Thoughtfulnesse*, and *Largenesse* married with a *Providence*, I may have leave to depart from this consideration of her *person*, and *personall circumstances*, lest by insisting longer upon them, I should seeme to pretend, to say all the good, that might bee said of her ; But that's not in my *purpose* ; yet, onely therefore, because it is not in my *power* ; For I would do her all *right*, and all you that good, if I could, to say all. But, I haste to an end, in consideration of some things, that appertaine more expressly to me, then these *personall*, or *civill*, or *morall* things doe.

In those, the next is, the *secundum promissa*, that shee

govern'd herself, *according to his promises*; his promises, laid downe in his *Scriptures*. For, as the *rule* of all her *civill Actions*, was *Religion*, so, the *rule* of her *Religion*, was the *Scripture*; And, her *rule*, for her particular understanding of the *Scripture*, was the *Church*. Shee never diverted towards the *Papist*, in undervaluing the *Scripture*; nor towards the *Separatist*, in undervaluing the *Church*. But in the *doctrine*, and *discipline* of that *Church*, in which, *God* seal'd her, to himselfe, in *Baptisme*, shee brought up her children, shee assisted her family, she dedicated her soule to *God* in her life, and surrendered it to him in her death; And, in that forme of *Common Prayer*, which is ordain'd by that *Church*, and to which she had accustom'd her selfe, with her family, twice every day, she joyn'd with that company, which was about her *death-bed*, in answering to every part thereof, which the Congregation is directed to answer to, with a *cleere understanding*, with a *constant memory*, with a *distinct voyce*, not two hours before she died.

According to this promise, that is, the will of God manifested in the *Scriptures*, She *expected*; Shee expected this, that she hath received; *Gods Physicke*, and Gods *Musicke*; a *Christianly death*. For, *death*, in the *old Testament* was a *Commination*; but in the new Testament, death is a *Promise*; When there was a *Super-dying*, a *death* upon the *death*, a *Morte* upon the *Morieris*, a *Spirituall* death after the *bodily*, then wee died *according to Gods threatening*; Now, when by the *Gospell*, that *second death* is taken off, though wee die still, yet we die *according to his Promise*, That's a part of his *mercy*, and his *Promise*, which his *Apostle* gives us from him, That

wee shall *all bee changed* ; For, after that *promise*, that 1Cor.15.51.
change, follow's that triumphant *Acclamation, O death
where is thy sting, O grave where is thy victory ?* Consider
us fallen in *Adam*, and wee are miserable, that wee must
die ; but consider us restor'd, and redintegrated in
Christ, wee were more miserable if we might not die ;
Wee lost the *earthly Paradise* by death then ; but wee
get not *Heaven*, but by *death*, now. This shee expected
till it came, and embrac't it when it came. How may we
thinke, shee was joy'd to see that face, that *Angels* delight
to looke upon, the face of her *Saviour*, that did not abhor
the face of his fearfullest *Messenger*, Death ? Shee
shew'd no feare of his face, in any change of her owne ;
but died without any change of *countenance*, or *posture* ;
without any *strugling*, any *disorder* ; but her *Death-bed*
was as quiet, as her *Grave*. To another *Magdalen*,
Christ said upon earth, *Touch me not, for I am not ascended*.
Being ascended now, to his glory, and she being gone up
to him, after shee had awaited his leisure, so many yeeres,
as that more, would soone have growne to bee *vexation*,
and *sorrow*, as her last words here, were, *I submit my will
to the will of God* ; so wee doubt not, but the first word
which she heard there, was that *Euge*, from her *Saviour,
Well done good and faithfull servant ; enter into thy
masters joy.*

Shee expected that ; dissolution of body, and soule ;
and rest in both, from the incumbrances, and tentations
of this world. But yet, shee is in *expectation* still ; Still
a *Reversionarie* ; and a *Reversionary* upon a long life ;
the whole world must die, before she come to a *possession*
of this *Reversion* ; which is a *Glorified body in the Resur-*

rection. In which *expectation*, she return's to her former *charity* ; shee will not have that, till *all wee*, shall have it, as well as shee ; She eat not her morsels alone, in her life, Job 31. 17. (as *Job* speakes) She lookes not for the *glory* of the *Resurrection* alone, after her death. But when *all wee*, shall have been mellowd in the earth, many yeeres, or chang'd in the *Aire*, in the twinkling of an eye, (*God* knowes which) That *body* upon which you tread now, That *body* which now, whilst I speake, is mouldering, and crumbling into lesse, and lesse dust, and so hath some *motion*, though no *life*, That *body*, which was the *Tabernacle* of a *holy Soule*, and a *Temple* of the *holy Ghost*, That *body* that was eyes to the blinde, and hands, and feet to the lame, whilst it liv'd, and being dead, is so still, by having beene so *lively* an example, to teach others, to be so, That *body* at last, shall have her last expectation satisfied, and dwell *bodily*, with that *Righteousnesse*, in these *new Heavens*, and *new Earth*, for *ever*, and *ever*, and *ever*, and *infinite*, and *super-infinite evers*. Wee end all, with the *valediction* of the *Spouse* to *Christ* : *His* Cant. 8. 3. *left hand is under my head, and his right embraces mee*, was the *Spouses valediction*, and *good night* to *Christ* then, when she laid her selfe down to sleep in the strength of his *Mandrakes*, and in the power of his *Spices*, as it is exprest there ; that is, in the *influence* of his *mercies*. Beloved, every good *Soule* is the *spouse* of *Christ*. And this good *Soule*, being thus laid downe to sleepe in his peace, *His left hand under her head*, gathering, and composing, and preserving her *dust* for *future Glory* ; *His right hand embracing her*, assuming, and establishing her *soule* in present *Glory*, in his *name*, and in her *behalfe*,

I say that, to *all you*, which *Christ* sayes there, in the behalfe of that *Spouse*, *Adjuro vos*, *I adjure you*, *I charge you*, *O daughters of Jerusalem*, *that yee wake her not, till she please*. The words are directed to the *daughters*, rather than to the *sons* of *Jerusalem*, because for the most part, the aspersions that women receive, either in *Morall* or *Religious* actions, proceed from women themselves. Therefore, *Adjuro vos*, I charge you, O ye daughters of *Jerusalem*, wake her not, Wake her not, with any *halfe calumnies*, with any *whisperings*; But if you wil wake her, wake her, and keepe her awake with an active imitation, of her *Morall*, and her *Holy virtues*. That so her *example* working upon you, and the number of *Gods Saints*, being, the sooner, by this blessed *example*, fulfil'd, wee may all meet, and meet quickly in that *kingdome*, which *hers*, and *our Saviour*, hath purchac't for us all, with the inestimable price, of his incorruptible bloud. To which glorious Sonne of God, &c.

29. *Death of Elizabeth and Accession of James I.*

GODS hand hath been abundant towards us, in raising Ministers of State, so qualified, and so endowed; and such Princes as have fastned their friendships, and conferred their favors upon such persons. We celebrate, seasonably, opportunely, the thankful acknowledgement of these mercies, this day: This day, which God made for us, according to the pattern of his *first days* in the Creation; where, *Vesper & mane dies unus*, the evening first, and then the morning made up the day; for, here the saddest night, and the joyfullest morning, that ever the daughters of this Island saw, made up this day.

Consider the tears of *Richmond* this night, and the joys of *London*, at this place, at this time, in the morning ; and we shall find *Prophecy* even in that saying of the *Poet, Nocte pluit tota*, showers of rain all night, of weeping for our Sovereign ; and we would not be comforted, because she was not : And yet, *redeunt spectacula manè*, the same hearts, the same eyes, the same hands were all directed upon recognitions, and acclamations of her successor in the morning : And when every one of you in the City, were running up and down like Ants with their eggs bigger then themselves, every man with his bags, to seek where to hide them safely, Almighty God shed down his *Spirit* of *Unity*, and recollecting, and reposedness, and acquiescence upon you all. In the death of that Queen, unmatchable, inimitable in her sex ; that Queen, worthy, I will not say of *Nestors* years, I will not say of *Methusalems*, but worthy of *Adams* years, if *Adam* had never faln ; in her death we were all under one common flood, and depth of tears. *But the Spirit of God moved upon the face of that depth* ; and God said, *Let there be light, and there was light, and God saw that that light was good*. God took pleasure, and found a savor of rest, in our peaceful chearfulness, and in our joyful and confident apprehension of blessed days in his Government, whom he had prepared at first, and preserved so often for us.

As the Rule is true, *Cum de Malo principe posteri tacent, manifestum est vilem facere præsentem*, when men dare not speak of the vices of a Prince that is dead, it is certain that the Prince that is alive proceeds in the same vices ; so the inversion of the Rule is true too, *Cum de*

Matt. 2. 18.

Plinius ad Trajan.

bono principe loquuntur, when men may speak freely of the virtues of a dead Prince, it is an evident argument, that the present Prince practises the same virtues ; for, if he did not, he would not love to hear of them. Of *her*, we may say (that which was well said, and therefore it were pity it should not be once truly said, for, so it was not, when it was first said to the Emperor *Julian*) *Nihil humile, aut abjectum cogitavit, quia novit de se semper loquendum ;* she knew the world would talk of her after her death, and therefore she did such things all her life were worthy to be talked of. Of her glorious successor, and our gracious Soveraign, we may say ; *Onerosum est succedere bono Principi*, It would have troubled any king Ibid. but *him*, to have come in succession, and in comparison with such a *Queen*. And in them both we may observe the unsearchableness of the ways of God ; of them both, we may say, *Dominus fecit, It is the Lord that hath done it, and it is wonderful in our eyes* : First, that a *woman* Psalm 118. and a *maid* should have all the wars of Christendom in 23. her contemplation, and govern and ballance them all ; And then, that a *King*, born and bred in a *warlike Nation*, and so accustomed to the *sword*, as that it had been directed upon his own person, in the *strength* of his age, and in his *Infancy*, in his *Cradle*, in his *mothers belly*, should yet have the *blessed spirit of peace* so abundantly in him, as that by his Councils, and his authority, he should sheath all the swords of Christendom again.

30. *The Gunpowder Plot.*

Psal. 2. 1. QUARE *fremuerunt,* Why did these men rage, and imagine a vaine thing ? What they did historically, we know ; They made that house, which is *the hive* of the Kingdome, from whence all her *honey* comes ; that house where *Justice* herself is conceived, in their preparing of *Laws,* and inanimated, and quickned and borne by the Royall Assent, there given ; they made that whole house *one Murdring peece,* and charged that peece with Peers, with People, with Princes, with the King, and meant to discharge it upward at the face of heaven, to shoot God at the face of God, Him, of whom God hath said, *Dii estis,* You are Gods, at the face of God, that had said so, as though they would have reproached the God of heaven, and not have been beholden to him for such a King, but shoot him up to him, and bid him take his King again, with a *nolumus hunc regnare,* we will not have this King to reign over us.

31. *Preached to the Honourable Company of the Virginian Plantation,* 1622.

BELOVED in him, whose kingdome, and Ghospell you seeke to advance, in this Plantation, our *Lord* and *Saviour Christ Jesus,* if you seeke to establish a temporall kingdome there, you are not rectified, if you seeke to bee *Kings* in either acceptation of the word ; To be a *King* signifies *Libertie* and *independency,* and *Supremacie,* to bee under no man, and to be a *King* signifies *Abundance,* and *Omnisufficiencie,* to neede no man. If those that governe there, would establish such

a government, as should not depend upon this, or if
those that goe thither, propose to themselves an exemp-
tion from Lawes, to live at their libertie, this is to be
Kings, to devest *Allegeance*, to bee under no man : and
if those that adventure thither, propose to themselves
present benefit, and profit, a sodaine way to bee rich,
and an aboundance of all desirable commodities from
thence, this is to be sufficient of themselves, and to need
no man : and to bee under no man and to need no man,
are the two acceptations of being *Kings*. Whom liberty
drawes to goe, or present profit drawes to adventure,
are not yet in the right way. O, if you could once bring
a *Catechisme* to bee as good ware amongst them as
a Bugle, as a knife, as a hatchet : O, if you would be
as ready to hearken at the returne of a *Ship*, how many
Indians were converted to *Christ Jesus*, as what Trees,
or druggs, or Dyes that Ship had brought, then you were
in your right way, and not till then ; *Libertie* and
Abundance, are Characters of kingdomes, and a kingdome
is excluded in the *Text* ; the *Apostles* were not to looke
for it, in their employment, nor you in this your Plantation. . . .

God ment from the first howre, to people the whole
earth ; and *God* could have made men of clay, as fast
as they made Brickes of Clay in *Egypt* ; but he began
upon two, and when they had been multiplying and re-
plenishing the Earth One thousand six hundred yeares,
the *Flood* washed all that away, and God was almost
to begin againe upon eight persons ; and they have
serv'd to people *Earth* and *Heaven* too ; Be not you
discouraged, if the Promises which you have made to

your selves, or to others, be not so soone discharg'd ; though you see not your money, though you see not your men, though a *Flood*, a *Flood* of *bloud* have broken in upon them, be not discouraged. Great Creatures ly long in the wombe ; *Lyons* are litter'd perfit, but *Beare whelps* lick'd unto their shape ; actions which Kings undertake, are cast in a mould ; they have their perfection quickly ; actions of private men, and private purses, require more hammering, and more filing to their perfection. . . .

God sayes to you, *No Kingdome*, not *ease*, not *abundance* ; nay *nothing at all yet* ; the Plantation shall not discharge the Charges, not defray it selfe yet ; but yet already, now at first, it shall conduce to great uses ; It shall redeeme many a wretch from the Jawes of death, from the hands of the Executioner, upon whom, perchaunce a small fault, or perchance a first fault, or perchance a fault heartily and sincerely repented, perchance no fault, but malice, had otherwise cast a present, and ignominious death. It shall sweep your streets, and wash your dores, from idle persons, and the children of idle persons, and imploy them : and truely, if the whole Countrey were but such a *Bridewell*, to force idle persons to work, it had a good use. But it is already, not onely a *Spleene*, to draine the ill humours of the body, but a *Liver*, to breed good bloud ; already the imployment breeds Marriners ; already the place gives essayes, nay Fraytes of Marchantable commodities ; already it is a marke for the Envy, and for the ambition of our Enemies ; I speake but of our *Doctrinall*, not *Nationall* Enemies ; as they are *Papists*, they are sory we have this Countrey ;

and surely, twenty Lectures in matter of Controversie,
doe not so much vexe them, as one Ship that goes, &
strengthens that Plantation. Neither can I recommend
it to you by any better *Retorique*, then their malice. They
would gladly have it, and therefore let us bee glad to
hold it. . . .

Those of our profession that goe, you, that send them
who goe, do all an *Apostolicall* function. What action
soever, hath in the first intention thereof, a purpose
to propagate the Gospell of *Christ Jesus*, that is an
Apostolicall action. Before the ende of the world come,
before this mortality shall put on immortalitie, before
the Creature shall be delivered of the bondage of corruption under which it groanes, before the Martyrs under Rom. 3.
the Altar shall be silenc'd, before all things shall be
subdued to *Christ*, his kingdome, perfected, & the last
Enemy Death destroied, the Gospell must be preached
to those men to whom ye send ; to all men ; furder and
hasten you this blessed, this joyfull, this glorious consummation of all, and happie reunion of all bodies to their
Soules, by preaching the *Gospell* to those men. Preach
to them Doctrinally, preach to them Practically ;
Enamore them with your *Justice*, and (as farre as may
consist with your security), your *Civilitie* ; but inflame
them with your *godlinesse*, and your *Religion*. Bring them
to *love* and *Reverence* the name of that *King*, that sends
men to teach them the wayes of *Civilitie* in this world,
but to *feare* and *adore* the Name of that *King of Kings*,
that sends men to teach them the waies of Religion, for
the next world. Those amongst you, that are old now,
shall passe out of this world with this great comfort, that

you contributed to the beginning of that Common
Wealth, and of that Church, though they live not to see
the groath thereof to perfection : *Apollos* watred, but
Paul planted ; hee that begun the worke, was the greater
man. And you that are young now, may live to see the
Enemy as much empeach'd by that place, and your
friends, yea Children, as well accommodated in that
place, as any other. You shall have made this *Iland*,
which is but as the *Suburbs* of the old world, a Bridge,
a Gallery to the new ; to joyne all to that world that
shall never grow old, the Kingdome of heaven, You
shall add persons to this Kingdome, and to the Kingdome
of heaven, and adde names to the Bookes of our Chronicles,
and to the Booke of Life.

1 Cor. 3. 6.

To end all, as the *Orators* which declaimd in the
presence of the *Roman Emperors*, in their *Panegyriques*,
tooke that way to make those *Emperours* see, what they
were bound to doe, to say in those publique Orations,
that those *Emporors* had done so (for that increased the
love of the Subject to the Prince, to bee so tolde, that
hee had done those great things, and then it convayd
a Counsell into the Prince to do them after.) As their
way was to procure things to bee done, by saying they
were done, so beloved I have taken a contrary way :
for when I, by way of exhortation, all this while have
seem'd to tell you what should be done by you, I have,
indeed, but told the Congregation, what hath beene
done already : neither do I speake to move a wheele
that stood still, but to keepe the wheele in due motion ;
nor persuade you to begin, but to continue a good worke ;
nor propose foreigne, but your own Examples, to do still,

as you have done hitherto. For, for that, that which is especially in my contemplation, the conversion of the people, as I have receiv'd, so I can give this Testimony, that of those persons, who have sent in moneys, and conceal'd their names, the greatest part, almost all, have limited their devotion, and contribution upon that point, the propagation of Religion, and the conversion of the people; for the building and beautifying of the house of God, and for the instruction and education of their young Children. *Christ Jesus* himself *is yesterday, and to day, and the same for ever.* In the advancing of his glory, be you so to, yesterday, and to day, and the same for ever, here; and hereafter, when time shall be no more, no more yesterday, no more to day, yet for ever and ever, you shall enjoy that joy, and that glorie, which no ill accident can attaine to diminish, or Eclipse it.

32. *The Mission of England.*

CHRIST came *per mundam in mundum,* by a clean woman into an unclean world. And he came in a purpose, (as we do piously believe) to manifest himself in the Christian Religion to all the nations of the world; and therefore, *Lætentur Insulæ,* saies *David, The Lord reigneth let the Islands rejoice* the Islands who by reason of their situation, provision and trading, have most means of conveying Christ Jesus over the world. He hath carried us up to heaven, & set us at the right hand of God, & shal not we endeavour to carry him to those nations, who have not yet heard of his name ? shall we still brag that we have brought our clothes, and our hatchets, and our knives, and bread to this and this value and estimation amongst those poor ignorant Souls, and shall we never glory that we have brought the name, and Religion of Christ Jesus in estimation amongst them? shall we stay till other nations have planted a fals Christ among them? and then either continue in our sloth, or take more pains in rooting out a false Christ then would have planted the true? Christ is come into the world; we will do little, if we will not ferry him over, and propagate his name, as well as our own to other Nations.

33. *James I.*

WE say sometimes in scorn to a man, *God help you*, and *God send you wit*; and therein, though it have the sound of a prayer, wee call him foole. So wee have seen of late, some in obscure Conventicles, institute certain prayers, *That God would keep the King*, and *the Prince in the true Religion*; The prayer is always good, always usefull; but when that prayer is accompanied with circumstances, as though the King and the Prince were declining from that Religion, then even the prayer it selfe is libellous, and seditious; Saint *Paul*, in that former place, apparels a Subjects prayer well, when hee sayes, *Let prayers bee given with thanks*; Let our prayers bee for continuance of the blessings, which wee have, and let our acknowledgement of present blessings, bee an inducement for future: pray, and praise together; pray thankfully, pray not suspiciously; for, beloved in the bowels of Christ Jesus, before whose face I stand now, and before whose face, I shall not be able to stand amongst the righteous, at the last day, if I lie now, and make this Pulpit my Shop, to vent sophisticate Wares, In the presence of you, a holy part, I hope, of the Militant Church, of which I am, In the presence of the whole Triumphant Church, of which, by him, by whom I am that I am, I hope to bee, In the presence of the Head of the whole Church, who is All in all, I, (*and I thinke I have the Spirit of God,*) (I am sure, I have not resisted it in this point) I, (and I may bee allowed to know something in Civill affaires) (I am sure I have not been stupefied in this point) doe deliver that, which upon the truth of a Morall man, and a Christian man, and a Church man, beleeve to be true, That hee, who is *the Breath of our nostrils*, is in his heart, as farre from submitting us to that Idolatry, and superstition, which did heretofore oppresse us, as his immediate Predecessor, whose memory is justly precious to you, was : Their wayes may bee divers, and yet their end the same, that is, The glory of God ; And to a higher Comparison, then to her, I know not how to carry it.

*1 Cor.*7.44.

34. *Death of James I.*

WHEN you shall find that hand that had signed to one of you a *Patent* for *Title*, to another for *Pension*, to another for *Pardon*, to another for *Dispensation, Dead* : That hand that settled Possessions by his *Seale*, in the *Keeper*, and rectified *Honours* by the *sword*, in his *Marshall*, and distributed relief to the *Poore*, in his *Almoner*, and *Health* to the *Diseased*, by his *immediate Touch*, Dead : That Hand that ballanced his *own three Kingdomes* so equally, as that none of them complained of one another, nor of him, and carried the *Keyes* of all the Christian world, and locked up, and let out *Armies* in their due season, Dead ; how poore, how faint, how pale, how momentany, how transitory, how empty, how frivolous, how Dead things, must you necessarily thinke *Titles*, and *Possessions*, and *Favours*, and all, when you see that Hand, which was the *hand of Destinie*, of *Christian Destinie*, of the *Almighty God*, lie dead ? It was not so *hard* a hand when we touched it last, nor so *cold* a hand when we kissed it last : That hand which was wont *to wipe all teares from all our eyes*, doth now but presse and squeaze us as so many spunges, filled one with one, another with another cause of teares. Teares that can have no other banke to bound them, but the declared and manifested *will of God* : For, till our teares flow to that heighth, that they might be called a *murmuring* against the declared will of God, it is against our Allegiance, it is *Disloyaltie*, to give our teares any stop, any termination, any measure.

35. *The Plague*, 1625.

BELOVED, as God empayl'd a *Goshen* in *Egypt*, a place for the righteous amongst the wicked ; so there is an *Egypt* in every *Goshen*, neasts of Snakes in the fairest Gardens, and even in this City (which in the sense of the Gospel, we may call, *The holy City* ; as Christ called *Jerusalem*, though she had multiplied transgressions, *The Holy City*, because she had not cast away his Law, though she had disobeyed it : So howsoever your sins have provoked God, yet as you retain a zealous profession of the truth of his Religion, I may in his name, and do in the bowels of his mercy, call you,

The Holy City) even in this City, no doubt but the hand of God fell upon thousands in this deadly infection, who were no more affected with it, than those *Egyptians*, to cry out, *Omnes Moriemur*, We can but die, and we must die : And, *Edamus, & bibamus, cras moriemur, Let us eat and drink, and take our pleasure*, and make our profits, *for to-morrow we shall die*, and so were cut off by the hand of God, some even in their robberies, in half-empty houses ; and in their drunkenness in voluptuous and riotous houses ; and in their lusts and wantonness in licentious houses ; and so took in infection and death, like *Judas's* sop, death dipt and soaked in sin. Men whose lust carried them into the jaws of infection in lewd houses, and seeking one sore perished with another ; men whose rapine and covetousness broke into houses, and seeking the Wardrobes of others, found their own winding-sheet, in the infection of that house where they stole their own death ; men who sought no other way to divert sadness, but strong drink in riotous houses, and there drank up *Davids* cup of Malediction, the cup of Condemned men, of death, in the infection of that place. For these men that died in their sins, that sinned in their dying, that sought and hunted after death so sinfully, we have little comfort of such men, in the phrase of this Text, *They were dead* ; for they are dead still : As *Moses* said of the *Egyptians*, I am afraid we may say of these men, *We shall see them no more for ever*.

But God will give us the comfort of this phrase in the next House ; This next House is *Domus nostra*, our Dwelling-House, our Habitation, our Family ; and there, *They were dead* ; they were, but by Gods goodness

they are not. If this savor of death have been the savor
of life unto us; if this heavy weight of Gods hand
upon us have awakened us to a narrower survey, and
a better discharge of our duties towards all the parts of
our Families, we may say, to our comforts and his glory,
There was a son dead in disobedience and murmuring;
there was a daughter dead in a dangerous easiness of
conversation; there was a servant dead in the practice
of deceit and falsifying; *there was,* but the Lord hath
breath'd a new life into us, the Lord hath made even
his tempest a refreshing, and putrefaction a perfume
unto us. The same measure of wind that blows out
a candle, kindles a fire; this correction that hath hardned
some, hath entendred and mollified us; and howsoever
there were dead sons, and dead daughters, and dead
servants, this holy sense of Gods Judgements shall not
only preserve for the future, that we shall admit no
more such dead limbs into our Family, but even give
to them who were (in these kindes) formerly dead, a new
life, a blessed resurrection from all their sinful habits,
by the power of his grace, though reached to them with
a bloody hand, and in a bitter cup, in this heavy calamity;
and as Christ said of himself, they shall say in him, *I was
dead, but am alive;* and by that grace of God, I am
that I am. . . .

Lastly, in this fourth house, the house where we stand
now, the house of God, and of his Saints, God affords
us a fair beam of this consolation, in the phrase of this
Text also, *They were dead.* How appliable to you, in this
place, is that which God said to *Moses, Put off thy shoes,
for thou treadest on holy ground;* put off all confidence,

all standing, all relying upon worldly assurances, and consider upon what ground you tread ; upon ground so holy, as that all the ground is made of the bodies of Christians, and therein hath received a second consecration. Every puff of wind within these walls, may blow the father into the sons eys, or the wife into her husbands, or his into hers, or both into their childrens, or their childrens into both. Every grain of dust that flies here, is a piece of a Christian ; you need not distinguish your Pews by figures ; you need not say, I sit within so many of such a neighbour, but I sit within so many inches of my husbands, or wives, or childes, or friendes grave. Ambitious men never made more shift for places in Court, then dead men for graves in Churches ; and as in our later times, we have seen two and two almost in every Place and Office, so almost every Grave is oppressed with twins ; and as at Christs resurrection some of the dead arose out of their graves, that were buried again ; so in this lamentable calamity, the dead were buried, and thrown up again before they were resolved to dust, to make room for more.

36. *Difficult Times.*

AS in the *Arke* there were Lions, but the Lion shut his mouth, and clincht his paw, (the Lion hurt nothing in the Arke) and in the Arke there were Vipers and Scorpions, but the Viper shewed no teeth, nor the Scorpion no taile, (the Viper bit none, the Scorpion stung none in the Arke) (for, if they had occasioned any disorder there, their escape could have been but into the Sea, into irreparable ruine) so, in every State, (though

that State be an Arke of peace, and preservation) there
will be some kind of oppression in some Lions, some that
will abuse their power; but *Væ si scandalizemur*, woe
unto us if we be scandalized with that, and seditiously
lay aspersions upon the State and Government, because
there are some such in every Church, (though that Church
bee an Arke, for integrity and sincerity) there will bee
some Vipers, Vipers that will gnaw at their Mothers
belly, men that will shake the articles of Religion; But
Væ si scandalizemur, woe if we be so scandalized at that,
as to defame that Church, or separate our selves from
that Church which hath given us our Baptism, for that.
It is the chafing of the Lion, and the stirring of the Viper,
that aggravates the danger; The first blow makes the
wrong, but the second makes the fray; and they that
will endure no kind of abuse in State or Church, are
many times more dangerous then that abuse wch they
oppose. It was only Christ Jesus himself that could say
Mar. 4. 39. to the Tempest, *Tace, obmutesce*, peace, be still, not
a blast, not a sob more; onely he could becalm a Tempest
at once. It is well with us, if we can ride out a storm at
anchour; that is, lie still and expect, and surrender
our selves to God, and anchor in that confidence, till
the storm blow over. It is well for us if we can beat
out a storm at sea, with boarding to and again; that is,
maintain and preserve our present condition in Church,
and State, though we encrease not, that though we gain
no way, yet wee lose no way whilst the storm lasts. It
is well for us, if, though we be put to take in our sayls,
and to take down our masts, yet we can hull it out;
that is, if in storms of contradiction, or persecution,

the Church, or State, though they be put to accept
worse conditions then before, and to depart with some
of their outward splendor, be yet able to subsist and
swimme above water, and reserve it selfe for Gods
farther glory, after the storme is past ; onely Christ
could becalm the storme ; He is a good Christian that
can ride out, or board out, or hull out a storme, that by
industry, as long as he can, and by patience, when he
can do no more, over-lives a storm, and does not forsake
his ship for it, that is not scandalized with that State,
nor that Church, of which he is a member, for those
abuses that are in it. The Arke is peace, peace is good
dispositions to one another, good intepretations of one
another ; for, if our impatience put us from our peace,
and so out of the Arke, all without the Arke is sea ; The
bottomlesse and boundlesse Sea of Rome, will hope to
swallow us, if we dis-unite our selves, in uncharitable
mis-interpretations of one another.

37. *Polemical Preaching.*

THERE was a time but lately, when he who was in
his desire and intension, the Peace-maker of all
the Christian world, as he had a desire to have slumbred
all Field-drums, so had he also to have slumbred all
Pulpit-drums, so far, as to passe over all impertinent
handling of Controversies, meerly and professedly as
Controversies, though never by way of positive maintenance of Orthodoxall and fundamentall Truths ; That
so there might be no slackning in the defence of the truth
of our Religion, and yet there might bee a discreet and
temperate forbearing of personall, and especially of

Nationall exasperations. And as this way had piety, and peace in the worke it selfe, so was it then occasionally exalted, by a great necessity; He, who was then our hope, and is now the breath of our nostrils, and the Anointed of the Lord, being then taken in their pits, and, in that great respect, such exasperations the fitter to be forborne, especially since that course might well bee held, without any prevarication, or cooling the zeale of the positive maintenance of the religion of our Church. But things standing now in another state, and all peace, both Ecclesiasticall and Civill, with these men, being by themselves removed, and taken away, and hee whom we feared, returned in all kinde of safety, safe in body, and safe in soule too, whom though their Church could not, their Court hath chatechised in their religion, that is, brought him to a cleere understanding of their Ambition, (for Ambition is their Religion, and S. *Peters* Ship must saile in their Fleets, and with their winds, or it must sink, and the Catholique and Militant Church must march in their Armies, though those Armies march against Rome it selfe, as heretofore they have done, to the sacking of that Towne, to the holding of the Pope himselfe in so sordid a prison, for sixe moneths, as that some of his nearest servants about him died of the plague, to the treading under foot Priests, and Bishops, and Cardinals, to the dishonouring of Matrons, and the ravishing of professed Virgins, and committing such insolencies, Catholiques upon Catholiques, as they would call us Heretiques for beleeving them, but that they are their owne Catholique Authors that have written them) Things being now, I say, in this state, with these men,

since wee heare that Drums beat in every field abroad,
it becomes us also to returne to the brasing and beating
of our Drums in the Pulpit too, that so, as *Adam* did not
onely dresse Paradise, but keepe Paradise ; and as the
children of God, did not onely build, but build with
one hand, and fight with another ; so wee also may
employ some of our Meditations upon supplanting, and
subverting of error, as well as upon the planting, and
watering of the Truth.

38. *The World Decays.*

AS the world is the whole frame of the world, God *Mundus*
hath put into it a reproofe, a rebuke, lest it should *magnus.*
seem eternall, which is, a sensible decay and age in the
whole frame of the world, and every piece thereof. The
seasons of the yeare irregular and distempered ; the Sun
fainter, and languishing ; men lesse in stature, and shorter-
lived. No addition, but only every yeare, new sorts,
new species of wormes, and flies, and sicknesses, which
argue more and more putrefaction of which they are
engendred. And the Angels of heaven, which did so
familiarly converse with men in the beginning of the world,
though they may not be doubted to perform to us still
their ministeriall assistances, yet they seem so far to have
deserted this world, as that they do not appeare to us,
as they did to those our Fathers. S. *Cyprian* observed *Cyprian.*
this in his time, when writing to *Demetrianus,* who imputed all those calamities which afflicted the world then,
to the impiety of the Christians who would not joyne
with them in the worship of their gods, *Cyprian* went
no farther for the cause of these calamities, but *Ad*

senescentem mundum, To the age and impotency of the whole world ; And therefore, sayes he, *Imputent senes Christianis, quòd minùs valeant in senectutem* ; Old men were best accuse Christians, that they are more sickly in their age, then they were in their youth ; Is the fault in our religion, or in their decay ? *Canos in pueris videmus, nec ætas in senectute desinit, sed incipit à senectute* ; We see gray haires in children, and we do not die old, and yet we are borne old. Lest the world (as the world signifies the whole frame of the world) should glorifie it selfe, or flatter, and abuse us with an opinion of eternity, we may admit usefully (though we do not conclude peremptorily) this observation to be true, that there is a reproofe, a rebuke born in it, a sensible decay and mortality of the whole world.

39. *Imperfection.*

I NEED not call in new Philosophy, that denies a settlednesse, an acquiescence in the very body of the Earth, but makes the Earth to move in that place, where we thought the Sunne had moved ; I need not that helpe, that the Earth it selfe is in Motion, to prove this, That nothing upon Earth is permanent ; The Assertion will stand of it selfe, till some man assigne me some instance, something that a man may relie upon, and find permanent. Consider the greatest Bodies upon Earth, The Monarchies ; Objects, which one would thinke, Destiny might stand and stare at, but not shake ; Consider the smallest bodies upon Earth, The haires of our head, Objects, which one would thinke, Destiny would not observe, or could not discerne ; And yet,

Destiny, (to speak to a naturall man) And God, (to speake
to a Christian) is no more troubled to make a Monarchy
ruinous, then to make a haire gray. Nay, nothing needs
be done to either, by God, or Destiny; A Monarchy
will ruine, as a haire will grow gray, of it selfe. In
the Elements themselves, of which all sub-elementary
things are composed, there is no acquiescence, but a
vicissitudinary transmutation into one another; Ayre
condensed becomes water, a more solid body, And Ayre
rarified becomes fire, a body more disputable, and in-
apparant. It is so in the Conditions of men too; A
Merchant condensed, kneaded and packed up in a great
estate, becomes a Lord; And a Marchant rarified,
blown up by a perfidious Factor, or by a riotous Sonne,
evaporates into ayre, into nothing, and is not seen. And
if there were any thing permanent and durable in this
world, yet we got nothing by it, because howsoever
that might last in it selfe, yet we could not last to enjoy
it; If our goods were not amongst Moveables, yet we
our selves are; if they could stay with us, yet we cannot
stay with them; which is another Consideration in
this part.

The world is a great Volume, and man the Index of *Corpus*
that Booke; Even in the body of man, you may turne *hominis*
to the whole world; This body is an Illustration of all
Nature; Gods recapitulation of all that he had said
before, in his *Fiat lux*, and *Fiat firmamentum*, and in
all the rest, said or done, in all the six dayes. Propose
this body to thy consideration in the highest exaltation
thereof; as it is the *Temple of the Holy Ghost*: Nay,
not in a Metaphor, or comparison of a Temple, or any

other similitudinary thing, but as it was really and truly the very body of God, in the person of Christ, and yet this body must wither, must decay, must languish, must perish. When *Goliah* had armed and fortified this body, And *Iezabel* had painted and perfumed this body, And *Dives* had pampered and larded this body, As God said to *Ezekiel*, when he brought him to the *dry bones, Fili hominis, Sonne of Man, doest thou thinke these bones can live?* They said in their hearts to all the world, Can these bodies die? And they are dead. *Iezabels* dust is not Ambar, nor *Goliahs* dust *Terra sigillata*, Medicinall; nor does the Serpent, whose meat they are both, finde any better rellish in *Dives* dust, then in *Lazarus*.

40. *Man.*

Illis, qui nihil.
Esay. 40.15.

*M*AN is, sayes the Prophet *Esay, Quasi stilla situlæ, As a drop upon the bucket.* Man is not all that, not so much as that, as a drop upon the bucket, but *quasi*, something, some little thing towards it; and what is a drop upon the bucket, to a river, to a sea, to the waters above the firmament? Man to God? *Man is*, sayes the same Prophet in the same place, *Quasi momentum stateræ;* we translate it, *As small dust upon the balance*: Man is not all that, not that small graine of dust; but *quasi*, some little thing towards it: And what can a graine of dust work in governing the balance? What is man that God should be mindfull of him? Vanity seemes to be the lightest thing, that the Holy Ghost could name; and when he had named that, he sayes, and sayes, and sayes, often, very, very often, *All is vanity.* But when he

comes to waigh man with vanity it selfe, he findes man
lighter then vanity : *Take*, says he, *great men, and* Ps. 62. 9.
*meane men altogether, and altogether they are lighter then
vanity.* When that great Apostle sayes of himselfe,
that he was in *nothing behinde the very chiefest of the* 2Cor.12.11.
Apostles, and yet, for all that, sayes he was nothing ; who
can think himselfe any thing, for being a Giant in proportion, a Magistrate in power, a Rabbi in learning, an
Oracle in Counsell ?   Let man be something ; how
poore, and inconsiderable a ragge of this world, is man ?
Man, whom *Paracelsus* would have undertaken to have L. 1. *de*
made, in a Limbeck, in a Furnace : Man, who, if they *rerum ge-
neratione.*
were altogether, all the men, that ever were, and are,
and shall be, would not have the power of one Angel in
them all, whereas all the Angels, (who, in the Schoole
are conceived to be more in number, then, not onely all
the Species, but all the individualls of this lower world)
have not in them all, the power of one finger of Gods
hand : Man, of whom when *David* had said, (as the lowest
diminution that he could put upon him) *I am a worme* Ps. 22. 6.
and no man, He might have gone lower, and said, I am
a man and no worm ; for man is so much lesse then a
worm, as that wormes of his own production, shall feed
upon his dead body in the grave, and an immortall
worm gnaw his conscience in the torments of hell.

41. *Afflictions.*

ALL our life is a continuall burden, yet we must not
groane ; A continuall squeasing, yet we must not
pant ; And as in the tendernesse of our childhood, we

suffer, and yet are whipt if we cry, so we are complained of, if we complaine, and made delinquents if we call the times ill. And that which addes waight to waight, and multiplies the sadnesse of this consideration, is this, That still the best men have had most laid upon them. As soone as I heare God say, that he hath found *an upright man, that feares God, and eschews evill,* in the next lines I finde a Commission to Satan, to bring in Sabeans and Chaldeans upon his cattell, and servants, and fire and tempest upon his children, and loathsome diseases upon himselfe. As soone as I heare God say, That he hath found *a man according to his own heart,* I see his sonnes ravish his daughters, and then murder one another, and then rebell against the Father, and put him into straites for his life. As soone as I heare God testifie of Christ at Mat. 3. 17. his Baptisme, *This is my beloved Sonne in whom I am well* Matt. 4. 1. *pleased,* I finde that Sonne of his *led up by the Spirit, to be tempted of the Devill.* And after I heare God ratifie Matt. 17. 5. the same testimony againe, at his Transfiguration, (*This is my beloved Sonne, in whom I am well pleased*) I finde that beloved Sonne of his, deserted, abandoned, and given over to Scribes, and Pharisees, and Publicans, and Herodians, and Priests, and Souldiers, and people, and Judges, and witnesses, and executioners, and he that was called the beloved Sonne of God, and made partaker of the glory of heaven, in this world, in his Transfiguration, is made now the Sewer of all the corruption, of all the sinnes of this world, as no Sonne of God, but a meere man, as no man, but a contemptible worme. As though the greatest weaknesse in this world, were man, and the greatest fault in man were to be good, man is more

miserable then other creatures, and good men more
miserable then any other men.

But then there is *Pondus Gloriæ, An exceeding waight of* Afflictio
eternall glory, and that turnes the scale ; for as it makes spiritualis.
all worldly prosperity as dung, so it makes all worldly
adversity as feathers.

42. *Discontent.*

EVERY man is under that complicated disease, and
that ridling distemper, not to be content with the
most, and yet to be proud of the least thing hee hath ;
that when he lookes upon men, he dispises them, because
he is some kind of Officer, and when he looks upon
God, hee murmures at him, because he made him not
a King.

43. *The World a House.*

LET the whole world be in thy consideration as one
house ; and then consider in that, in the peacefull
harmony of creatures, in the peacefull succession, and
connexion of causes, and effects, the peace of Nature.
Let this Kingdome, where God hath blessed thee with
a being, be the Gallery, the best roome of that house,
and consider in the two walls of that Gallery, the Church
and the State, the peace of a royall, and a religious
Wisedome ; Let thine owne family be a Cabinet in this
Gallery, and finde in all the boxes thereof, in the severall
duties of Wife, and Children, and servants, the peace of
vertue, and of the father and mother of all vertues,
active discretion, passive obedience ; and then lastly,
let thine owne bosome be the secret box, and reserve in
this Cabinet, and then the best Jewell in the best Cabinet,

and that in the best Gallery of the best house that can be had, peace with the Creature, peace in the Church, peace in the State, peace in thy house, peace in thy heart, is a faire Modell, and a lovely designe even of the heavenly Jerusalem which is *Visio pacis*, where there in no object but peace.

44. *Mundus Mare.*

Mundus Mare.

THE world is a Sea in many respects and assimilations. It is a Sea, as it is subject to stormes, and tempests; Every man (and every man is a world) feels that. And then, it is never the shallower for the calmnesse, The Sea is as deepe, there is as much water in the Sea, in a calme, as in a storme; we may be drowned in a calme and flattering fortune, in prosperity, as irrecoverably, as in a wrought Sea, in adversity; So the world is a Sea. It is a Sea, as it is bottomlesse to any line, which we can sound it with, and endlesse to any discovery that we can make of it. The purposes of the world, the wayes of the world, exceed our consideration; But yet we are sure the Sea hath a bottome, and sure that it hath limits, that it cannot overpasse; The power of the greatest in the world, the life of the happiest in the world, cannot exceed those bounds, which God hath placed for them; So the world is a Sea. It is a Sea, as it hath ebbs and floods, and no man knowes the true reason of those floods and those ebbs. All men have changes and vicissitudes in their bodies, (they fall sick) And in their estates, (they grow poore) And in their minds, (they become sad) at which changes, (sicknesse, poverty, sadnesse) themselves wonder, and the cause is wrapped up in the purpose and judgement of God onely, and hid even from them that have them; and so the world is a Sea. It is a Sea, as the Sea affords water enough for all the world to drinke, but such water as will not quench the thirst. The world affords conveniences enow to satisfie Nature, but these encrease our thirst with drinking, and our desire growes and enlarges it selfe with our abundance, and though we sayle in a full Sea, yet we lacke water; So the world is a Sea. It is a Sea, if we consider the Inhabitants. In the Sea, the greater fish devoure the lesse; and so doe the men of this world too. And as fish, when they mud themselves, have no hands to make themselves cleane, but the current of the waters must worke that; So have the men of this world no means to cleanse themselves from those sinnes which they have contracted in the world, of themselves, till a new flood, waters of repentance, drawne up, and sanctified by the Holy Ghost, worke that blessed effect in them.

All these wayes the world is a Sea, but especially it is a Sea in this respect, that the Sea is no place of habitation, but a passage to our habitations. So the Apostle expresses the world, *Here we have no continuing City, but we seeke* Heb.13.14. *one to come*; we seeke it not here, but we seeke it whilest we are here, els we shall never finde it. Those are the two great works which we are to doe in this world; first to know, that this world is not our home, and then to provide us another home, whilest we are in this world. Therefore the Prophet sayes, *Arise, and depart, for this is* Mic. 2. 10. *not your rest*. Worldly men, that have no farther prospect, promise themselves some rest in this world, (*Soule*, Luk. 12.19.

thou hast much goods laid up for many yeares, take thine
ease, eate, drinke, and be merry, sayes the rich man) but
this is not your rest ; indeed no rest ; at least not yours.
You must depart, depart by death, before yee come to
that rest ; but then you must arise, before you depart ;
for except yee have a resurrection to grace here, before
you depart, you shall have no resurrection to glory in
the life to come, when you are departed.

Status
navigan-
tium.

    Now, in this Sea, every ship that sayles must necessarily
have some part of the ship under water ; Every man that
lives in this world, must necessarily have some of his life,
some of his thoughts, some of his labours spent upon
this world ; but that part of the ship, by which he sayls,
is above water ; Those meditations, and those endevours
which must bring us to heaven, are removed from this
world, and fixed entirely upon God. And in this Sea,
are we made fishers of men ; Of men in generall ; not
of rich men, to profit by them, nor of poore men, to
pierce them the more sharply, because affliction hath
opened a way into them ; Not of learned men, to be
over-glad of their approbation of our labours, Nor of
ignorant men, to affect them with an astonishment, or
admiration of our gifts : But we are fishers of men, of
all men, of that which makes them men, their soules.
And for this fishing in this Sea, this Gospel is our net.

Rete Euan-
gelium.

    Eloquence is not our net ; Traditions of men are not
our nets ; onely the Gospel is. The Devill angles with
hooks and bayts ; he deceives, and he wounds in the
catching ; for every sin hath his sting. The Gospel of
Christ Jesus is a net ; It hath leads and corks ; It hath
leads, that is, the denouncing of Gods judgements, and

a power to sink down, and lay flat any stubborne and rebellious heart, And it hath corks, that is, the power of absolution, and application of the mercies of God, that swimme above all his works, means to erect an humble and contrite spirit, above all the waters of tribulation, and affliction. . . .

With this net S. *Peter* caught three thousand soules Acts 2. 41. in one day, at one Sermon, and five thousand in another. 4. 4. With this net S. *Paul* fished all the Mediterranean Sea, and caused the Gospel of Christ Jesus to abound from Jerusalem round about to Illyricum. This is the net, Rom.15.19. with which if yee be willing to bee caught, that is, to lay downe all your hopes and affiances in the gracious promises of his Gospel, then you are fishes reserved for that great Mariage-feast, which is the Kingdome of heaven; where, whosoever is a dish, is a ghest too; whosoever is served in at the table, sits at the table; whosoever is caught by this net, is called to this feast; and there your soules shall be satisfied as with marrow, and with fatnesse, in an infallible assurance, of an ever-lasting and undeterminable terme, in inexpressible joy and glory. Amen.

45. *The Indifference of Nature.*

A FOUNTAINE breaks out in the wildernesse, but that fountaine cares not, whether any Man come to fetch water, or no; A fresh, and fit gale blowes upon the Sea, but it cares not whether the Mariners hoise saile or no; A rose blowes in your garden, but it calls you not to smell to it.

46. *Wealth*.

RICHES is the Metaphor, in which, the Holy Ghost hath delighted to expresse God and Heaven to us ; *Despise not the riches of his goodnesse*, sayes the Apostle ; And againe, *O the depth of the riches of his wisdome* ; And so, after, *The unsearchable riches of Christ* ; And for the consummation of all, *The riches of his Glory*, Gods goodnesse towards us in generall, our Religion in the way, his Grace here, his Glory hereafter, are all represented to us in Riches. With poverty God ordinarily accompanies his comminations ; he threatens feeblenesse, and warre, and captivity, and poverty every where, but he never threatens men with riches.

Ordinary poverty, (that is a difficulty, with all their labors, and industry to sustaine their family, and the necessary duties of their place) is a shrewd, and a slippery tentation. But for that street-beggery, which is become a Calling, (for Parents bring up their children to it, nay they doe almost take prentises to it, some expert beggers teach others what they shall say, how they shall looke, how they shall lie, how they shall cry) for these, whom our lawes call Incorrigible, I must say of them (in a just accommodation of our Saviours words, *It is not meet to take the childrens bread, and to cast it to dogs*) It is not meet, that this vermin should devoure any of that, which belongs to them who are truely poore. Neither is there any measure, any proportion of riches, that exposes man naturally to so much sin, as this kinde of beggery doth. Rich men forget, or neglect the duties of their Baptisme ; but of these, how many are there,

Rom. 2. 4.
11. 33.
Ephes. 3. 8.
ver. 16.

Matt. 25.
26.

that were never baptized ? Rich men sleepe out Sermons, but these never come to Church : Rich men are negligent in the practice, but these are ignorant in all knowledge.

It would require a longer disquisition, then I can afford to it now, whether Riches, or Poverty (considered in lesser proportions, ordinary riches, ordinary poverty) open us to more, and worse sins ; But consider them in the highest and in the lowest, abundant riches, beggerly poverty, and it will scarce admit doubt, but that the incorrigible vagabond is farther from all wayes of goodnesse, then the corruptest rich man is. And therefore labour wee all earnestly in the wayes of some lawfull calling, that we may have our portion of this world by good meanes.

47. *A London Merchant.*

THE Lord was with him in all these steps ; with him *In vita.* in his life ; with him in his death ; He is with him in his funerals, and he shall be with him in his Resurrection ; and therefore, because the Lord was with him, our Brother is not dead. He was with him in the beginning of his life, in this manifestation, That though he were of Parents of a good, of a great Estate, yet his possibility and his expectation from them, did not slacken his own industry ; which is a Canker that eats into, nay that hath eat up many a family in this City, that relying wholly upon what the Father hath done, the Sonne does nothing for himselfe. And truly, it falls out too often, that he that labours not for more, does not keepe his own. God imprinted in him an industrious disposition, though such hopes from such parents might

have excused some slacknesse, and God prospered his
industry so, as that when his Fathers estate came to
a distribution by death, he needed it not. God was
Psal.81.11. with him, as with *David* in a Dilatation, and then in
a Repletion ; God enlarged him, and then he filled him ;
He gave him a large and a comprehensive understanding,
and with it, A publique heart ; And such as perchance
in his way of education, and in our narrow and contracted
times, in which every man determines himselfe in himselfe, and scarce looks farther, it would be hard to finde
many Examples of such largenesse. You have, I thinke,
a phrase of Driving a Trade ; And you have, I know,
a practise of Driving away Trade, by other use of money ;
And you have lost a man, that drove a great Trade,
the right way in making the best use of our home-
commodity. To fetch in Wine, and Spice, and Silke,
is but a drawing of Trade ; The right driving of trade,
is, to vent our owne outward ; And yet, for the drawing
in of that, which might justly seeme most behoofefull,
that is, of Arts, and Manufactures, to be imployed upon
our owne Commodity within the Kingdome, he did his
part, diligently, at least, if not vehemently, if not passion-
ately. This City is a great Theater, and he Acted great
and various parts in it ; And all well ; And when he
went higher, (as he was often heard in Parliaments, at
Councell tables, and in more private accesses to the
late King of ever blessed memory) as, for that compre-
hension of those businesses, which he pretended to understand, no man doubts, for no man lacks arguments and
evidences of his ability therein, So for his manner of
expressing his intentions, and digesting and uttering his

purposes, I have sometimes heard the greatest Master of Language and Judgement, which these times, or any other did, or doe, or shall give, (that good and great King of ours) say of him, That he never heard any man of his breeding, handle businesses more rationally, more pertinently, more elegantly, more perswasively; And when his purpose was, to do a grace to a Preacher, of very good abilities, and good note in his owne Chappell, I have heard him say, that his language, and accent, and manner of delivering himselfe, was like this man. This man hath God accompanied all his life; and by performance thereof seemes to have made that Covenant with him, which he made to *Abraham, Multiplicabo te vehe-* Gen. 17. 2. *menter, I will multiply thee exceedingly.* He multiplied his estate so, as was fit to endow many and great Children; and he multiplied his Children so, both in their number, and in their quality, as they were fit to receive a great Estate. God was with him all the way, In *a Pillar of Fire,* in the brightnesse of prosperity, and in the *Pillar of Clouds* too, in many darke, and sad, and heavy crosses: So great a Ship, required a great Ballast, So many blessings, many crosses; And he had them, and sailed on his course the steadier for them; The *Cloud* as well as the *Fire,* was a *Pillar* to him; His crosses, as well as his blessings established his assurance in God; And so, in all the course of his life, *The Lord was here,* and therefore *our Brother is not dead*; not dead in the evidences and testimonies of life; for he, whom the world hath just cause to celebrate, for things done, when he was alive, is alive still in their celebration.

The Lord was here, that is, with him at his death too. *In morte.*

He was served with the Processe here in the City, but his cause was heard in the Country; Here he sickned, There he languished, and dyed there. In his sicknesse there, those that assisted him, are witnesses, of his many expressings, of a religious & a constant heart towards God, and of his pious joyning with them, even in the holy declaration of kneeling, then, when they, in favour of his weakenesse, would disswade him from kneeling. I must not defraud him of this testimony frõ my selfe, that into this place where we are now met, I have observed him to enter with much reverence, & compose himselfe in this place with much declaration of devotion. And truly it is that reverence, which those persons who are of the same ranke that he was in the City, that reverence that they use in this place, when they come hither, is that that makes us, who have now the administration of this Quire, glad, that our Predecessors, but a very few yeares before our time, (and not before all our times neither) admitted these Honourable and worshipfull Persons of this City, to sit in this Quire, so, as they do upon Sundayes: The Church receives an honour in it; But the honour is more in their reverence, then in their presence; though in that too: And they receive an honour, and an ease in it; and therefore they do piously towards God, and prudently for themselves, and gratefully towards us, in giving us, by their reverent comportment here, so just occasion of continuing that honour, and that ease to them here, which to lesse reverend, and unrespective persons, we should be lesse willing to doe. To returne to him in his sicknesse; He had but one dayes labour, and all the rest were Sabbaths,

one day in his sicknesse he converted to businesse ; Thus ;
He called his family, and friends together ; Thankfully
he acknowledged Gods manifold blessings, and his owne
sins as penitently : And then, to those who were to have
the disposing of his estate, joyntly with his Children,
he recommended his servants, and the poore, and the
Hospitals, and the Prisons, which, according to his
purpose, have beene all taken into consideration ; And
after this (which was his Valediction to the world) he
seemed alwaies loath to returne to any worldly businesse,
His last Commandement to Wife and Children was
Christs last commandement to his Spouse the Church,
in the Apostles, *To love one another.* He blest them, and
the Estate devolved upon them, unto them : And by
Gods grace shall prove as true a Prophet to them in that
blessing, as he was to himselfe, when in entring his last
bed, two dayes before his Death, he said, *Help me off with
my earthly habit, & let me go to my last bed.* Where, in
the second night after, he said, *Little know ye what paine
I feele this night, yet I know, I shall have joy in the morning* ;
And in that morning he dyed. The forme in which he
implored his Saviour, was evermore, towards his end, this,
*Christ Iesus, which dyed on the Crosse, forgive me my
sins ; He have mercy upon me :* And his last and dying
words were the repetition of the name of Jesus ; And when
he had not strength to utter that name distinctly and
perfectly, they might heare it from within him, as from
a man a far off ; even then, when his hollow and remote
naming of Jesus, was rather a certifying of them, that he
was with his Jesus, then a prayer that he might come to
him. And so *The Lord was here,* here with him in his

Death ; and because *the Lord was here, our Brother is not dead* ; not dead in the eyes and eares of God ; for as the blood of *Abel* speaks yet, so doth the zeale of Gods Saints ; and their last prayers (though we heare them not) God continues still ; and they pray in Heaven, as the Martyrs under the Altar, even till the Resurrection.

In funere.   He is with him now too ; Here in his Funerals. Buriall, and Christian Buriall, and Solemne Buriall are all evidences, and testimonies of Gods presence. God forbid we should conclude, or argue an absence of God, from the want of Solemne Buriall, or Christian Buriall, or any Buriall ; But neither must we deny it, to be an evidence of his favour and presence, where he is pleased to afford these. So God

Gen. 15.   makes that the seale of all his blessings to *Abraham, That he should be buried in a good age* ; God established *Iacob*

Gen. 46.   with that promise, *That his Son Ioseph should have care of his Funerals :* And *Ioseph* does cause his servants,

Gen. 50.   *The Physitians, to embalme him, when he was dead.* Of

Esay 11.10. Christ it was Prophecied, *That he should have a glorious Buriall* ; And therefore Christ interprets well that profuse, and prodigall piety of the Woman that poured

Matt. 26.   out the Oyntment upon him, *That she did it to Bury him* ; And so shall *Ioseph* of Arimathea be ever celebrated, for his care in celebrating Christs Funerals. If we were to send a Son, or a friend, to take possession of any place in Court, or forraine parts, we would send him out in the best equipage : Let us not grudge to set downe our friends, in the Anti-chamber of Heaven, the Grave, in as good manner, as without vaine-gloriousnesse, and wastfulnesse we may ; And, in inclining them, to whom that care belongs, to expresse that care as they doe this day, *The Lord is with him*, even in this Funerall; And because *The Lord is here, our brother is not dead*; Not dead in the memories and estimation of men.

And lastly, that we may have God present in all his *In resurrectione.* Manifestations, *Hee that was, and is, and is to come*, was with him, in his life and death, and is with him in this holy Solemnity, and shall bee with him againe in the Resurrection. God sayes to *Iacob, I will goe downe with* Gen. 46. 4. *thee into Egypt, and I will also surely bring thee up againe.* God goes downe with a good man into the Grave, and will surely bring him up againe. When? The Angel promised to returne to *Abraham* and *Sarah*, for the assurance of Gen. 18. 10. the birth of *Isaac, according to the time of life*; that is, in such time, as by nature a woman may have a childe. God will returne to us in the Grave, *according to the time of life*; that is, in such time, as he, by his gracious Decree, hath fixed for the Resurrection. And in the meane time, no more then the God-head departed from the dead body of our Saviour, in the grave, doth his power, and his presence depart from our dead bodies in that darknesse; But that which *Moses* said to the whole Congregation, I say to you all, both to you that heare me, and to him that does not, *All ye that did cleave* Deut. 4. 4. *unto the Lord your God, are alive, every one of you, this day*; Even hee, whom wee call dead, is alive this day. In the presence of God, we lay him downe; In the power of God, he shall rise; In the person of Christ, he is risen already. And so into the same hands that have received his soule, we commend his body; beseeching his blessed Spirit, that as our charity enclines us to hope confidently of his good estate, our faith may assure us of the same happinesse, in our owne behalfe ; And that for all our sakes, but especially for his own glory, he will be pleased to hasten the consummation of all, in that kingdome which that Son of God hath purchased for us, with the inestimable price of his incorruptible blood. *Amen.*

48. *Sickness.*

PUT all the miseries, that man is subject to, together, *sicknesse* is more then all. It is the *immediate* sword of God. *Phalaris* could invent a Bull ; and others have invented Wheels and Racks ; but no persecutor could ever invent a *sicknesse* or a way to inflict a *sicknesse* upon a condemned man : To a *galley* he can send him, and to the *gallows*, and command execution that hour ; but to a *quartane fever*, or to a *gout*, hee cannot condemn him. In *poverty* I lack but other things ; In *banishment* I lack but other men ; But in *sicknesse*, I lack my *self*. And, as the greatest misery of war, is, when our own Country is made the seat of the war ; so is it of *affliction*, when *mine own Body* is made the subject thereof. How shall I put a just value upon Gods great *blessings* of *Wine*, and *Oyle*, and *Milke*, and *Honey*, when my tast is gone, or of *Liberty*, when the *gout* fetters my feet ?

49. *Public Opinion.*

THE shame of men, is one bridle, that is cast upon us. It is a morall obduration, and in the suburbs, next doore to a spirituall obduration, to be Voyce-proofe, Censure-proofe, not to be afraid, nor ashamed, what the world sayes. He that relyes upon his *Plaudo domi*, Though the world hisse, I give my selfe a Plaudite at home, I have him at my Table, and her in my bed, whom I would have, and I care not for rumor; he that rests in such a Plaudite, prepares for a Tragedy, a Tragedy in the Amphitheater, the double Theater, this world, and the next too.

50. *Joy.*

JOY is peace for having done that which we ought to have done .... To have something to doe, to doe it, and then to Rejoyce in having done it, to embrace a calling, to performe the Duties of that calling, to joy and rest in the peacefull testimony of having done so; this is Christianly done, Christ did it; Angelically done, Angels doe it; Godly done, God does it.

51. *Women.*

FOR, howsoever some men out of a petulancy and wantonnesse of wit, and out of the extravagancy of Paradoxes, and such singularities, have called the faculties, and abilities of women in question, even in the roote thereof, in the reasonable and immortall soul, yet that one thing alone hath been enough to create a doubt, (almost an assurance in the negative) whether S. *Ambroses* Commentaries upon the Epistles of S. *Paul,* be truly his or no, that in that book there is a doubt made, whether the woman were created according to Gods Image; Therefore, because that doubt is made in that book, the book it self is suspected not to have had so great, so grave, so constant an author as S. *Ambrose* was; No author of gravity, of piety, of conversation in the Scriptures could admit that doubt, whether woman were created in the Image of God, that is, in possession of a reasonable and an immortall soul.

The faculties and abilities of the soul appeare best in affaires of State, and in Ecclesiasticall affaires; in matter of government, and in matter of religion; and in neither of these are we without examples of able women. For, for State affaires, and matter of government, our age hath given us such a Queen, as scarce any former King hath equalled; And in the Venetian Story, I remember, that certain Matrons of that City were sent by Commission, in quality of Ambassadours, to an Empresse with whom that State had occasion to treate; And in the Stories of the Eastern parts of the World, it is said to be in ordinary practise to send women for Ambassadours. And then, in matters of Religion, women have evermore had a great hand, though sometimes on the left, as well as on the right hand. Sometimes their abundant wealth, sometimes their personall affections to some Church-men, sometimes their irregular and indiscreet zeale hath made them great assistants of great Heretiques; as S. *Hierome* tels us of *Helena* to *Simon Magus*, and so was *Lucilia* to *Donatus*, so another to *Mahomet*, and others to others. But so have they been also great instruments for the advancing of true Religion, as S. *Paul* testifies in their behalf, at *Thessolonica*, *Of the chiefe women, not a few*; Great, and Many. For, many times women have the proxies of greater persons then themselves, in their bosomes; many times women have voices, where they should have none; many times the voices of great men, in the greatest of Civill, or Ecclesiasticall Assemblies, have been in the power and disposition of women. . . .

Women of quality may be up and ready early enough

Hieron.

Acts 17. 4.

for Gods service, if they will. If they be not, let them
but seriously aske themselves that question, whether
upon no other occasion, no entertainment, no visit, no
letter to or from another, they could have made more
haste ; And if they finde they could, I must say in that
case, as *Tertullian* said, They have put God and that man   Tertul.
into the balance, and waighed them together, and found
God too light. That Mighty, that waighty, that pon-
derous God, that blasts a State with a breath, that melts
a Church with a looke, that molders a world with a touch,
that God is waighed downe with that man ; That man,
whose errand, if it be but conversation, is vanity, but,
if it be sin, is nothing, waighs downe God. The world
will needs thinke one of these *Maries*, (*Magdalen*) to
have been guilty of such entertainments as these, of
Incontinency, and of that in the lowest (that is, the
highest) kinde, Prostitution ; perchance she was ; But,
I would there were that necessity of thinking so, that
because she was a Woman, and is called a sinner, therefore
that must be her sin, as though they were capable of
no other sin ; Alas, it is not so. There may be women,
whom even another sin, the sin of Pride, and over-
valuation of themselves may have kept from that sin,
and yet may well be called sinners too ; There may be
found women, whom only their scorne of others, hath
kept honest, and yet are sinners, though not in that sin.

52. *Cosmetics*.

CERTAINLY the limits of adorning and beautifying
the body are not so narrow, so strict, as by some
sowre men they are sometimes conceived to be. Differ-

ences of Ranks, of Ages, of Nations, of Customes, make
great differences in the enlarging, or contracting of these
limits, in adorning the body; and that may come neare sin
at some time, and in some places, which is not so alwaies,
nor every where. Amongst the women there, the Jewish
women, it was so generall a thing to helpe themselves
with aromaticall Oyles, and liniments, as that that which
is said by the Prophets poore Widow, to the Prophet
2 King 4. *Elisha, That she had nothing in the house but a pot of Oyle*,
is very properly by some collected from the Originall
word, that it was not Oyle for meate, but Oyle for
unction, aromaticall Oyle, Oyle to make her looke better;
she was but poore, but a Widow, but a Prophets Widow,
(and likely to be the poorer for that) yet she left not that.
We see that even those women, whom the Kings were
to take for their Wives, and not for Mistresses, (which
is but a later name for Concubines) had a certaine, and
a long time assigned to be prepared by these aromaticall
unctions, and liniments for beauty. Neither do those
that consider, that when *Abraham* was afraid to lose his
wife *Sara* in Egypt, and that every man that saw her,
would fall in love with her, *Sara* was then above threescore; And when the King *Abimelech* did fall in love
with her, and take her from *Abraham*, she was fourescore
and ten, they doe not assigne this preservation of her
complexion, and habitude to any other thing, then the
use of those unctions, and liniments, which were ordinary
to that Nation. But yet though the extent and limit of
this adorning the body, may be larger then some austere
persons will allow, yet it is not so large, as that it should be
limited onely, by the intention and purpose of them that

doe it ; So that if they that beautifie themselves, meane no harme in it, therefore there should be no harme in it ; for, except they could as well provide, that others should take no harme, as that they should meane no harme, they may participate of the fault. And since we finde such an impossibility in rectifying and governing our owne senses, (we cannot take our owne eye, nor stop our owne eare, when we would) it is an unnecessary, and insupportable burden, to put upon our score, all the lascivious glances, and the licentious wishes of other persons, occasioned by us, in over-adorning our selves.

53. *The Skin.*

*C*ORRUPTION *in the skin,* says *Iob* ; In the outward *In pelle.* beauty, These be the Records of velim, these be the parchmins, the endictments, and the evidences that shall condemn many of us, at the last day, our *own skins* ; we have the book of God, the Law, written in our own hearts ; we have the image of God imprinted in our own souls ; wee have the character, and seal of God stamped in us, in our baptism ; and, all this is bound up in this velim, in this parchmin, in this skin of ours, and we neglect book, and image, and character, and seal, and all for the covering. It is not a clear case, if we consider the originall words properly, *That Iesabel* 2 *Reg.*9.30. *did paint* ; and yet all translators, and expositors have taken a just occasion, out of the ambiguity of those words, to cry down that abomination of painting. It is not a clear case, if we consider the propriety of the words, That *Absolon was hanged by the hair of the head* ; 2 *Sam.*18.9. and yet the Fathers and others have made use of that

indifferency, and verisimilitude, to explode that abomination, of cherishing and curling haire, to the enveagling,
and ensnaring, and entangling of others; *Iudicium*
patietur æternum, says *Saint Hierome*, Thou art guilty of
a murder, though no body die; *Quia vinum attulisti, si*
fuisset qui bibisset; Thou hast poyson'd a cup, if any
would drink, thou hast prepar'd a tentation, if any would
swallow it. *Tertullian* thought he had done enough,
when he had writ his book *De Habitu muliebri*, against
the excesse of women in clothes, but he was fain to adde
another with more vehemence, *De cultu fœminarum*,
that went beyond their clothes to their skin. And he
concludes, *Illud ambitionis crimen*, there's vain-glory
in their excesse of clothes, but, *Hoc prostitutionis*, there's
prostitution in drawing the eye to the skin. *Pliny* says,
that when their thin silke stuffes were first invented at
Rome, *Excogitatum ad fœminas denudandas*; It was but
an invention that women might go naked in clothes,
for their skins might bee seen through those clothes,
those thinne stuffes: Our women are not so carefull,
but they expose their nakednesse professedly, and paint
it, to cast bird-lime for the passengers eye. Beloved,
good dyet makes the best Complexion, and a good
Conscience is a continuall feast; A cheerfull heart makes
the best blood, and peace with God is the true cheerfulnesse of heart, Thy Saviour neglected his skin so much,
as that at last, hee scarce had any; all was torn with the
whips, and scourges; and thy skin shall come to that
absolute corruption, as that, though a hundred years
after thou art buryed, one may find thy bones, and say,
this was a *tall* man, this was a *strong* man, yet we shall

(margin note: Hieron.)

(margin note: Tertul.)

soon be past saying, upon any relique of thy skinne, This was a *fair* man; Corruption seises the skinne, all outward beauty quickly, and so it does the body, the whole frame and constitution, which is another consideration; *After my skinne, my Body.*

If the whole body were an eye, or an ear, where were the body, says Saint *Paul*; but, when of the whole body there is neither eye nor ear, nor any member left, where is the body? And what should an eye do there, where there is nothing to be seen but loathsomnesse; or a nose there, where there is nothing to be smelt, but putrefaction; or an ear, where in the grave they doe not praise God? Doth not that body that boasted but yesterday of that priviledge above all creatures, that it onely could goe upright, lie to day as flat upon the earth as the body of a horse, or of a dogge? And doth it not to morrow lose his other priviledge, of looking up to heaven? Is it not farther remov'd from the eye of heaven, the Sunne, then any dogge, or horse, by being cover'd with the earth, which they are not? Painters have presented to us with some horrour, the *sceleton*, the frame of the bones of a mans body; but the state of a body, in the dissolution of the grave, no pencil can present to us.

In corpore.
1Cor.12.17.

54. *Mud Walls.*

BEHOLD God hath walled us with mud walls, and wet mud walls, that waste away faster, then God meant at first, they should. And by sinnes, this flesh, that is but the loame and plaster of thy Tabernacle, thy body, *that*, *all*, that, *that* in the intire substance is

corrupted. Those Gummes, and spices, which should
embalme thy flesh, when thou art dead, are spent upon
that diseased body whilest thou art alive : Thou seemest,
in the eye of the world, to walk in *silks*, and thou doest
but walke in *searcloth* ; Thou hast a desire to please
some *eyes*, when thou hast much to doe, not to displease
every *Nose* ; and thou wilt solicite an adulterous entrance
into their beds, who, if they should but see thee goe into
thine own bed, would need no other mortification, nor
answer to thy solicitation. Thou pursuest the works
of the flesh, and hast none, for thy flesh is but dust held
together by plaisters : Dissolution and putrefaction is
gone over thee alive ; Thou hast over liv'd thine own
death, and art become thine own ghost, and thine own
hell.

55. *Ignorance.*

THE Schooles have made so many Divisions, and sub-
divisions, and re-divisions, and post-divisions of
Ignorance, that there goes as much learning to understand ignorance, as knowledg. One, much elder then al
they, & elder (as some will have it) then any but some of
the first Secretaries of the Holy Ghost in the Bible, that
is *Trismegistus*, hath said as much as all, *Nequitia animæ
Ignorantia*, Ignorance is not onely the drousinesse, the
sillinesse, but the wickednesse of the soule : Not onely
dis-estimation in this world, and damnification here, but
damnation in the next world, proceeds from ignorance.
And yet, here in this world, knowledge is but as the
earth, and ignorance as the Sea ; there is more sea then
earth, more ignorance then knowledge ; and as if the sea
do gaine in one place, it loses in another, so is it with

knowledge too ; if new things be found out, as many,
and as good, that were knowne before, are forgotten and
lost. What Anatomist knowes the body of man thorowly,
or what Casuist the soule ?   What Politician knowes the
distemper of the State thorowly ; or what Master, the
disorders of his owne family ? Princes glory *in Arcanis*,
that they have secrets which no man shall know, and, God
knowes, they have hearts which they know not themselves ;
Thoughts and purposes indigested fall upon them and
surprise them.   It is so in naturall, in morall, in civill
things ; we are ignorant of more things then we know ;·
And it is so in divine and supernaturall things too ; for,
for them, the Scripture is our onely light, and of the
Scripture, S. *Augustine* professes, *Plura se nescire quam
scire*, That there are more places of Scripture, that he
does not, then that he does understand.

Hell is darknesse ; & the way to it, is the cloud of
Ignorance ; hell it self is but condensed Ignorance,
multiplied Ignorance.

56. *The Imperfection of Knowledge.*

HOW imperfect is all our knowledge ?   What one
thing doe we know perfectly ? Whether wee consider
Arts, or Sciences, the servant knows but according to
the proportion of his Masters knowledge in that Art, and
the Scholar knows but according to the proportion of
his Masters knowledge in that Science ; Young men
mend not their sight by using old mens Spectacles ; and
yet we looke upon Nature, but with *Aristotles* Spectacles,
and upon the body of man, but with *Galens*, and upon
the frame of the world, but with *Ptolomies* Spectacles.

Almost all knowledge is rather like a child that is embalmed to make Mummy, then that is nursed to make a Man; rather conserved in the stature of the first age, then growne to be greater; And if there be any addition to knowledge, it is rather a new knowledge, then a greater knowledge; rather a singularity in a desire of proposing something that was not knowne at all before, then an emproving, an advancing, a multiplying of former inceptions; and by that meanes, no knowledge comes to be perfect. One Philosopher thinks he is dived to the bottome, when he sayes, he knows nothing but this, That he knows nothing; and yet another thinks, that he hath expressed more knowledge then he, in saying, That he knows not so much as that, That he knows nothing. S. *Paul* found that to be all knowledge, To know Christ; And Mahomet thinks himselfe wise therefore, because he knows not, acknowledges not Christ, as S. *Paul* does. Though a man knew not, that every sin casts another shovell of Brimstone upon him in Hell, yet if he knew that every riotous feast cuts off a year, and every wanton night seaven years of his seventy in this world, it were some degree towards perfection in knowledge. He that purchases a Mannor, will thinke to have an exact Survey of the Land: But who thinks of taking so exact a survey of his Conscience, how that money was got, that purchased that Mannor? We call that a mans meanes, which he hath; But that is truly his meanes, what way he came by it. And yet how few are there, (when a state comes to any great proportion) that know that; that know what they have, what they are worth? We have seen great Wills, dilated into glorious uses, and into pious uses, and then too narrow an estate to reach to it ; And we have seen Wills, where the Testator thinks he hath bequeathed all, and he hath not knowne halfe his own worth. When thou knowest a wife, a sonne, a servant, a friend no better, but that that wife betrayes thy bed, and that sonne thine estate, and that servant thy credit, and that friend thy secret, what canst thou say thou knowest ?

57. *Change of Mind.*

*T*HEY *changed their minds, and said, That he was a God,* Acts xxviii. 6. .... Neither have these men of Malta (consider them in what quality you will) so much honour afforded them, in the Originall, as our translation hath given them. We say, *they changed their minds*; the Original says only this, *they changed,* and no more. Alas, they, we, men of this world, wormes of this dunghil, whether Basilisks or blind wormes, whether Scarabs or Silkworms, whether high or low in the world, have no minds to change. The Platonique Philosophers did not only acknowledge *Animā in homine,* a soule in man, but *Mentem in anima,* a minde in the soul of man. They meant by the minde, the superiour faculties of the soule, and we never come to exercise them. Men and women call one another inconstant, and accuse one another of having changed their minds, when, God knowes, they have but changed the object of their eye, and seene a better white or red. An old man loves not the same sports that he did when he was young, nor a sicke man the same meats that hee did when hee was well: But these men have not changed their mindes; The old man hath changed his fancy, and the sick man his taste ; neither his minde.

The Mind implies consideration, deliberation, conclusion upon premisses ; and wee never come to that ;
wee never put the soule home ; wee never bend the soule
up to her height ; we never put her to a tryall what she
is able to doe towards discerning a tentation, what towards
resisting a tentation, what towards repenting a tentation ;
we never put her to tryall what she is able to doe by her
naturall faculties, whether by them shee cannot be as
good as a *Plato*, or a *Socrates*, who had no more but those
naturall faculties ; what by vertue of Gods generall
grace, which is that providence, in which he inwraps
all his creatures, whether by that she cannot know her
God, as well as the Oxe knowes his Crib, and the Stork
her nest ; what by vertue of those particular graces,
which God offers her in his private inspirations at home,
and in his publique Ordinances here, whether by those
she cannot be as good an houre hence, as she is now ;
and as good a day after, as that day that she receives
the Sacrament ; we never put the soule home, we never
bend the soule up to her height ; and the extent of the
soule is this minde. When *David* speaks of the people,
he sayes, *They imagine a vaine thing* ; It goes no farther,
then to the fancy, to the imagination ; it never comes
so neare the minde, as Consideration, Reflection, Examination, they onely imagine, fancy a vain thing, which is
but a waking dreame, for the fancy is the seat, the scene,
the theatre of dreames.

Psal. 2. 2.

58. *Reason and Faith*.

THEY had a precious composition for *lamps*, amongst the *ancients*, reserved especially for *Tombes*, which kept light for many hundreds of yeares ; we have had *in our age* experience, in some casuall openings of ancient vaults, of finding such lights, as were kindled, (as appeared by their inscriptions) *fifteen* or *sixteen hundred* years before ; but, as soon as that light comes to our light, it vanishes. So this *eternall*, and this *supernaturall light*, *Christ* and *faith*, enlightens, warmes, purges, and does all the profitable offices of *fire*, and *light*, if we keep it in the right spheare, in the proper place, (that is, if wee consist in *points necessary* to salvation, and *revealed* in the Scripture) but when wee bring this light to the common light of *reason*, to our inferences, and conse-quencies, it may be in danger to vanish it selfe, and perchance extinguish our reason too ; we may search so far, and reason so long of *faith* and *grace*, as that we may lose not onely *them*, but even our reason too, and sooner become *mad* then *good*. Not that we are bound to believe any thing *against reason*, that is, to believe, we know not why. It is but a slacke opinion, it is not *Beliefe*, that is not grounded upon reason. He that should come to a *Heathen man*, a meere naturall man, uncatechized, uninstructed in the rudiments of the Christian Religion, and should at first, without any preparation, present him first with this necessitie ; Thou shalt burn in fire and brimstone eternally, except thou believe *a Trinitie of Persons, in an unitie of one God*, Except thou believe the *Incarnation* of the second

Person of the Trinitie, the Sonne of God, Except thou believe that *a Virgine had a Sonne*, and the same Sonne that God had, and that God was Man too, and being the immortall God, yet died, he should be so farre from working any spirituall cure upon this poore soule, as that he should rather bring Christian Mysteries into scorne, then *him* to a beliefe. For, that man, if you proceed so, Believe all, or you burne in Hell, would finde an easie, an obvious way to escape all ; that is, first not to believe *Hell* it selfe, and then nothing could binde him to believe the rest.

The *reason* therefore of Man, must first be satisfied ; but the way of such satisfaction must be *this*, to make him see, That this World, a frame of so much harmony, so much concinnitie and conveniencie, and such a correspondence, and subordination in the parts thereof, must necessarily have had a workeman, for nothing can make it selfe : That no such workeman would deliver over a frame, and worke, of so much Majestie, to be governed by *Fortune*, casually, but would still retain the Administration thereof in his owne hands : That if he doe so, if he made the World, and *sustaine* it still by his watchfull Providence, there belongeth a worship and service to him, for doing so : That therefore he hath certainly revealed to man, what kinde of worship, and service, shall be acceptable to him : That this manifestation of his Will, must be permanent, it must be *written*, there must be a *Scripture*, which is his *Word* and his *Will* : And that therefore, from that Scripture, from that Word of God, all Articles of our Beliefe are to bee drawne.

If then his *Reason* confessing all this, aske farther

proofe, how he shall know that *these Scriptures* accepted by the Christian Church, are the true Scriptures, let him bring any other Booke which pretendeth to be the Word of God, into comparison with these; It is true, we have not a *Demonstration*; not such an Evidence as that one and two, are three, to prove these to be Scriptures of God; God hath not proceeded in that manner, to drive our Reason into a pound, and to force it by a peremptory necessitie to accept these for Scriptures, for then, here had been no exercise of our *Will*, and our assent, if we could not have resisted. But yet these Scriptures have so orderly, so sweet, and so powerfull a working upon the reason, and the understanding, as if any third man, who were utterly discharged of all preconceptions and anticipations in matter of Religion, one who were altogether *neutrall*, disinterested, unconcerned in either party, nothing towards a *Turke*, and as little toward a *Christian*, should heare a *Christian* pleade for his Bible, and a *Turke* for his Alcoran, and should weigh the evidence of both; the Majesty of the *Style*, the punctuall accomplishment of the *Prophecies*, the harmony and concurrence of the *foure Evangelists*, the consent and unanimity of the *Christian Church* ever since, and many other such reasons, he would be drawne to such an Historicall, such a Grammaticall, such a Logicall beliefe of our Bible, as to preferre it before any other, that could be pretended to be the Word of God. He would believe it, and he would know *why* he did so. For let no man thinke that *God* hath given him so much ease here, as to save him by believing he knoweth not what, or why. *Knowledge* cannot save us, but we cannot be saved without Knowledge ; Faith is not on this side Knowledge, but beyond it ; we must necessarily come to *Knowledge* first, though we must not stay at it, when we are come thither. For, a regenerate Christian, being now a *new Creature*, hath also *a new facultie of Reason :* and so believeth the Mysteries of Religion, out of another Reason, then as a meere naturall Man, he believed naturall and morall things. He believeth them for their own sake, by *Faith,* though he take *Knowledge* of them before, by that common Reason, and by those humane Arguments, which worke upon other men, in naturall or morall things. Divers men may walke by the Sea side, and the same beames of the Sunne giving light to them all, one gathereth by the benefit of that light pebles, or speckled shells, for curious vanitie, and another gathers precious Pearle, or medicinall Ambar, by the same light. So the common light of reason illumins us all ; but one imployes this light upon the searching of impertinent vanities, another by a better use of the same light, finds out the Mysteries of Religion ; and when he hath found them, loves them, not for the lights sake, but for the naturall and true worth of the thing it self. Some men by the benefit of this light of Reason, have found out things profitable and usefull to the whole world ; As in particular, *Printing,* by which the learning of the whole world is communicable to one another, and our minds and our inventions, our wits and compositions may trade and have commerce together, and we may participate of one anothers understandings, as well as of our Clothes, and Wines, and Oyles, and other Merchandize : So by the benefit of this light of reason, they have found out *Artillery*, by which warres come to quicker ends then heretofore, and the great expence of bloud is avoyded : for the numbers of men slain now, since the invention of Artillery, are much lesse then before, when the sword was the executioner. Others, by the benefit of this light have searched and found the secret corners of gaine, and profit, wheresoever they lie. They have found wherein the weakenesse of another man consisteth, and made their profit of that, by circumventing him in a bargain : They have found his riotous, and wastefull inclination, and they have fed and fomented that disorder, and kept open that leake, to their advantage, and the others ruine. They have found where was the easiest, and most accessible way, to sollicite the Chastitie of a woman, whether *Discourse*, *Musicke*, or *Presents*, and according to that discovery, they have pursued *hers*, and *their* own eternall destruction. By the benefit of this light, men see through the darkest, and most impervious places, that are, that is, *Courts of Princes*, and the greatest *Officers* in Courts ; and can submit themselves to second, and to advance the humours of men in great place, and so make their profit of the weakenesses which they have discovered in these great men. All the wayes, both of *Wisdome*, and of *Craft* lie open to this light, this light of naturall reason : But when they have gone all these wayes by the benefit of this light, they have got no further, then to have walked by a tempestuous Sea, and to have gathered pebles, and speckled cockle shells. Their light seems to be great out of the same reason, that a Torch in a misty night, seemeth greater then in a clear, because it hath

kindled and inflamed much thicke and grosse Ayre round
about it.   So the light and wisedome of worldly men,
seemeth great, because he hath kindled an admiration,
or an applause in Aiery flatterers, not because it is so
in deed.

But, if thou canst take this light of reason that is in
thee, this poore snuffe, that is almost out in thee, thy
faint and dimme knowledge of God, that riseth out of
this light of nature, if thou canst in those embers, those
cold ashes, finde out one small coale, and wilt take the
paines to kneell downe, and blow that coale with thy
devout *Prayers*, and light thee a *little candle*, (a *desire*
to reade that Booke, which they call the Scriptures, and
the Gospell, and the Word of God ;) If with that little
candle thou canst creep humbly into low and poore
places, if thou canst finde thy Saviour in a *Manger*, and
in his *swathing clouts*, in his humiliation, and blesse God
for that beginning, if thou canst finde him flying into
Egypt, and finde in thy selfe a disposition to accompany
him in a persecution, in a banishment, if not a bodily
banishment, a locall banishment, yet a *reall*, *a spirituall
banishment*, a banishment from those sinnes, and that
sinnefull conversation, which thou hast loved more then
thy *Parents*, or *Countrey*, or thine owne body, which
perchance thou hast consumed, and destroyed with that
sinne ; if thou canst finde him contenting and containing
himselfe at home in his fathers house, and not breaking
out, no not about the worke of our salvation, till the
due time was come, when it was to be done.   And if
according to that example, thou canst contain thy selfe
in that station and vocation in which God hath planted

thee, and not, through a hasty and precipitate *zeale*, breake out to an imaginary, and intempestive, and unseasonable *Reformation*, either in *Civill* or *Ecclesiasticall* businesse, which belong not to thee; if with this little poore light, these *first degrees* of *Knowledge* and *Faith*, thou canst follow him into the *Garden*, and gather up some of the droppes of his precious Bloud and sweat, which he shed for thy soule, if thou canst follow him to *Jerusalem*, and pick up some of those *teares*, which he shed upon that City, and upon thy soule; if thou canst follow him to the place of his scourging, and to his crucifying, and provide thee some of that balme, which must cure thy soule; if after all this, thou canst turne this little light inward, and canst thereby discerne where thy diseases, and thy wounds, and thy corruptions are, and canst apply those teares, and blood and balme to them, (all this is, That if thou attend the light of naturall reason, and cherish that, and exalt that, so that that bring thee to a *love of the Scriptures*, and that *love to a beleefe* of the truth thereof, and that *historicall faith* to a *faith of application, of appropriation*, that as all those things were certainly done, so they were certainly done *for thee*) thou shalt never envy the lustre and glory of the great lights of worldly men, which are great by the infirmity of others, or by their own opinion, great because others think them great, or because they think themselves so, but thou shalt finde, that howsoever they magnifie their lights, their wit, their learning, their industry, their fortune, their favour, and *sacrifice to their owne nets*, yet thou shalt see, *Habak* 1. that thou by thy small light hast gathered *Pearle* and *Amber*, and they by their great lights nothing but shels and pebles; they have determined the light of nature, upon the booke of nature, this world, and thou hast carried the light of nature higher, thy naturall reason, and even *humane arguments*, have brought thee to reade the Scriptures, and to that *love*, God hath set to the seale of *faith*. Their light shall set at noone; even in their heighth, some heavy crosse shall cast a damp upon their soule, and cut off all their succours, and devest them of all comforts, and thy light shall grow up, from a *faire hope*, to a modest assurance and *infallibility*, that that light shall never go out, nor the *works of darknesse*, nor the *Prince of darknesse* ever prevaile upon thee, but as thy light of *reason* is exalted by *faith* here, so thy light of *faith* shall be exalted into the light *of glory*, and fruition in the Kingdome of heaven. Before the sunne was made, there was *a light* which did that office of distinguishing night and day; but when the sunne was created, that did all the offices of the former light, and more. *Reason* is that first, and primogeniall light, and goes no farther in a naturall man; but in a man regenerate by faith, that light does all that reason did, *and more*; and all his *Morall*, and *Civill*, and *Domestique*, and indifferent actions, (though they be never done *without Reason*) yet their principall scope, and marke is the glory of God, and though they seeme but *Morall*, or *Civill*, or *domestique*, yet they have a deeper tincture, a heavenly nature, a relation *to God*, in them.

59. *True Knowledge.*

BLESSED are they that inanimate all their knowledge, consummate all in Christ Jesus. The University is a Paradise, Rivers of knowledge are there, Arts and Sciences flow from thence. Counsell Tables are *Horti conclusi*, (as it is said in the Canticles) *Gardens that are walled in*, and they are *Fontes signati*, *Wells that are sealed up*; bottomlesse depths of unsearchable Counsels there. But those *Aquæ quietudinum*, which the Prophet speaks of, *The waters of rest*, they flow *à magistro bono*, from this good master, and flow into him again; All knowledge that begins not, and ends not with his glory, is but a giddy, but a vertiginous circle, but an elaborate and exquisite ignorance.

60. *Terrible Things.*

IN the frame and constitution of al Religions, these Materials, these Elements have ever entred; Some words of a remote signification, not vulgarly understood, some actions of a kinde of halfe-horror and amazement, some places of reservation and retirednesse, and appropriation to some sacred persons, and inaccessible to all others. Not to speake of the services, and sacrifices of the Gentiles, and those selfe-manglings and lacerations of the Priests of *Isis*, and of the Priests of *Baal*, (faintly counterfaited in the scourgings and flagellations in the Roman Church) In that very discipline which was delivered from God, by *Moses*, the service was full of mysterie, and horror, and reservation, *By terrible things*, (Sacrifices of blood in manifold effusions) *God answered them*, then. So, the matter of Doctrine was delivered mysteriously, and with much reservation, and in-intelligiblenesse, as *Tertullian* speaks. The Joy and Glory of Heaven was not easily understood by their temporall abundances of Milke, and Honey, and Oyle, and Wine ; and yet, in these (and scarce any other way) was Heaven presented, and notified to that people by *Moses*. Christ, a Messias, a Saviour of the World, by shedding his blood for it, was not easily discerned in their Types and Sacrifices ; And yet so, and scarce any other way was Christ revealed unto them. God sayes, *I have multiplied visions, and used similitudes, by the ministery of the Prophets.* They were Visions, they were Similitudes, not plaine and evident things, obvious to every understanding, that God led his people by. . . .

Hos.12.10.

So that God in the Old, and Christ in the New Testament, hath conditioned his Doctrine, and his Religion (that is, his outward worship) so, as that evermore there should be preserved a Majesty, and a reverentiall feare, and an awfull discrimination of Divine things from Civill, and evermore something reserved to be inquired after, and laid up in the mouth of the Priest, that the People might acknowledge an obligation from him, in the exposition, and application thereof. Nay, this way of *answering us by terrible things*, (that is, by things that imprint a holy horror, and a Religious reverence) is much more in the Christian Church, then it can have beene in any other Religion ; Because, if wee consider the Jews, (which is the onely Religion, that can enter into any comparison with the Christian, in this kinde) yet, we looke more directly and more immediately upon

God in Christ, then they could, who saw him but by
way of Prophecie, a future thing that should be done
after ; we looke upon God, in History, in matter of fact,
upon things done, and set before our eyes ; and so that
Majesty, and that holy amazement, is more to us then
ever it was to any other Religion, because we have
a nearer approximation, and vicinity to God in Christ,
then any others had, in any representions of their Gods ;
and it is a more dazeling thing to looke upon the Sun,
in a direct, then in an oblique or side line. And therefore,
the love of God, which is so often proposed unto us,
is as often seasoned with the feare of God ; nay, all our
Religious affections are reduced to that one, To a reverentiall feare ; If he be a *Master*, he cals for *feare*, and, Mal. 1. 6.
If he be a *Father*, he calls for *honor* ; And honour implies
a reverentiall feare. And that is the Art that *David*
professes to teach, *Artem timendi, Come ye children, and* Psal. 34. 12.
hearken unto me, and I will teach you the feare of the Lord.
That you thinke not Divinity an Occupation, nor
Church-Service a recreation ; but still remember, That
the God of our Salvation (God working in the Christian
Church) *will answer you* ; but yet, *by terrible things* ;
that is, by not being over-fellowly with God, nor over-
homely with places, and acts of Religion ; which, it
may be an advancement to your Devotion and edification,
to consider, in some particulars in the Christian Church.

And first, consider we it, in our manners, and conversa- *In moribus.*
tion. Christ sayes, *Henceforth I call you not servants,* Iohn 15. 14.
but friends. But, howsoever Christ called him *friend*,
that was come to the feast without the wedding garment,
he *cast him out*, because he made no difference of that Mat. 22. 12.

place from another. First then, remember by what terrible things God answers thee in the Christian Church, when he comes to that round and peremptory issue, *Qui non crediderit, damnabitur*, He that beleeves not every Article of the Christian faith, and with so stedfast a belief, as that he would dye for it, *Damnabitur*, (no modification, no mollification, no going lesse) He shal be damned. Consider too the nature of Excōmunication, That it teares a man from the body of Christ Jesus ; That that man withers that is torne off, and Christ himselfe is wounded in it. Consider the insupportable penances that were laid upon sinners, by those penitentiall Canons, that went through the Church in those Primitive times ; when, for many sins which we passe through now, without so much as taking knowledge that they are sins, men were not admitted to the Communion all their lives, no, nor easily upon their death-beds. Consider how dangerously an abuse of that great doctrine of Predestination may bring thee to thinke, that God is bound to thee, and thou not bound to him, That thou maiest renounce him, and he must embrace thee, and so make thee too familiar with God, and too homely with Religion, upon presumption of a Decree. Consider that when thou preparest any uncleane action, in any sinfull nakednesse, God is not onely present with thee in that roome then, but then tels thee, That at the day of Judgement thou must stand in his presence, and in the presence of all the World, not onely naked, but in that foule, and sinfull, and uncleane action of nakednesse, which thou committedst then ; Consider all this and confesse, that for

Marke 16. 16.

matters of manners, and conversation, *The God of thy Salvation answers thee by terrible things.* And so it is also, if we consider Prayer in the Church.

Gods House is the house of Prayer; It is his Court of *In oratione.* Requests; There he receives petitions, there he gives Order upon them. And you come to God in his House, as though you came to keepe him company, to sit downe, and talke with him halfe an houre; or you come as Ambassadors, covered in his presence, as though ye came from as great a Prince as he. You meet below, and there make your bargaines, for biting, for devouring Usury, and then you come up hither to prayers, and so make God your Broker. You rob, and spoile, and eat his people as bread, by Extortion, and bribery, and deceitfull waights and measures, and deluding oathes in buying and selling, and then come hither, and so make God your Receiver, and his house a den of Thieves. His house is *Sanctum Sanctorum*, The holiest of holies, and you make it onely *Sanctuarium*; It should be a place sanctified by your devotions, and you make it onely a Sanctuary to priviledge Malefactors, A place that may redeeme you from the ill opinion of men, who must in charity be bound to thinke well of you, because they see you here. *Offer this to one of your Princes*, (as God argues in the Prophet) and see, if he will suffer his house to be prophaned by such uncivill abuses; And, *Terribilis* Psal. 47. 3. *Rex, The Lord most high is terrible, and a great King over all the earth*; and, *Terribilis super omnes Deos, More* 96. 4. *terrible then all other Gods.* Let thy Master be thy god, or thy Mistresse thy god, thy Belly be thy god, or thy Back be thy god, thy fields be thy god, or thy chests be thy god, *Terribilis super omnes Deos*, The Lord is terrible

95. 3. above all gods, *A great God, and a great King above all gods.* You come, and call upon him by his name here, But

Deut.28.58. *Magnum & terribile, Glorious and fearefull is the name of the Lord thy God.* And, as if the Son of God were but the Son of some Lord, that had beene your Schoole-fellow in your youth, and so you continued a boldnesse to him ever after, so, because you have beene brought up with Christ from your cradle, and catechized in his name, his name becomes lesse reverend unto you, And

Psal.111.4. *Sanctum & terribile*, Holy, and reverend, Holy and terrible should his name be.

61. *The Fate of the Heathen.*

Pagani.   AND as those blessed Fathers of tender bowels, enlarged themselves in this distribution, and apportioning the mercy of God, that it consisted best with the nature of his mercy, that as his Saints had suffered temporall calamities in this world, in this world they should be recompenced with temporall abundances, so did they inlarge this mercy farther, and carry it even to the Gentiles, to the Pagans that had no knowledge of Christ in any established Church. You shall not finde a *Trismegistus*, a *Numa Pompilius*, a *Plato*, a *Socrates*, for whose salvation you shall not finde some Father, or some Ancient and Reverend Author, an Advocate. In which liberality of Gods mercy, those tender Fathers proceed partly upon that rule, That in *Trismegistus*, and in the rest, they finde evident impressions, and testimonies, that they knew the Son of God, and knew the Trinity; and then, say they, why should not these good men, beleeving a Trinity, be saved? and partly they goe upon that rule, which goes through so many of the Fathers, *Facienti quod in se est*, That to that man who does as much as he can, by the light of nature, God never denies grace; and then, say they, why should not these men that doe so be saved? And, upon this ground, S. *Dionyse*, the Areopagite sayes, That from the beginning of the world, God hath called some men of all Nations, and of all sorts, by the ministry of Angels, though not by the ministry of the Church. To me, to whom God hath revealed his Son, in a Gospel, by a Church, there can be no way of salvation, but by applying that Son of God, by that Gospel, in that Church. Nor is there any other foundation for any, nor other name by which any can be saved, but the name of Jesus. But how this foundation is presented, and how this name of Jesus is notified to them, amongst whom there is no Gospel preached, no Church established, I am not curious in inquiring. I know God can be as mercifull as those tender Fathers present him to be; and I would be as charitable as they are. And therefore humbly imbracing that manifestation of his Son, which he hath afforded me, I leave God, to his unsearchable waies of working upon others, without farther inquisition.

62. *The Church a Company.*

THE Key of *David* openeth and no man shutteth; The Spirit of Comfort shineth upon us, and would not be blown out. Monasterie, and Ermitage, and Anchorate, and such words of singularitie are not *Synonyma* with those plurall words *Concio, Cœtus, Ecclesia, Synagoga*

& *Congregatio*, in which words God delivereth himselfe
to us. A Church is a Company, Religion is Religation,
a binding of men together in one manner of Worship ;
and Worship is an exteriour service ; and that exteriour
service is the *Venite exultemus*, to come and rejoyce
in the presence of God.

63. *God Proceeds Legally.*

GOD proceeds legally ; Publication before Judgement.
God shall condemn no man, for not beleeving in
Christ, to whom Christ was never manifested. ʼ*Tis
true*, that God is said to have come to *Eliah* in that
still small voice, and not in the *strong wind*, not in the
Earth-quake, not in the *fire*. So God says, *Sibilabo
populum meum*, I will but hisse, I will but whisper for
my people, and gather them so. So Christ tells us things
in *darknesse* ; And so Christ speakes to us in our *Ear* ; And
these low voices, and holy whisperings, and halfe-silences,
denote to us, the inspirations of his Spirit, *as his Spirit
beares witnesse with our spirit* ; as the Holy Ghost insinu-
ates himselfe into our soules, and works upon us so,
by his *private motions*. But this is not Gods ordinary
way, to be whispering of secrets. The first thing that
God made, was *light* ; The last thing, that he hath reserved
to doe ; is the manifestation of the light of his Essence
in our Glorification. And for Publication of himselfe
here, by the way, he hath constituted a *Church*, in
a Visibility, in an eminency, *as a City upon a hill* ; And
in this Church, his Ordinance is Ordinance indeed ; his
Ordinance of preaching batters the soule, and by that
breach, the Spirit enters ; His Ministers are an *Earth-*

*1 Reg.*19.12.
Zech. 10. 8.
Mat. 10.27.

quake, and shake an earthly soule ; They are the *sonnes of thunder*, and scatter a cloudy conscience ; They are as the fall of waters, and carry with them whole Congregations ; 3000 at a Sermon, 5000 at a Sermon, a whole City, such a City as Niniveh at a Sermon ; and they are as the roaring of a Lion, where the Lion of the tribe of Juda, cries down the Lion that seekes whom he may devour ; that is, Orthodoxall and fundamentall truths, are established against clamorous, and vociferant innovations. Therefore what Christ tels us in the darke, he bids us speake in the light ; and what he saies in our eare, he bids us preach on the house top. Nothing is Gospell, not *Evangelium*, good message, if it be not put into a Messengers mouth, and delivered by him ; nothing is conducible to his end, nor available to our salvation, except it be avowable doctrine, doctrine that may be spoke alowd, though it awake them, that sleep in their sinne, and make them the more froward, for being so awaked.

God hath made all things in a *Roundnesse*, from the round superficies of this earth, which we tread here, to the round convexity of those heavens, w^ch (as long as they shal have any beeing) shall be our footstool, when we come to heaven, God hath wrapped up all things in Circles, and then a Circle hath no *Angles* ; there are no *Corners* in a Circle. Corner Divinity, clandestine Divinity are incompatible termes ; If it be Divinity, it is avowable. *The heathens* served their Gods in Temples, *sub dio*, without roofs or coverings, in a free opennesse ; and, where they could, in Temples made of *Specular stone*, that was transparent as glasse, or crystall, so as they which walked without in the streets, might see all that was done within. And even nature it self taught the naturall man, to make that one argument of a man truly religious, *Aperto vivere voto*, That he durst pray aloud, and let the world heare, what he asked at Gods hand ; which duty is best performed, when we joyne with the Congregation in publique prayer. *Saint Augustine*, hath made that note upon the *Donatists*, That they were *Clancularii*, clandestine Divines, Divines in Corners. And in *Photius*, we have such a note almost upon all Heretiques ; as the *Nestorian* was called *Coluber*, a snake, because though he kept in the garden, or in the meadow, in the Church, yet he lurked and lay hid, to doe mischief. And the *Valentinian* was called a Grashopper, because he leaped and skipped from place to place ; and that creature, the Grashopper, you may hear as you passe, but you shall hardly find him at his singing ; you may hear a Conventicle Schismatick, heare him in his Pamphlets, heare him in his Disciples, but hardly surprize him at his exercise. Publication is a fair argument of truth. That tasts of *Luthers* holy animosity, and zealous vehemency, when he says, *Audemus gloriari Christum à nobis primo vulgatum* ; other men had made some attempts at a Reformation, and had felt the pulse of some persons, and some Courts, and some Churches, how they would relish a Reformation ; But *Luther* rejoyces with a holy exultation, That he first published it, that he first put the world to it. So the Apostles proceeded ; when they came in their peregrination, to a new State, to a new Court, to Rome it selfe, they did not enquire, how stands the Emperour affected to Christ, and to the preaching

of his Gospel; Is there not *a Sister*, or *a Wife* that might
be wrought upon to further the preaching of Christ?
Are there not some persons, great in power and place,
that might be content to hold a party together, by
admitting the preaching of Christ? This was not their
way; They only considered who sent them; Christ
Jesus: And what they brought; *salvation* to every soul
that embraced Christ Jesus. That they preached; and
still begunne with a *Væ si non*; Never tell us of displeasure, or disgrace, or detriment, or death, for preaching
of Christ. For, *woe be unto us*, if we preach him not:
And still they ended with a *Qui non crediderit, Damnabitur*,
Never deceive your own souls, He, to whom Christ hath
been preached, and beleeves not, shall be damned. All
Divinity that is bespoken, and not ready made, fitted
to certaine turnes, and not to generall ends; And all
Divines that have their *soules* and *consciences*, so disposed,
as their Libraries may bee, (At that end stand Papists,
and at that end Protestants, and he comes in in the
middle, as neare one as the other) all these have a brackish
taste; as a River hath that comes near the Sea, so have
they, in comming so neare the Sea of Rome.

64. *The Church.*

AS Waspes make combs, but empty ones, so do
Heretiques Churches, but frivolous ones, ineffectuall
ones. And, as we told you before, That errors and
disorders are as well in wayes, as in ends, so may we
deprive our selves of the benefit of this judgement, The
Church, as well in circumstances, as in substances, as
well in opposing discipline, as doctrine. The holy Ghost

reproves thee, convinces thee, *of judgement*, that is, offers thee the knowledge that such a Church there is ; A Jordan to wash thine originall leprosie in Baptisme ; A City upon a mountaine, to enlighten thee in the works of darknesse ; a continuall application of all that Christ Jesus said, and did, and suffered, to thee. Let no soule say, she can have all this at Gods hands immediatly, and never trouble the Church ; That she can passe her pardon between God and her, without all these formalities, by a secret repentance. It is true, beloved, a true repentance is never frustrate : But yet, if thou wilt think thy selfe a little Church, a Church to thy selfe, because thou hast heard it said, That thou art a little world, a world in thy selfe, that figurative, that meta-phoricall representation shall not save thee. Though thou beest a world to thy self, yet if thou have no more corn, nor oyle, nor milk, then growes in thy self, or flowes from thy self, thou wilt starve ; Though thou be a Church in thy fancy, if thou have no more seales of grace, no more absolution of sin, then thou canst give thy self, thou wilt perish. *Per solam Ecclesiam sacrificium libenter accipit Deus :* Thou maist be a Sacrifice in thy chamber, but God receives a Sacrifice more cheerefully at Church. *Sola, quæ pro errantibus fiducialiter intercedit,* Only the Church hath the nature of a surety ; Howsoever God may take thine own word at home, yet he accepts the Church in thy behalfe, as better security. Joyne therefore ever with the Communion of Saints ; *Et cum membrum sis ejus corporis, quod loquitur omnibus linguis, crede te omnibus linguis loqui,* Whilst thou art a member of that Congregation, that speaks to God with a thousand

Gregor.

August.

7

tongues, beleeve that thou speakest to God with all
those tongues. And though thou know thine own
prayers unworthy to come up to God, because thou
liftest up to him an eye, which is but now withdrawne
from a licentious glancing, and hands which are guilty
yet of unrepented uncleannesses, a tongue that hath
but lately blasphemed God, a heart which even now
breaks the walls of this house of God, and steps home,
or runs abroad upon the memory, or upon the new
plotting of pleasurable or profitable purposes, though
this make thee thinke thine own prayers uneffectuall,
yet beleeve that some honester man then thy selfe stands
by thee, and that when he prayes with thee, he prayes
for thee ; and that, if there be one righteous man in
the Congregation, thou art made the more acceptable
to God by his prayers ; and make that benefit of this
reproofe, this conviction of the holy Ghost, That he
convinces thee *De judicio*, assures thee of an orderly
Church established for thy reliefe, and that the application of thy self to this judgement, The Church, shall
enable thee to stand upright in that other judgement,
the last judgement, which is also enwrapped in the
signification of this word of our Text, *Iudgement*, and
is the conclusion for this day.

As God begun all with judgement, (for he made all *Iudicium*
things in measure, number, and waight) as he proceeded *finale.*
Sap. 11.
with judgement, in erecting a judiciall seat for our
direction, and correction, the Church, so he shall end
all with judgement, The finall, and generall judgement,
at the Resurrection ; which he that beleeves not, beleeves
nothing ; not God ; for, *He that commeth to God* (that Heb. 11. 6.

makes any step towards him) *must beleeve, Deum remunera-
torem*, God, and God in that notion, as he is a Rewarder ;
Therefore there is judgement. But was this work left
for the Holy Ghost ? Did not the naturall man that
knew no Holy Ghost, know this ? Truly, all their
fabulous Divinity, all their Mythology, their Minos, and
their Rhadamanthus, tasted of such a notion, as a judgement. And yet the first planters of the Christian Religion
found it hardest to fixe this roote of all other articles
That Christ should come againe to judgement. Miserable
and froward men ! They would beleeve it in their fables,
and would not beleeve it in the Scriptures ; They would
beleeve it in the nine Muses, and would not beleeve it
in the twelve Apostles ; They would beleeve it by Apollo,
and they would not beleeve it by the Holy Ghost ;
They would be saved Poetically, and fantastically, and
would not reasonably, and spiritually ; By Copies, and
not by Originals ; by counterfeit things at first deduced
by their Authors, out of our Scriptures, and yet not by
the word of God himself.

65. *Reverence in Church.*

THE rituall and ceremoniall, the outward worship
of God, the places, the times, the manner of meetings, [which] are in the disposition of Christian Princes,
and by their favours of those Churches, which are in their
government : and not to rejoyce in the peacefull exercise
of those spirituall helps, not to be glad of them, is a transgression. Now the Prophet expresses this rejoycing thus,
Venite exultemus, let us come and rejoyce. We must
doe both. And therefore they who out of a thraldome to

another Church abstaine from these places of these exercises, that doe not come, or if they doe come, doe not rejoyce, but though they be here brought by necessity of law, or of observation, yet had rather they were in another Chappell, or at another kinde of service then in this : and they also who abstain out of imaginary defects in this church, & think they cannot perform *Davids De profundis*, they cannot call upon God out of the depth, except it be in a Conventicle in a cellar, nor acknowledge *Solomons Excelsis Excelsior*, that God is *Eccles.* 5. 8. higher then the highest, except it be in a Conventicle in a garret, & when they are here wink at the ornaments, & stop their ears at the musique of the Church, in which manner she hath always expressed her rejoycing in those helps of devotion ; or if there bee a third sort who abstain, because they may not be here at so much ease, and so much liberty, as at their own houses, all these are under this transgression. Are they in the Kings house at so much liberty as in their own ? and is not this the King of Kings house ? Or have they seene the King in his owne house, use that liberty to cover himselfe in his ordinary manner of covering, at any part of Divine Service ? Every Preacher will look, and justly, to have the Congregation uncovered at the reading of his Text : and is not the reading of the Lesson, at time of Prayer, the same Word of the same God, to be received with the same reverence ? The service of God is one entire thing ; and though we celebrate some parts with more, or with lesse reverence, some kneeling, some standing, yet if we afford it no reverence, we make that no part of Gods service. And therefore I must humbly intreat them, who make this Quire the place of their Devotion, to testifie their devotion by more outward reverence there; wee know our parts in this place, and we doe them; why any stranger should think himself more priviledged in this part of Gods House, then we, I know not. I presume no man will mis-interpret this that I say here now; nor, if this may not prevaile, mis-interpret the service of our Officers, if their continuing in that unreverent manner give our Officers occasion to warn them of that personally in the place, whensoever they see them stray into that uncomely negligence. They should not blame me now, they must not blame them then, when they call upon them for this reverence in this Quire; neither truly can there be any greater injustice, then when they who will not do their duties, blame others for doing theirs.

66. *Going to Church.*

BETWEENE that fearefull occasion of comming to Church, which S. *Augustine* confesses and laments, That they came to make wanton bargaines with their eyes, and met there, because they could meet no where else; and that more fearfull occasion of comming, when they came onely to elude the Law, and proceeding in their treacherous and traiterous religion in their heart, and yet communicating with us, draw God himselfe into their conspiracies, and to mocke us, make a mocke of God, and his religion too: betweene these two, this licencious comming, and this treacherous comming, there are many commings to Church, commings for company, for observation, for musique: And all these indispositions are ill at prayers; there they are unwholesome, but at the Sacrament, deadly: He that brings any collaterall respect to prayers, looses the benefit of the prayers of the Congregation; and he that brings that to a Sermon, looses the blessing of Gods ordinance in that Sermon; hee heares but the Logique, or the Retorique, or the Ethique, or the poetry of the Sermon, but the Sermon of the Sermon he heares not; but he that brings this disposition to the Sacrament, ends not in the losse of a benefit, but he acquires, and procures his owne damnation.

67. *Prayer.*

I BRING not a *Star-chamber* with me up into the Pulpit, to punish a *forgery*, if you counterfeit a zeale in coming hither now; nor an *Exchequer*, to punish usurious contracts, though made in the Church; nor a high *Commission*, to punish incontinencies, if they be promoted by wanton interchange of looks, in this place. Onely by my prayers, which he hath promised to accompany and prosper in his service, I can diffuse his overshadowing Spirit over all the corners of this Congregation, and pray that *Publican*, that stands below afar off, and dares not lift up his eyes to heaven, to receive a chearfull confidence, that his sinnes are forgiven him; and pray that *Pharisee*, that stands above, and onely thanks God, that he is not like other men, to believe himself to be, if not a rebellious, yet an unprofitable servant.

68. *Prayer.*

PRAYER is our whole service to God. Earnest Prayer hath the nature of Importunity; Wee presse, wee importune God in Prayer; Yet that puts not God to a morosity, to a frowardnesse; God flings not away from that; Gods suffers that importunity, and more. Prayer hath the nature of Impudency; Wee threaten God in Prayer; as *Gregor: Nazi:* adventures to expresse it; He saies, his Sister, in the vehemence of her Prayer, would threaten God, *Et honesta quadam impudentia, egit impudentem*; She came, saies he, to a religious impudency with God, and to threaten him, that she would never depart from his Altar, till she had her Petition granted; And God suffers this Impudency, and more. Prayer hath the nature of Violence; In the publique Prayers of the Congregation, we besiege God, saies *Tertul:* and we take God Prisoner, and bring God to our Conditions; and God is glad to be straitned by us in that siege. This Prophet here executes before, what the Apostle counsailes after, *Pray incessantly*; Even in his singing he prayes; And as S. *Basil* saies, *Etiam somnia justorum preces sunt*, A Good mans dreames are Prayers, he prayes, and not sleepily, in his sleepe, so *Davids* Songs are Prayers.

69. *The Time of Prayer.*

THE comfort of being presented to God as innocent as *Adam*, then when God breathed a soule into him, yea as innocent as Christ Jesus himselfe, when he breathed out his soule to God; oh how blessed is that soule that enjoyes it, and how bold that tongue that goes about to expresse it! This is the blessednesse which the godly attaine to by prayer, but not by every sudden *Lord, Lord,* or every occasionall holy interjection, but by serious prayer, invested, as with the former, so with that other circumstance that remains, *In tempore opportuno, In a time when thou mayest be found.*

This time is not those *Horæ stativæ, Horæ canonicæ,* *In tempore.* those fixed houres in the Romane Church, where men are bound to certaine prayers at certaine houres. Not that it is inconvenient for men to binde themselves to certaine fixed times of prayer in their private Exercises; and though not by such a vow, as that it shall be an impiety, yet by so solemne a purpose, as that it shall be a levity to breake it. I have known the greatest Christian Prince, (in Style and Title) even at the Audience of an Ambassador, at the sound of a Bell, kneele downe in our presence and pray; and God forbid, he should be blamed for doing so; But to place a merit in observing those times, as they doe, is not a right understanding of this time of finding. Nor is it those transitory and inter-locutory prayers, which out of custome and fashion we make, and still proceed in our sin; when we pretend to speake to God, but like Comedians upon a stage, turne over our shoulder, and whisper to the Devill. . . .

The Manifestation of the Gospel, that is, the helpes *Prosperi-* which God offers us, more then Jews, or Gentils, in the *tas.* Ministery of the Gospel, and the Ordinances of his Church, is the time of finding God; And woe unto us, if we seeke him not whilest he affords us these helpes; And then the time of affliction, when God threatens

to hide his face, but hath not yet hidden it, but awakens
us by a calamity, is a time of finding God. But the best
and the clearest time is in the Sun-shine, then when
he appeares to us in the warme and chearefull splendor
of temporall blessings upon us; Then when thou hast
a good estate, and good children to let it descend upon;
Then when thou hast good health, and a good profession
to exercise thy strength, and thy labors in; Then when
the dishes upon thy table are doubled, and thy cup
overflows, and the hungry and thirsty soules of the poore
doe not onely feed upon the crums under thy table, and
lick up the overflowings of thy cup, but divide dishes
with thee, and enter into the midst of thy Bolls; Then
when thou hast temporall blessings, (that is Gods silver)
and his grace to use those blessings well, (that is Gods
gold) then is the best time of finding the Lord, for then
he looks upon thee in the Sun-shine, and then thy
thankfull acknowledgement of former blessings is the
most effectuall prayer thou canst make, for the continuance, and enlargement of them.

70. *At Table and Bed.*

THEREFORE, beloved, since every master of a family,
who is a *Bishop in his house*, should call his family
together, to humble, and powre out their soules to God,
let him consider, that when he comes to kneele at the
side of his table, to pray, he comes to build a Church
there; and therefore should sanctifie that place, with
a due, and penitent consideration how voluptuously
he hath formerly abused Gods blessings at that place,
how superstitiously, and idolatrously he hath flatter'd

and humour'd some great and useful ghests invited by
him to that place, how expensively, he hath served his
owne ostentation and vain-glory, by excessive feasts
at that place, whilest *Lazarus* hath lien panting, and
gasping at the gate ; and let him consider what a dangerous Mockery this is to Christ *Jesus*, if he pretend by
kneeling at that table, fashionally to build Christ a Church
by that solemnity at the table side, and then crucifie
Christ again, by these sinnes, when he is sat at the table.
When thou kneelest down at thy *bed side*, to shut up
the day at night, or to beginne it in the morning, thy
servants, thy children, thy little flock about thee, there
thou buildest a Church too : And therefore sanctifie
that place ; wash it with thy tears, and with a repentant
consideration ; That in that bed thy children were
conceived in sinne, that in that bed thou hast turned
mariage which God afforded thee for remedy, and
physique to voluptuosnesse, and licenciousnesse ; That
thou hast made that bed which God gave thee for rest,
and for reparation of thy weary body, to be as thy
dwelling, and delight, and the bed of idlenesse, and
stupidity.

71. *Unconscious Prayer.*

THAT soule, that is accustomed to direct her selfe
to God, upon every occasion, that, as a flowre at
Sun-rising, conceives a sense of God, in every beame of
his, and spreads and dilates it selfe towards him, in
a thankfulnesse, in every small blessing that he sheds
upon her ; that soule, that as a flowre at the Suns
declining, contracts and gathers in, and shuts up her

selfe, as though she had received a blow, when soever she
heares her Saviour wounded by a oath, or blasphemy,
or execration ; that soule, who, whatsoever string be
strucken in her, base or treble, her high or her low
estate, is ever tun'd toward God, that soule prayes
sometimes when it does not know that it prayes.

72. *Sermons.*

GOD directs the tongue of his Ministers, as he doth
his showres of rain : They fall upon the face of
a large compasse of earth, when as all that earth did not
need that rain. The whole Congregation is, oftentimes,
in common entendment, conformable, and well setled
in all matters of Doctrine, and all matters of Discipline.
And yet God directs us sometimes to extend our discourse
(perchance with a zeale and a vehemence, which may
seem unnecessary, and impertinent, because all in the
Church are presumed to be of one minde) in the proofe
of our doctrine against Papists, or of our discipline against
Nonconformitans. For, Gods eye sees, in what seat
there sits, or in what corner there stands some one man
that wavers in matters of Doctrine, and enclines to
hearken after a Seducer, a Jesuit, or a Semi-Jesuit,
a practising Papist, or a Sesqui-Jesuit, a Jesuited Lady ;
And Gods eye sees in what seat there sits, or in what
corner there stands some weak soul that is scandalized,
with some Ceremony, or part of our Discipline, and in
danger of falling from the unity of the Church : And
for the refreshing of that one span of ground, God lets
fall a whole showre of rain ; for the rectifying of that
one soul, God poures out the Meditations of the Preacher,

into such a subject, as perchance doth little concern the rest of the Congregation. S. *Matthew* relates Christs Sermon at large, and S. *Luke* but briefly, and yet S. *Luke* remembers some things that S. *Matthew* had left out. If thou remember not all that was presented to thy faith, all the Citations of places of Scriptures, nor all that was presented to thy reason, all the deducements, and inferences of the Schooles, nor all that was presented to thy spirituall delight, all the sentences of ornament produced out of the Fathers, yet if thou remember that which concerned thy sin, and thy soul, if thou meditate upon that, apply that, thou hast brought away all the Sermon, all that was intended by the Holy Ghost to be preached to thee. And if thou have done so, as at a donative at a Coronation, or other solemnity, when mony is throwne among the people, though thou light but upon one shilling of that money, thou canst not think that all the rest is lost, but that some others are the richer for it, though thou beest not; so if thou remember, or apply, or understand but one part of the Sermon, doe not think all the rest to have been idly, or unnecessarily, or impertinently spoken, for thou broughtest a feaver, and hast had thy Julips, another brought a fainting, and a diffident spirit, and must have his Cordials. . . .

This excuses no mans ignorance, that is not able to preach seasonably, and to break, and distribute the bread of life according to the emergent necessities of that Congregation, at that time; Nor it excuses no mans lazinesse, that will not employ his whole time upon his calling; Nor any mans vain-glory, and ostentation, who

having made a Pye of Plums, without meat, offers it
to sale in every Market, and having made an Oration
of Flowres, and Figures, and Phrases without strength,
sings it over in every Pulpit : It excuses no mans ignorance, nor lazinesse, nor vain-glory, but yet it reproaches
their itching and curious eares, to whom any repetition
of the same things is irksome and fastidious. You may
have heard an answer of an Epigrammatist applyable to
this purpose ; When he read his Epigrams in an Auditory,
one of the hearers stopped him, and said, Did not I heare
an Epigram to this purpose from you, last yeare ? Yes,
sayes he, it is like you did ; but is not that vice still in
you this yeare, which last yeares Epigram reprehended ?
If your curiosity bring you to say to any Preacher, Did
not I heare this Point thus handled in your Sermon,
last yeare ? Yes, must he say, and so you must next
yeare againe, till it appeare in your amendment, that
you did heare it. The Devill maintaines a Warre good
cheap, if he may fight with the same sword, and we may
not defend with the same buckler ; If he can tempt
a Son with his Fathers covetousnesse, and a Daughter
with her Mothers wantonnesse, if he need not vary
the sin, nor the tentation, must wee vary our Doctrine ?
This is indeed to put new Wine into old vessels, new
Doctrine into eares, and hearts not disburdened of old
Cant. 7.13. sins. We say, as the Spouse sayes, *Vetera & nova*, we
prepare old and new, all that may any way serve your
holy taste, and conduce to your spirituall nourishment ;
And he is not a Preacher sufficiently learned, that must
of necessity preach the same things againe, but he is not
a Preacher sufficiently discreet neither, that forbeares

any thing therefore, because himselfe, or another in that place, hath handled that before. Christ himselfe varied his Sermon very little, if this in S. *Matthew*, and that in S. *Luke*, were divers Sermons.

73. *New Doctrines.*

NEW fashions in men, make us doubt new manners; and new terms in Divinity were ever suspicious in the Church of God, that new Doctrines were hid under them. *Resistibility*, and *Irresistibility* of grace, which is every Artificers wearing now, was a stuff that our Fathers wore not, a language that pure antiquity spake not. They knew Gods ordinary proceeding. They knew his Common Law, and they knew his Chancery. They knew his Chief Justice *Moses*, that denounced his Judgements upon transgressors of the Law; and they knew his Chancellor Christ Jesus, into whose hands he had put all Judgements, to mitigate the rigor and condemnation of the Law. They knew Gods law, and his Chancery: but for Gods prerogative, what he could do of his absolute power, they knew Gods pleasure, *Nolumus disputari*: It should scarce be disputed of in Schools, much less serv'd in every popular pulpit to curious and itching ears; least of all made table-talke, and household-discourse. Christ promises to come to the door, and to knock at the door, and to stand at the door, and to enter if any man open; but he does not say, he will break open the door: it was not his pleasure to express such an earnestness, such an Irresistibility in his grace, so. Let us cheerfully rely upon that; his purpose shall not be frustrated; his ends shall not be prevented; his ways

Revel. 3.

shall not be precluded : But the depth of the goodness of God, how much good God can do for man ; yea the depth of the illness of man, how much ill man can do against God, are such seas, as, if it be not impossible, at least it is impertinent, to go about to sound them.

74. *Papist and Puritan.*

BELOVED, there are some things in which all Religions agree ; The worship of God, The holinesse of life ; And therefore, if when I study this holinesse of life, and fast, and pray, and submit my selfe to discreet, and medicinall mortifications, for the subduing of my body, any man will say, this is Papisticall, Papists doe this, it is a blessed Protestation, and no man is the lesse a Protestant, nor the worse a Protestant for making it, Men and brethren, I am a Papist, that is, I will fast and pray as much as any Papist, and enable my selfe for the service of my God, as seriously, as sedulously, as laboriously as any Papist. So, if when I startle and am affected at a blasphemous oath, as at a wound upon my Saviour, if when I avoyd the conversation of those men, that prophane the Lords day, any other will say to me, This is Puritanicall, Puritans do this, It is a blessed Protestation, and no man is the lesse a Protestant, nor the worse a Protestant for making it, Men and Brethren, I am a Puritan, that is, I wil endeavour to be pure, as my Father in heaven is pure, as far as any Puritan.

75. *Theological Dissensions.*

PSALME 11. 3. *If the Foundations be destroyed, what can the righteous doe ? . . .*

For, as wee, at last, shall commend our Spirits, into the hands of *God*, *God* hath commended our Spirits, not onely our civill peace, but our Religion too, into the *hand* of the *Magistrate*. And therefore, when the *Apostle* sayes, *Studie to bee quiet*, it is not quiet in the blindnesse of the *Eye*, nor quiet in the *Deafenesse* of the *Eare*, nor quiet in the *Lamenesse* of the *Hand* ; the iust discharge of the dueties of our severall places, is no *disquieting* to any man. But when *private* men will spend all their thoughts upon their *Superiours* actions, this must necessarily disquiet them ; for they are off of their owne *Center*, and they are *extra Sphæram Activitatis*, out of their owne *Distance*, and *Compasse*, and they cannot possibly discerne the *Ende*, to which their *Superiours* goe. And to such a iealous man, when his jealousie is not a tendernesse towards his owne actions, which is a holy and a wholesome jealousie, but a suspition of his *Superiours* actions, to this Man, every *Wheele* is a *Drumme*, and every *Drumme* a *Thunder*, and every *Thunder-clapp* a dissolution of the whole frame of the World : If there fall a broken tyle from the house, hee thinkes *Foundations are destroyed* ; if a crazie woman, or a disobedient childe, or a needie servant fall from our *Religion*, from our *Church*, hee thinkes the whole *Church* must necessarily fall, when all this while there are no *Foundations destroyed* ; and *till foundations bee destroyed, the righteous should be quiet.*

K 2

Hence have wee just occasion, first to *condole* amongst *our selves*, who, for matters of *Foundations* professe one and the same *Religion*, and then to complain of our *Adversaries*, who are of another. First, that amongst our selves, for matters not *Doctrinall*, or if *Doctrinall*, yet not *Fundamentall*, onely because we are sub-divided in divers *Names*, there should be such Exasperations, such Exacerbations, such Vociferations, such Ejulations, such Defamations of one another, as if all *Foundations* were destroyed. Who would not tremble, to heare those *Infernall* words, spoken by men, to men, of one and the same Religion fundamentally, as *Indiabolificata*, *Perdiabolificata*, and *Superdiabolificata*, that the *Devill*, and all the *Devills* in Hell, and worse then the *Devill* is in their *Doctrine*, and in their *Divinitie*, when, *God* in heaven knowes, if their owne uncharitablenesse did not exclude him, there were roome enough for the *Holy Ghost*, on both, and on either side, in those *Fundamentall* things, which are unanimely professed by both; And yet every *Mart*, wee see more Bookes written by these men against one another, then by them both, for *Christ*.

But yet though this *Torrent* of uncharitablenesse amongst them, bee too violent, yet it is within some bankes; though it bee a *Sea*, and too tempestuous, it is limitted within some bounds : The poynts are certaine, knowen, limitted, and doe not grow upon us every yeare, and day. But the uncharitablenesse of the *Church* of *Rome* towards us all, is not a *Torrent*, nor it is not a *Sea*, but a *generall Flood*, an universall *Deluge*, that swallowes all the world, but that *Church*, and *Church-yard*, that *Towne*, and *Suburbes*, themselves, and those that depend

upon them ; and will not allowe possibilitie of Salvation to
the whole *Arke*, the whole *Christian Church*, but to one
Cabin in that *Arke*, the *Church* of *Rome* ; and then
denie us this Salvation, not for any *Positive* Errour, that
ever they charged us to affirme ; not because we affirme
any thing, that they denie, but because wee denie some
things, which they in their afternoone are come to
affirme.

76. *Despair.*

WHO ever comes into a Church to denounce an
excommunication against himselfe ? And shall any
sad soule come hither, to gather arguments, from our
preaching, to *excommunicate* it selfe, or to pronounce an
impossibility upon her owne salvation ? *God did a new* Nunb. 16.
thing, says *Moses*, a strange thing, a thing never done 30.
before, when the earth opened her mouth and *Dathan*,
and *Abiram* went downe quicke into the pit. Wilt thou
doe a stranger thing then that ? To teare open the
jawes of Earth, and Hell, and cast thy self actually
and really into it, out of a mis-imagination, that God
hath cast thee into it before ? Wilt thou force God to
second thy irreligious *melancholy*, and to condemne thee
at last, because thou hadst precondemned thy selfe, and
renounced his mercy ?

77. *The Sociablenesse of God.*

OUR first step then in this first part, is, the *sociable-* 1 Part.
nesse, the *communicablenesse* of God ; He loves holy
meetings, he loves the *communion of Saints*, the *houshold
of the faithfull* : *Deliciæ ejus*, says *Solomon*, *his delight is
to be with the Sons of men*, and that the Sons of men

should be with him : Religion is not a *melancholy* ; the spirit of God is not a *dampe* ; the Church is not a *grave* : it is a *fold*, it is an *Arke*, it is a *net*, it is a *city*, it is a *kingdome*, not onely a house, but a house that hath *many mansions* in it : still it is a *plurall* thing, consisting of *many* : and very good *grammarians* amongst the *Hebrews*, have thought, and said, that that *name*, by which God notifies himself to the world, in the very beginning of *Genesis*, which is *Elohim*, as it is a *plurall word* there, so it hath no *singular* : they say we cannot name God, but *plurally* : so sociable, so communicable, so extensive, so derivative of himself, is God, and so manifold are the beames, and the emanations that flow out from him.

78. *God a Circle.*

ONE of the most convenient Hieroglyphicks of God, is a Circle ; and a Circle is endlesse ; whom God loves, hee loves to the end : and not onely to their own end, to their death, but to his end, and his end is, that he might love them still. His hailestones, and his thunderbolts, and his showres of bloud (emblemes and instruments of his Judgements) fall downe in a direct line, and affect and strike some one person, or place : His Sun, and Moone, and Starres, (Emblemes and Instruments of his Blessings) move circularly, and communicate themselves to all. His Church is his chariot ; in that, he moves more gloriously, then in the Sun ; as much more, as his begotten Son exceeds his created Sun, and his Son of glory, and of his right hand, the Sun of the firmament ; and this Church, his chariot, moves in that communicable motion, circularly ; It began in the East, it came to us,

and is passing now, shining out now, in the farthest
West.

79. *God's Mirror.*

THERE is not so poore a creature but may be thy
glasse to see God in. The greatest flat glasse that
can be made, cannot represent any thing greater then
it is : If every gnat that flies were an Arch-angell, all
that could but tell me, that there is a God ; and the
poorest worme that creeps, tells me that. If I should
aske the Basilisk, how camest thou by those killing eyes,
he would tell me, Thy God made me so ; And if I should
aske the Slow-worme, how camest thou to be without
eyes, he would tell me, Thy God made me so. The
Cedar is no better a glasse to see God in, then the Hyssope
upon the wall ; all things that are, are equally removed
from being nothing ; and whatsoever hath any beeing,
is by that very beeing, a glasse in which we see God, who
is the roote, and the fountaine of all beeing. The whole
frame of nature is the Theatre, the whole Volume of
creatures is the glasse, and the light of nature, reason, is
our light.

80. *God's Names.*

FIRST then, lest any man in his dejection of spirit, *Vmbra*
or of fortune, should stray into a jealousie or suspi-   *Alarum.*
tion of Gods power to deliver him, As God hath spangled
the firmament with starres, so hath he his Scriptures
with names, and Metaphors, and denotations of power.
Sometimes he shines out in the name of a *Sword*, and of
a *Target*, and of a *Wall*, and of a *Tower*, and of a *Rocke*,
and of a *Hill* ; And sometimes in that glorious and

manifold constellation of all together, *Dominus exercituum*, *The Lord of Hosts*. God, as God, is never represented to us, with Defensive Armes; He needs them not. When the Poets present their great Heroes, and their Worthies, they alwayes insist upon their Armes, they spend much of their invention upon the description of their Armes; both because the greatest valour and strength needs Armes, (*Goliah* himselfe was armed) and because to expose ones selfe to danger unarmed, is not valour, but rashnesse. But God is invulnerable in himselfe, and is never represented armed; you finde no shirts of mayle, no Helmets, no Cuirasses in Gods Armory.

81. *God's Mercies.*

Psal.101.1. *I WILL sing of thy mercy and judgement*, sayes *David*; when we fixe our selves upon the meditation and modulation of the mercy of God, even his judgements cannot put us out of tune, but we shall sing, and be chearefull, even in them. As God made grasse for beasts, before he made beasts, and beasts for man, before he made man : As in that first generation, the Creation, so in the regeneration, our re-creating, he begins with that which was necessary for that which followes, Mercy before Judgement. Nay, to say that mercy was first, is but to post-date mercy; to preferre mercy but so, is to diminish mercy; The names of first or last derogate from it, for first and last are but ragges of time, and his mercy hath no relation to time, no limitation in time, it is not first, nor last, but eternall, everlasting; Let the Devill make me so far desperate as to conceive a time when there was no mercy, and he hath made me so far an

Atheist, as to conceive a time when there was no God ;
if I despoile him of his mercy, any one minute, and say,
now God hath no mercy, for that minute I discontinue his
very Godhead, and his beeing. Later Grammarians have
wrung the name of mercy out of misery ; *Misericordia
præsumit miseriam*, say these, there could be no subsequent
mercy, if there were no precedent misery ; But the true
roote of the word mercy, through all the Prophets, is
Racham, and *Racham* is *diligere*, to love ; as long as there
hath been love (and *God is love*) there hath been mercy :
And mercy considered externally, and in the practise and
in the effect, began not at the helping of man, when man
was fallen and become miserable, but at the making of man,
when man was nothing. So then, here we consider not
mercy as it is radically in God, and an essentiall attribute
of his, but productively in us, as it is an action, a working
upon us, and that more especially, as God takes all
occasions to exercise that action, and to shed that mercy
upon us : for particular mercies are feathers of his wings,
and that prayer, *Lord let thy mercy lighten upon us, as
our trust is in thee*, is our birdlime ; particular mercies
are that cloud of Quailes which hovered over the host of
Israel, and that prayer, *Lord let thy mercy lighten upon us*,
is our net to catch, our Gomer to fill of those Quailes.
The aire is not so full of Moats, of Atomes, as the Church
is of Mercies ; and as we can suck in no part of aire,
but we take in those Moats, those Atomes ; so here in
the Congregation we cannot suck in a word from the
preacher, we cannot speak, we cannot sigh a prayer to
God, but that that whole breath and aire is made of
mercy. But we call not upon you from this Text, to

consider Gods ordinary mercy, that which he exhibites to all in the ministery of his Church; nor his miraculous mercy, his extraordinary deliverances of States and Churches; but we call upon particular Consciences, by occasion of this Text, to call to minde Gods occasionall mercies to them; such mercies as a regenerate man will call mercies, though a naturall man would call them accidents, or occurrences, or contingencies; A man wakes at midnight full of unclean thoughts, and he heares a passing Bell; this is an occasionall mercy, if he call that his own knell, and consider how unfit he was to be called out of the world then, how unready to receive that voice, *Foole, this night they shall fetch away thy soule.* The adulterer, whose eye waites for the twy-light, goes forth, and casts his eyes upon forbidden houses, and would enter, and sees a *Lord have mercy upon us* upon the doore; this is an occasionall mercy, if this bring him to know that they who lie sick of the plague within, passe through a furnace, but by Gods grace, to heaven; and hee without, carries his own furnace to hell, his lustfull loines to everlasting perdition. What an occasionall mercy had *Balaam*, when his Asse Catechized him? What an occasionall mercy had one Theefe, when the other catechized him so, *Art not thou afraid being under the same condemnation?* What an occasionall mercy had all they that saw that, when the Devil himself fought

Act. 19. 14. for the name of Jesus, and wounded the sons of *Sceva* for exorcising in the name of Jesus, with that indignation, with that increpation, *Iesus we know, and Paul we know, but who are ye?* If I should declare what God hath done (done occasionally) for my soule, where he instructed me

for feare of falling, where he raised me when I was fallen,
perchance you would rather fixe your thoughts upon my
illnesse, and wonder at that, then at Gods goodnesse,
and glorifie him in that; rather wonder at my sins,
then at his mercies, rather consider how ill a man I was,
then how good a God he is. If I should inquire upon
what occasion God elected me, and writ my name in
the book of Life, I should sooner be afraid that it were
not so, then finde a reason why it should be so. God
made Sun and Moon to distinguish seasons, and day, and
night, and we cannot have the fruits of the earth but in
their seasons : But God hath made no decree to distinguish the seasons of his mercies ; In paradise, the fruits
were ripe, the first minute, and in heaven it is alwaies
Autumne, his mercies are ever in their maturity. We
ask *panem quotidianum*, our daily bread, and God never
sayes you should have come yesterday, he never sayes
you must againe to morrow, but *to day if you will heare
his voice*, to day he will heare you. If some King of the
earth have so large an extent of Dominion, in North,
and South, as that he hath Winter and Summer together
in his Dominions, so large an extent East and West, as
that he hath day and night together in his Dominions,
much more hath God mercy and judgement together :
He brought light out of darknesse, not out of a lesser
light ; he can bring thy Summer out of Winter, though
thou have no Spring ; though in the wayes of fortune,
or understanding, or conscience, thou have been benighted
till now, wintred and frozen, clouded and eclypsed,
damped and benummed, smothered and stupified till
now, now God comes to thee, not as in the dawning of

the day, not as in the bud of the spring, but as the Sun at noon to illustrate all shadowes, as the sheaves in harvest, to fill all penuries, all occasions invite his mercies, and all times are his seasons.

82. *God not Cruel.*

NEVER propose to thy self such a God, as thou wert not bound to imitate : Thou mistakest God, if thou make him to be any such thing, or make him to do any such thing, as thou in thy proportion shouldst not be, or shouldst not do. And shouldst thou curse any man that had never offended, never transgrest, never trespast thee ? Can God have done so ? Imagine God, as the Poet saith, *Ludere in humanis,* to play but a *game at Chesse* with this world ; to sport himself with making little things great, and great things nothing : Imagine God to be but at play with us, but a gamester ; yet will a gamester *curse,* before he be in danger of losing any thing ? Will God curse man, before man have sinned ?

83. *The Voice of God.*

Audivit.

HOW often does God speake, and nobody heares the voyce ? He speaks in his Canon, in Thunder, and he speaks in our Canon, in the rumour of warres. He speaks in his musique, in the harmonious promises of the Gospel, and in our musique, in the temporall blessings of peace, and plenty ; And we heare a noyse in his Judgements, and wee heare a sound in his mercies ; but we heare no voyce, we doe not discern that this noyse, or this sound comes from any certain person ; we do not feele them to be mercies, nor to be judgements

uttered from God, but naturall accidents, casuall occur-
rencies, emergent contingencies, which as an Atheist
might think, would fall out though there were no God,
or no commerce, no dealing, no speaking between God
and Man. Though *Saul* came not instantly to a perfect
discerning who spoke, yet he saw instantly, it was a Person
above nature, and therefore speakes to him in that phrase
of submission, *Quis es Domine?* *Lord who art thou?*
And after, with trembling and astonishment, (as the Text
sayes) *Domine quid me vis facere?* *Lord what wilt thou
have me to do?* Then we are truliest said to hear, when
we know from whence the voyce comes. Princes are
Gods Trumpet, and the Church is Gods Organ, but
Christ Jesus is his voyce. When he speaks in the Prince,
when he speaks in the Church, there we are bound to
heare, and happy if we doe hear. Man hath a natural
way to come to God, by the eie, by the creature; So
Visible things shew the *Invisible God*: But then, God
hath super-induced a supernaturall way, by the eare.
For, though hearing be naturall, yet that faith in God
should come by hearing a man preach, is supernatural.
God shut up the naturall way, in *Saul*, Seeing; He
struck him blind; But he opened the super-naturall
way, he inabled him to heare, and to heare him. God
would have us beholden to grace, and not to nature, and
to come for our salvation, to his Ordinances, to the
preaching of his Word, and not to any other meanes.

84. *God's Language.*

Psal. 19. 2.

GOD multiplies his mercies to us, in his divers ways of speaking to us. *Cœli enarrant*, says *David*, *The heavens declare the glory of God* ; and not onely by showing, but by *saying* ; there is a *language* in the heavens ; for it is *enarrant*, a verball declaration ; and, as it followes literally, *Day unto day uttereth speech*. This is the true harmony of the Spheares, which every man may heare. Though he understand no tongue but his owne, he may heare God in the motions of the same, in the seasons of the yeare, in the vicissitudes and revolutions of Church, and State, in the voice of Thunder, and lightnings, and other declarations of his power. This is Gods *English* to thee, and his *French*, and his *Latine*, and *Greek*, and *Hebrew* to others. God once confounded languages ; that conspiring men might not understand one another, but never so, as that all men might not understand *him*. When the holy Ghost fell upon the Apostles, they spoke so, as that all men understood them, *in their owne tongues*. When the holy Ghost fell upon the waters, in the Creation, God spoke so, in his language of *Workes*, as that all men may understand them. For, in this language, the language of *workes*, the *Eye* is the *eare*, *seeing* is *hearing*. How often does the holy Ghost call upon us, in the Scriptures, *Ecce, quia os Domini locutum, Behold, the mouth of the Lord hath spoken it* ? he calls us to *behold*, (which is the office of the *eye*) and that that we are to behold, is the *voice* of God, belonging to the *eare* ; seeing is hearing, in Gods first language, the language of *works*. But then God translates himself, in particular *works* ; *nationally*, he speaks in particular judgments, or deliverances to one nation ; &, *domestically*, he speaks that language to a particular family ; & so *personally* too, he speaks to every particular soul. God will speak unto me, in that voice, and in that way, which I am most delighted with, & hearken most to. If I be *covetous*, God wil tel me that heaven is a pearle, a treasure. If cheerfull and affected with mirth, that heaven is all *Joy*. If ambitious, and hungry of preferment, that it is all *Glory*. If sociable, and conversable, that it is a *communion of Saints*. God will make a *Fever* speake to me, and tell me his minde, that there is no health but in *him* ; God will make the *disfavour*, and frowns of *him* I depend upon, speake to me, and tell me his minde, that there is no safe dependence, no assurance but in *him* ; God will make a *storme* at Sea, or a *fire* by land, speake to me, and tell mee his minde, that there is no perpetuity, no possession but in *him* ; nay, God will make my *sinne* speake to me, and tell me his minde ; even my sinne shall bee a Sermon, and a Catechisme to me ; God shall suffer mee me to fall into some such sinne, as that by some circumstances in the sinne, or consequences from the sinne, I shall be drawn to hearken unto him ; and whether I heare *Hosannaes*, acclamations, and commendations, or *Crucifiges*, exclamations and condemnations from the world, I shall stil finde the voice and tongue of God, though in the mouth of the Devill, and his instruments. God is a declaratory God. The whole yeare, is, to his Saints, a continuall *Epiphany*, one day of manifestation. In every minute that strikes upon the *Bell* is a syllable, nay a syllogisme from God. And, and in my *last Bell*, God

shall speake too ; that Bell, when it tolls, shall tell me
I am going, and when it rings out, shall tell you I am gone
into the hands of that God, who is the God of the living
and not of the dead, for, they dye not that depart in him.

85. *God's Anger.*

HONOUR not the malice of thine enemy so much,
as to say, thy misery comes from him : Dishonour
not the complexion of the times so much, as to say, thy
misery comes from them ; justifie not the *Deity* of
Fortune so much, as to say, thy misery comes from her ;
Finde God pleased with thee, and thou hast a hook in
the *nostrils* of every *Leviathan*, power cannot shake thee,
Iob 40. 19. Thou hast a wood to cast into the waters of *Marah*, the
bitternesse of the times cannot hurt thee, thou hast
Exod. 15. 23. a Rock to dwell upon, and the dream of a *Fortunes wheel*,
cannot overturn thee. But if the Lord be angry, he
needs no Trumpets to call in Armies, if he doe but
sibilare muscam, hisse and whisper for the flye, and the
Bee, there is nothing so little in his hand, as cannot
discomfort thee, discomfit thee, dissolve and powr out,
attenuate and annihilate the very marrow of thy soul.

86. *God's Faults.*

GOD in the Scriptures is often by the Holy Ghost
invested, and represented in the qualities and affections of man ; and to constitute a commerce and familiar-
ity between God and man, God is not onely said to have
bodily lineaments, eyes and eares, and hands, and feet,
and to have some of the naturall affections of man, as
Deut. 30. 9. Joy, in particular, (*The Lord will rejoyce over thee for*

good, *as he rejoyced over thy Fathers*) And so, pity too,
(*The Lord was with Ioseph, and extended kindnesse unto* Gen.39.21.
him) But some of those inordinate and irregular passions
and perturbations, excesses and defects of man, are
imputed to God, by the Holy Ghost in the Scriptures.
For so, lazinesse, drowsinesse is imputed to God ; (*Awake* Psal.44.23.
Lord, why sleepest thou?) So corruptiblenesse, and
deterioration, and growing worse by ill company, is
imputed to God ; (*Cum perverso perverteris,* God is said   18. 26.
to grow froward with the froward, and that hee learnes
to go crookedly with them that go crookedly) And
prodigality and wastfulnesse is imputed to God ; (*Thou*   44. 12.
sellest thy people for naught, and doest not increase thy
wealth by their price) So sudden and hasty choler ; (*Kisse*   2. 12.
the Son lest he be angry, and ye perish In ira brevi, though
his wrath be kindled but a little) And then, illimited and
boundlesse anger, a vindicative irreconciliablenesse is
imputed to God ; (*I was but a little displeased,* (but it Zech. 1. 15.
is otherwise now) *I am very sore displeased*) So there is
Ira devorans ; (*Wrath that consumes like stubble*) So there Exod.15.4.
is *Ira multiplicata,* (*Plagues renewed, and indignation* Iob 10. 17.
increased) So God himselfe expresses it, (*I will fight* Ier. 21. 5.
against you in anger and in fury) And so for his inexorable-
nesse, his irreconciliablenesse, (*O Lord God of Hosts,* Psal. 80. 4.
Quousque, how long wilt thou be angry against the prayer
of thy people?) Gods owne people, Gods own people
praying to their owne God, and yet their God irreconci-
liable to them. Scorne and contempt is imputed to
God ; which is one of the most enormious, and dispro-
portioned weakenesses in man ; that a worme that
crawles in the dust, that a graine of dust, that is hurried

with every blast of winde, should find any thing so much, inferiour to it selfe as to scorne it, to deride it, to contemne it ; yet scorne, and derision, and contempt is imputed

Psal. 2. 4. to God, (*He that sittest in the Heavens shall laugh, the*
Prov. 1. 26. *Lord shall have them in derision*) and againe, (*I will laugh at your calamity, I will mock you when your feare commeth.*) Nay beloved, even inebriation, excesse in that kinde, Drunkennesse, is a Metaphor which the Holy Ghost hath mingled in the expressing of Gods proceedings with man ; for God does not onely threaten to make his enemies drunke, (and to make others drunke is a circumstance of drunkennesse) (so Jerusalem being in his

Lam. 3. 15. displeasure complaines, *Inebriavit absynthio,* (*He hath made me drunke with wormewood*) and againe, (*They*
Esay 49. 26. *shall be drunke with their owne blood, as with new Wine*) Nor onely to expresse his plentifull mercies to his friends and servants, does God take that Metaphore,

Ier. 31. 14. (*Inebriabo animam Sacerdotis, I will make the soule of*
Ver. 25. *the Priest drunke ;* fill it, satiate it) and againe, (*I will make the weary soule, and the sorrowfull soule drunke*) But not onely all this, (though in all this God have a hand) not onely towards others, but God in his owne behalfe

Esay 43. 24. complaines of the scant and penurious Sacrificer, *Non inebriasti me, Thou hast not made me drunke with thy Sacrifices.* And yet, though for the better applying of God to the understanding of man, the Holy Ghost impute to God these excesses, and defects of man (lazinesse and drowsiness, deterioration, corruptiblenesse by ill conversation, prodigality and wastfulnesse, sudden choler, long irreconciablenesse, scorne, inebriation, and many others) in the Scriptures, yet in no place of the Scripture

is God, for any respect said to be proud ; God in the
Scriptures is never made so like man, as to be made
capable of Pride ; for this had not beene to have God
like man, but like the devill.

87. *God's Judgements.*

HOW desperate a state art thou in, if nothing will
convert thee, but a speedie execution, after which,
there is no possibility, no room left for a Conversion !
God is *the Lord of Hosts*, and he can proceed by Martial
Law : he can hang thee upon the next tree ; he can
choak thee with a crum, with a drop, at a voluptuous
feast ; he can sink down the Stage and the Player, The bed
of wantonness, and the wanton actor, into the jaws of
the earth, into the mouth of hell : he can surprise thee,
even in the act of sin ; and dost thou long for such a speedy
execution, for such an expedition ? Thou canst not lack
Examples, that he hath done so upon others, and will no
proof serve thee, but a speedy judgement upon thyself ?
Scatter thy thoughts no farther then ; contract them in
thy self, and consider Gods speedy execution upon thy
soul, and upon thy body, and upon thy soul and body
together. Was not Gods judgement executed speedily
enough upon thy soul, when in the same instant that it
was created, and conceiv'd, and infus'd, it was put to
a necessity of contracting Original sin, and so submitted
to the penalty of *Adam's* disobedience, the first minute ?
Was not Gods judgement speedily enough executed upon
thy body, if before it had any temporal life, it had a
spiritual death ; a sinful conception, before any inanima-
tion ? If hereditary diseases from thy parents, Gouts

and Epilepsies, were in thee, before the diseases of thine own purchase, the effects of thy licentiousness and thy riot ; and that from the first minute that thou beganst to live, thou beganst to die too ? Are not the judgements of God speedily enough executed upon thy soul and body together, every day, when as soon as thou commitst a sin, thou are presently left to thine Impenitence, to thine Insensibleness, and Obduration ? Nay, the judgement is more speedy then so : for, that very sin it self, was a punishment of thy former sins.

88. *Terrible Things.*

Terribilis. THOUGH there be a difference between *timor*, and *terror*, (fearc and terror) yet the difference is not so great, but that both may fall upon a good man ; Not onely a feare of God must, but a terror of God may fall Gen.15.12. upon the Best. When God talked with *Abraham*, *a horror of great darknesse fell upon him*, sayes that Text. The Father of lights, and the God of all comfort present, and present in an action of Mercy, and yet, a horror of great darknesse fell upon *Abraham*. When God talked person- Exod.13.6. ally, and presentially with *Moses*, *Moses hid his face, for* (sayes that Text) *he was afraid to looke upon God*. When I look upon God, as I am bid to doe in this Text, in those terrible Judgements, which he hath executed upon some men, and see that there is nothing between mee and the same Judgement, (for I have sinned the same sinnes, and God is the same God) I am not able of my selfe to dye that glasse, that spectacle, thorow which I looke upon this God, in what colour I will ; whether this glasse shall be black, through my despaire, and so I shall see God in

the cloud of my sinnes, or red in the blood of Christ
Jesus, and I shall see God in a Bath of the blood of his
Sonne, whether I shall see God as a Dove with an Olive
branch, (peace to my soule) or as an Eagle, a vulture to
prey, and to prey everlastingly upon mee, whether in
the deepe floods of Tribulation, spirituall or temporall,
I shall see God as an Arke to take mee in, or as a Whale to
swallow mee ; and if his Whale doe swallow mee, (the
Tribulation devour me) whether his purpose bee to restore
mee, or to consume me, I, I of my selfe cannot tell.
I cannot look upon God, in what line I will, nor take
hold of God, by what handle I will ; Hee is a terrible
God, I take him so ; And then I cannot discontinue,
I cannot breake off this terriblenesse, and say, Hee hath
beene terrible to that man, and there is an end of his
terror ; it reaches not to me. Why not to me ? In me
there is no merit, nor shadow of merit ; In God there
is no change, nor shadow of change. I am the same
sinner, he is the same God ; still the same desperate
sinner, still the same terrible God.

89. *God's Malediction.*

THERE is a malediction deposited in the Scriptures,
denounced by the Church, ratified by God, brought
into execution, yet it may be born, men doe bear it.
How men do bear it, we know not ; what passes between
God and those men, upon whom the curse of God lieth,
in their dark *horrours at midnight*, they would not have
us know, because it is part of their curse, to envy God
that glory. But we may consider in some part the insup-
portablenesse of that weight, if we proceed but so farre,

as to accommodate to God, that which is ordinarily said of naturall things. *Corruptio optimi pessima*; when the best things change their nature, they become worst. When God, who is all sweetnesse, shall have learned frowardnesse from us, as *David* speaks; and being all rectitude, shall have learned perversenesse and crooked-nesse from us, as *Moses* speaks; and being all providence, shall have learned negligence from us : when God who is all Blessing, hath learned to curse of us, and being of himself spread as an universall Hony-combe over All, takes in an impression, a tincture, an infusion of gall from us, what extraction of Wormwood can be so bitter, what exaltation of fire can be so raging, what multiplying of talents can be so heavy, what stifnesse of destiny can be so inevitable, what confection of gnawing worms, of gnashing teeth, of howling cries, of scalding brimstone, of palpable darknesse, can be so, so insupportable, so inexpressible, so in-imaginable, as the curse and male-diction of God ? *And therefore* let not us by our works provoke, nor by our words teach God to curse.

90. *God's Power.*

AS some *Schoolemasters* have usd that *Discipline*, to correct the Children of great Persons, whose personall correction they finde reason to forbeare, by correcting other Children in their *names*, and in their *sight*, and have wrought upon *good Natures*, that way, So did *Almightie God* correct the *Jewes* in the *Ægyptians*; for the *ten plagues of Egypt*, were as *Moses Decem Verba*, as the *ten Commandements to Israel*, that they should not provoke God. Every *Judgment* that falls upon another, should

be a *Catechisme* to me. But when this *Discipline* pre-
vaild not upon them, *God sold* them away, *gave* them
away, *cast* them away, in the tempest, in the whirlewinde,
in the inundation of his indignation, and scatterd them
as so much dust in a windy day, as so many broken
strawes upon a wrought Sea. With one *word*, *One
Fiat* (*Let there bee a world*,) nay with one *thought* of *God*
cast toward it, (for *Gods* speaking in the *Creation*, was
but a *thinking*) *God* made all of *Nothing*. And is any one
rationall Ant, (the wisest *Phylosopher* is no more) Is any
roaring Lyon (the most ambitious and devouring *Prince*
is no more) Is any *hive of Bees*, (The wisest *Councels*,
and *Parliaments* are no more) Is any of these so establishd,
as that, that *God* who by a *word*, by a *thought*, made them
of *nothing*, cannot, by recalling that *word*, and withdrawing
that *thought*, in sequestring his *Providence*, reduce them
to *nothing* againe ? That Man, that *Prince*, that *State*
thinks Past-board Canon-proofe, that thinkes Power,
or Policy a Rampart, when the *Ordinance* of *God* is
planted against it. *Navyes* will not keepe off *Navies*, if
God be not the *Pilot*, Nor *Walles* keepe out *Men*, if *God*
be not the *Sentinell*. If they could, if wee were walld
with a *Sea* of fire and brimstone without, and walld
with with Brasse within, yet we cannot ciel the Heavens
with a roofe of Brasse, but that *God* can come downe in
Thunder that way, Nor pave the Earth with a floare
of Brasse, but that *God* can come up in *Earthquakes*
that way. *God* can call up *Damps*, & *Vapors* from below,
and powre down putride *defluxions* from above, and bid
them meet and condense into a *plague*, a plague that shall
not be onely uncureable, uncontrollable, unexorable, but

undisputable, unexaminable, unquestionable; A *plague* that shall not onely not admit a *remedy*, when it is come, but not give a *reason* how it did come.

91. *Access to God.*

DAVID knew he could not retyre himselfe from God in his bedchamber; Guards and Ushers could not keepe him out. He knew he could not defend himselfe from God in his Army; for *the Lord of Hosts is Lord of his Hosts.* If he *fled to Sea, to Heaven, to Hell,* he was sure to meet *God there*; and there thou shalt meet him too, if thou fly from God, to the reliefe of outward comforts, of musicke, of mirth, of drinke, of cordialls, of Comedies, of conversation. Not that such recreations are unlawfull; the minde hath her physick as well as the body; but when thy sadnesse proceeds from a sense of thy sinnes, (which is Gods key to the doore of his mercy, put into thy hand) it is a new, and a greater sin, to goe about to overcome that holy sadnesse, with these prophane diversions; to fly *Ad consolatiunculas creaturulæ* (as that elegant man *Luther* expresses it, according to his naturall delight in that elegancy of Diminutives, with which he abounds above all Authors) to the little and contemptible comforts of little and contemptible creatures. And as *Luther* uses the physick, *Iob* useth the Physitian; *Luther* calls the comforts, Miserable comforts; and *Iob* calls them that minister them, *Onerosos consolatores, Miserable comforters are you all.* *David* could not drowne his adultery in blood; never thinke thou to drowne thine in wine. The Ministers of God are Sonnes of Thunder, they are falls of waters, trampling of horses,

and runnings of Chariots; and if these voyces of these
Ministers, cannot overcome thy musick, thy security, yet
the Angels trumpet will; That *Surgite qui dormitis,
Arise yee that sleepe in the dust, in the dust of the grave*, is
a Treble that over-reaches all; That *Ite maledicti, Goe
yee accursed into Hell fire*, is a Base that drowns all.
There is no recourse but to God, no reliefe but in God;
and therefore *David* applied himselfe to the right method,
to make his first accesse to God.

92. *The Image of God in Man.*

NO image, but the image of God, can fit our soul;
every other seal is too narrow, too shallow for it.
The magistrate is sealed with the *Lion*; the *Wolf* will
not fit that seal: the magistrate hath a *power* in his
hand, but not *oppression*. Princes are sealed with the
Crown; the *Mitre* will not fit that seal. Powerfully, and
graciously they protect the Church, and are supream
heads of the Church; but they minister not the Sacraments of the Church: they give preferments; but they
give not the capacitie of preferments: they give order
who shall have, but they have not Orders by which
they are enabled to have that they have. Men of inferiour
and laborious callings in the world are sealed with the
Crosse; a *Rose*, or a *bunch of Grapes* will not answer that
seal: ease and plentie in age must not be looked for
without crosses, and labour, and industrie in youth.
All men, Prince, and people; Clergie, and Magistrate,
are sealed with the image of God, with a conformitie
to him; and worldly seals will not answer that, nor fill
up that seal. We should wonder to see a mother in the

midst of many sweet children, passing her time in making babies and puppets for her own delight. We should wonder to see a man, whose chambers and galleries were full of curious master-pieces, thrust in a village fayre, to look upon sixpenie pictures, & three-farthing prints. We have all the image of God at home ; and we all make babies, fancies of honour in our ambitions. The master-piece is our own, in our own bosome ; and we thrust in countrey fayres, that is, we endure the distempers of any unseasonable weather, in night-journeys and watch-ings ; we endure the oppositions, and scorns, and triumphs of a rivall, and competitour, that seeks with us, and shares with us. We endure the guiltinesse and re-proach of having deceived the trust which a confident friend reposes in us, and solicit his wife or daughter. We endure the decay of fortune of bodie, of soul, of honour, to possesse lovers pictures ; pictures that are not originals, not made by that hand of God, Nature ; but artificiall beauties : and for that bodie we give a soul ; and for that drug, which might have been bought where they bought it, for a shilling, we give an estate. The image of God is more worth then all substances ; and we give it for colours, for dreams, for shadows.

93. *Man God's Enemy.*

Inimicus. AMONGST *naturall Creatures,* because howsoever they differ in bignesse, yet they have some proportion to one another, we consider that some very little creatures, contemptible in themselves, are yet called enemies to great creatures, as the Mouse is to the Elephant. (For the greatest Creature is not *Infinite,* nor the least is not

Nothing.) But shall man, betweene whom and nothing, there went but a word, *Let us make Man,* That Nothing, which is infinitely lesse then a Mathematicall point, then an imaginary Atome, shall this Man, this yesterdayes Nothing, this to morrow worse then Nothing, be capable of that honour, that *dishonourable honour,* that confounding honour, to be the enemy of God, of God who is not onely a multiplied Elephant, millions of Elephants multiplied into one, but a multiplied World, a multiplied All, All that can be conceived by us, infinite many times over; Nay, (if we may dare to say so,) a multiplyed God, a God that hath the Millions of the Heathens gods in himselfe alone, shall this man be an enemy to this God? Man cannot be allowed so high a sinne, as enmity with God. The Devill himselfe is but a *slave* to God, and shall Man be called his enemy? It is true, if we consider the infinite disproportion between them, he cannot; but to many sad purposes, and in many heavy applications Man is an enemy to God.

94. *The Atheist.*

POORE intricated soule! Riddling, perplexed, labyrinthicall soule! Thou couldest not say, that thou beleevest not in God, if there were no God; Thou couldest not beleeve in God, if there were no God; If there were no God, thou couldest not speake, thou couldest not thinke, not a word, not a thought, no not against God; Thou couldest not blaspheme the Name of God, thou couldest not sweare, if there were no God: For, all thy faculties, how ever depraved, and perverted by thee, are from him; and except thou canst seriously beleeve, that thou art nothing, thou canst not beleeve that there is no God. If I should aske thee at a Tragedy, where thou shouldest see him that had drawne blood, lie weltring, and surrounded in his owne blood, Is there a God now ? If thou couldst answer me, No, These are but Inventions, and Representations of men, and I beleeve a God never the more for this ; If I should ask thee at a Sermon, where thou shouldest heare the Judgements of God formerly denounced, and executed, re-denounced, and applied to present occasions, Is there a God now ? If thou couldest answer me, No, These are but Inventions of State, to souple and regulate Congregations, and keep people in order, and I beleeve a God never the more for this ; Bee as confident as thou canst, in company ; for company is the Atheists Sanctuary ; I respit thee not till the day of Judgement, when I may see thee upon thy knees, upon thy face, begging of the hills, that they would fall downe and cover thee from the fierce wrath of God, to aske thee then, Is there a God now ? I respit thee not till the day of thine own death, when thou shalt have evidence enough, that there is a God, though no other evidence, but to finde a Devill, and evidence enough, that there is a Heaven, though no other evidence, but to feele Hell ; To aske thee then, Is there a God now ? I respit thee but a few houres, but six houres, but till midnight. Wake then ; and then darke, and alone, Heare God aske thee then, remember that I asked thee now, Is there a God ? and if thou darest, say No.

95. *The Angels.*

THAT there are distinct orders of *Angels*, assuredly I beleeve; but what they are, I cannot tell; *Dicant qui possunt*; *si tamen probare possunt quod dicunt*, saies that Father, Let them tell you that can, so they be able to prove, that they tell you true. They are Creatures, that have not so much of a Body as *flesh* is, as *froth* is, as a *vapor* is, as a *sigh* is, and yet with a touch they shall molder a rock into lesse Atomes, then the sand that it stands upon; and a milstone into smaller flower, then it grinds. They are Creatures *made*, and yet not a minute elder now, then when they were first made, if they were made before all measure of time began; nor, if they were made in the beginning of Time, and be now six thousand yeares old, have they one wrinckle of Age in their face, or one sobbe of wearinesse in their lungs. They are *primogeniti Dei*, Gods eldest sonnes; They are super-elementary meteors, they hang between the nature of God, and the nature of man, and are of middle Condition; And, (if we may offencelessely expresse it so) they are *ænigmata Divina*, The Riddles of Heaven, and the perplexities of speculation.

96. *The Devil.*

SOME of the ancient Fathers, delivering the mercies *Illis omnibus.* of God, so, as the articles of our Church enjoyne them to bee delivered, that is, generally, as they are delivered in the Scriptures, have delivered them so over-generally, that they have seemed loth to thinke the devill himselfe excluded from all benefit of Christs

comming. Some of the later Authors in the Roman
Church, (who, as pious as they pretend to be towards
the Fathers, are apter to discover the nakednesse of the
Fathers, then we are) have noted in *Iustin Martyr*, and
in *Epiphanius*, and in *Clement* of Alexandria, and in
Oecumenius, (and *Oecumenius* is no single Father, but
Pater patratus, a manifold Father, a complicated father,
a Father that collected Fathers) and even in S. *Ierome*
himselfe, and S. *Ambrose* too, some inclinations towards
that opinion, that the devill retaining still his faculty
of free will, is therefore capable of repentance, and so of
benefit by this comming of Christ ; And those Authors
of the Roman Church, that modifie the matter, and
excuse the Fathers herein, excuse them no other way but
this, that though that opinion and doctrine of those
Fathers, bee not true in it selfe, yet it was never condemned
by any Councell, nor by any ancient Father. So very
far, did very many goe in enlarging the mercies of God
in Christ, to all. But waiving this over-large extention
and profusion thereof, and directing it upon a more
possible, and a more credible object, that is, Man ;
S. *Cyril* of Alexandria, speaking of the possibility of the
salvation of all men, saies, by way of objection to himselfe,
Omnes non credunt, How can all be saved since all doe not
beleeve ? but, saies he, Because actually they do not
beleeve, is it therefore impossible they should beleeve ?
And for actuall beleefe, saies he, though all doe not, yet
so many doe, *ut facilè qui pereant, superent*, that, by Gods
goodnesse, more are saved, then lost, saies that Father of
tender and large bowels, S. *Cyril.* And howsoever he
may seeme too tender, and too large herein, yet it is

a good peece of counsaile, which that Rabbi whom I named before, gives, *Ne redarguas ea falsitatis, de quorum contrariis nulla est demonstratio*, Be not apt to call any opinion false, or hereticall, or damnable, the contrary whereof cannot be evidently proved.

97. *The Creation.*

THERE is but one God ; but yet was that one God ever *alone* ? There were more *generations* (infinitely infinite) before the world was made, then there have been *minutes*, since it was made : all that while, there were no *creatures* ; but yet was God alone, any one minute of al this ? was there not alwais a *Father* and a *Son*, & a *holy Ghost* ? And had not they, always an acquiescence in one another, an exercise of *Affection*, (as we may so say) a love, a delight, and a complacency towards one another ? So, as that the Father could not be without the *Son* and the *holy Ghost*, so as neither *Sonne*, nor *holy Ghost* could be without the *Father*, nor without one another ; God was from all eternity collected into *one God*, yet from all eternity he derived himselfe into *three persons* : God could not be so alone, but that there have been three persons, as long as there hath been one God.

Had God company enough of himselfe ; was he satisfied in the *three Persons* ? We see he proceeded further ; he came to a *Creation* ; And as soon as he had made *light*, (which was his first Creature) he took a pleasure in it ; he said *it was good* ; he was glad of it ; glad of the *Sea*, glad of the *Earth*, glad of the *Sunne*, and *Moone*, and *Starres*, and he said of every one, *It is good* ; But when he had made *All*, peopled the whole world, brought all creatures together, then he was *very glad*, and then he said, not onely, that *it was good*, but that *it was very good* : God was so far from being *alone*, as that he found not the fulnesse of being well, till *all* was made, till all Creatures met together, in *an Host*, as *Moses* calls it ; then the *good* was extended into *very good*.

Angeli.

Did God satisfie himselfe with this *visible* and discernible world ; with all on earth, and all between that, and him ? were those *foure Monarchies*, the *foure Elements*, and all the subjects of those foure Monarchies, (if all the foure Elements have Creatures) company enough for God ? was that *Heptarchie*, the *seven kingdomes* of the *seven Planets*, conversation enough for him ? Let every Starre in the firmament, be (so some take them to be) a severall world, was all this enough ? we see, God drew persons nearer to him, then Sunne, or Moon, or Starres, or any thing, which is *visible*, and discernible to us, he created *Angels* ; How many, how great ? Arithmetique lacks *numbers* to to expresse them, proportion lacks *Dimensions* to figure them ; so far was God from being *alone*.

Homines.

And yet God had not shed himselfe far enough ; he had the *Leviathan*, the Whale in the Sea, and *Behemoth* and the *Elephant* upon the land ; and all these great *heavenly bodies* in the way, and *Angels* in their infinite numbers, and manifold offices, in heaven ; But, because *Angels*, could not propagate, nor make more *Angels*, he enlarged his love, in making *man*, that so he might enjoy all natures at once, and have the nature of *Angels*, and the nature of *earthly Creatures*, in one Person. God would not be without man, nor he would not come single, not alone to the making of man ; but it is *Faciamus hominem, Let us, us, make man*; God, in his whole counsail, in his whole Colledge, in his whole society, in the whole Trinity, makes man, in whom the whole nature of all the world should meet.

98. *The Heavens and Earth.*

NEVER such a frame so soon set up, as this in this chapter : For, for the thing it self, there is no other thing to compare it with ; for it is all, it is the whole world. And for the time, there was no other time to compare it with ; for this was the beginning of time, *In the beginning God created heaven and earth.* That earth, which in some thousands of yeares men could not look over, nor discern what form it had (for neither *Lactantius*, almost three hundred yeares after Christ ; nor *S. Augustine*, more then one hundred yeares after him, would beleeve the earth to be round) That earth, which no man in his person is ever said to have compassed till our age : That earth which is too much for man yet, (for, as yet a very great part of the earth is unpeopled) That earth, which, if we will cast it all but into a Map, costs many moneths labour to grave it ; nay, if we will cast but a piece of an acre of it into a garden, costs many yeares labour to fashion and furnish it ; all that earth : And then that heaven, which spreads so farre, as that subtill men have, with some appearance of probabilitie, imagined, that in that heaven, in those manifold Spheres of the Planets and the Starres, there are many earths, many worlds, as big as this which we inhabit : That earth and that heaven, which spent God himself, Almightie God, six dayes in finishing ; Moses sets up in a few syllables, in one line, *In principio, In the beginning God created heaven and earth.* If a *Livie* or a *Guicciardine,* or such extensive and voluminous authours had had this story in hand, God must have made another world, to have made them a library to hold their books, of the making of this world. Into what wire would they have drawn out this earth! Into what leaf-gold would they have beat out these heavens! It may assist our conjecture herein, to consider, that amongst those men, who proceed with a sober modestie and limitation in their writing, & make a conscience not to clog the world with unnecessary books; yet the volumes which are written by them, upon the beginning of Genesis, are scarce lesse than infinite. God did no more but say, Let this & this be done; and Moses doth no more but say, that upon Gods saying it was done. God required not Nature to help him to do it; Moses required not Reason to help him to beleeve.

99. *The Creation of a Harmonious World.*

GOD made this whole world in such an uniformity, such a correspondency, such a concinnity of parts, as that it was an Instrument, perfectly in tune: we may say, the trebles, the highest strings were disordered first; the best understandings, Angels and Men, put this instrument out of tune. God rectified all again, by putting in a new string, *semen mulieris,* the seed of the woman, the *Messias*: And onely by sounding that string in your ears, become we *musicum carmen,* true musick, true harmony, true peace to you. If we shall say, that Gods first string in this instrument, was Reprobation, that Gods first intention, was, for his glory to damn

man ; and that then he put in another string, of creating
Man, that so he might have some body to damn ; and
then another of enforcing him to sin, that so he might
have a just cause to damne him ; and then another, of
disabling him to lay hold upon any means of recovery :
there's no musick in all this, no harmony, no peace in
such preaching. But if we take this instrument, when
Gods hand tun'd it the second time, in the promise of
a *Messias*, and offer of the love & mercy of God to all that
will receive it in him ; then we are truely *musicum carmen*,
as a love-song, when we present the love of God to you,
and raise you to the love of God in Christ Jesus : for,
for the musick of the Sphears, whatsoever it be, we cannot
hear it ; for the decrees of God in heaven, we cannot say we
have seen them ; our musick is onely that salvation which is
declared in the Gospel to all them, and to them onely, who
take God by the right hand, as he delivers himself in Christ.

100. *God and Adam and Eve.*

WHO hath divided heaven into shires or parishes,
or limited the territories or jurisdictions there,
that God should not have and exercise *judicium dis-
cretionis*, the power of discerning all actions in all places,
when there was no more to be seen nor considered upon
the whole earth, but the garden of Paradise ? for from
the beginning, *Deliciæ ejus esse cum filiis hominum,
Gods delight was to be with the sonnes of men* ; and man
was only there. Shall we diminish God, or speak too
vulgarly of him, to say that he hovered like a falcon
over Paradise, and that from that height of heaven the
piercing eye of God saw so little a thing as the forbidden

fruit, and what became of that ? and the reaching eare of God heard the hissing of the serpent, and the whispering of the woman, and what was concluded upon that ? shall we think it little to have seen things done in Paradise, when there was nothing else to divert his eye, nothing else to distract his counsels, nothing else done upon the face of the earth ? take the earth now as it is replenished, and take it either as it is torn and crumbled in rags and shivers, not a kingdome, not a family, not a man agreeing with himself ; or take it in that concord which is in it, as all the kings of the earth set themselves, and all the rulers of the earth take counsel together against the Lord ; take it in this union, or this disunion ; in this concord, or this disconcord ; still the Lord that sitteth in the heavens discerns all, looks at all, laughs at all, and hath them in derision. Earthly judges have their districtions, and so their restrictions ; some things they cannot know : what mortall man can know all ? some things they cannot take knowledge of, for they are bounded : no cloud, no darkness, no disguise keeps him from discerning and judging all our actions.

101. *The World since the Fall.*

Morietur. WHEN *Paradise* should have extended, as man should have multiplied, and every holy family, every religious Colony have constituted a new Paradise, that as it was said of *Egypt*, when it abounded with Hermitages in the Primitive persecutions, That *Egypt* was a continuall *City of Hermitages* ; so all the world should have been a continuall Garden of Paradises, when all affections should have been subjects, and all creatures servants,

and all wives helpers, then life was a sincere blessing.
But, but a mixt blessing now, when all these are so much
vitiated; onely a possible blessing; a disputable, a con-
ditionable, a circumstantiall blessing now. If there
were any other way to be saved and to get to Heaven,
then by being born into this life, I would not wish to
have come into this world. And now that God hath
made this life a *Bridge* to Heaven; it is but a giddy, and
a vertiginous thing, to stand long gazing upon so narrow
a bridge, and over so deep and roaring waters, and desperate whirlpools, as this world abounds with: *So teach* Psal.90.12.
us to number our dayes, saith *David, that we may apply our
hearts unto wisedome :* Not to number them so, as that
we place our happinesse, in the increase of their number.

102. *Silkworms.*

SHALL we that are but wormes, but *silke-wormes,* but
glow-wormes at best, chide God that hee hath made
slow-wormes, and other venimous creeping things ? shall
we that are nothing but boxes of poyson in our selves,
reprove God for making Toads and Spiders in the world ?
shall we that are all discord, quarrell the harmony of
his Creation, or his providence ? Can an Apothecary
make a Soveraign triacle of Vipers, and other poysons,
and cannot God admit offences, and scandals into his
physick ? scandals, and offences, tentations, and tribula-
tions, are our leaven that ferment us, and our lees that
preserve us. Use them to Gods glory, and to thine own
establishing, and then thou shall be a particular exception
to that generall Rule, the *Væ mundo à scandalis,* shall
be an *Euge tibi à scandalis,* thou shalt see that it was

well for thee, that there were scandals and offences in the world, for they shall have exercised thy patience, they shall have occasioned thy victory, they shall have assured thy triumph.

103. *Original Sin.*

SCARCE any man considers the weight of Originall sinne; And yet, as the strongest tentations fall upon us when wee are weakest, in our *death-bed,* so the heavyest sinne seises us, when wee are weakest ; as soon as wee are any thing, we are sinners, and there, where there can be no more tentations ministred to us, then was to the Angels that fell in heaven, that is, in *our mothers womb,* when no world, nor flesh, nor Devill could present a provocation to sinne to us, when no faculty of ours is able to embrace, or second a provocation to sin, yet there, in that weaknesse, we are under the weight of Originall sin. And truly, if at this time, God would vouchsafe mee my choice, whether hee should pardon me all those actual and habituall sins, which I have committed in my life, or extinguish Originall sinne in me, I should chuse to be delivered from Originall sin, because, though I be delivered from the *imputation* thereof, by *Baptism,* so that I shall not fall under a condemnation for Originall sin onely, yet it still remains in me, and practices upon me, and occasions all the other sins, that I commit : now, for all my actuall and habituall sins, I know God hath instituted meanes in his Church, the *Word,* and the *Sacraments,* for my reparation ; But with what a holy alacrity, with what a heavenly joy, with what a cheerfull peace, should I come to the participation of these meanes

and seals of my reconciliation, and pardon of all my
sins, if I knew my selfe to be delivered from Originall
sinne, from that snake in my bosome, from that poyson
in my blood, from that leaven and tartar in all my actions,
that casts me into Relapses of those sins which I have
repented ? And what a cloud upon the best serenity
of my conscience, what an interruption, what a dis-
continuance from the sincerity and integrity of that
joy, which belongs to a man truly reconciled to God,
in the pardon of his former sins, must it needs be still
to know, and to know by lamentable experiences, that
though I wash my selfe with Soap, and Nitre, and Snow-
water, mine own cloathes will defile me again, though
I have washed my selfe in the tears of Repentance, and
in the blood of my Saviour, though I have no guiltinesse
of any former sin upon me at that present, yet I have
a sense of a *root* of sin, that is not grub'd up, of *Originall
sinne*, that will cast me back again. Scarce any man
considers the weight, the oppression of Originall sinne.
No man can say, that an Akorn weighs as much as an
Oak ; yet in truth, there is an Oak in that Akorn : no
man considers that Originall sinne weighs as much as
Actuall, or Habituall, yet in truth, all our Actuall and
Habituall sins are in Originall. Therefore Saint *Pauls*
vehement, and frequent prayer to God, to that purpose,
could not deliver him from Originall sin, and that
stimulus carnis, that provocation of the flesh, that
Messenger of Satan, which rises out of that, God would
give him *sufficient grace*, it should not worke to his
destruction, but yet he should have it : Nay, the infinite
merit of Christ Jesus himself, that works so upon all

actuall and habituall sins, as that after that merit is
applyed to them, those sins are no sins, works not so upon
Originall sin, but that, though I be eased in the *Dominion*,
and *Imputation* thereof, yet the same Originall sin is
in me still; and though God doe deliver me from
eternall death, due to mine actuall and habituall sins, yet
from the temporall death, due to Originall sin, he
delivers not his dearest Saints.

104. *Original Sin.*

MISERABLE man! a Toad is a bag of Poyson, and
a Spider is a blister of Poyson, and yet a Toad and
a Spider cannot poyson themselves; Man hath a dram
of poyson, originall-Sin, in an invisible corner, we know
not where, and he cannot choose but poyson himself
and all his actions with that; we are so far from being
able to begin without Grace, as then where we have the
first Grace, we cannot proceed to the use of that,
without more.

105. *The Heart of the Sinner.*

THE holyest man cannot at all times finde his own
heart, (his heart may be bent upon Religion, and yet
he cannot tell in which Religion; and upon Preaching,
and yet he cannot tell which Preacher; and upon Prayer,
and yet he shall finde strayings and deviations in his
Prayer) much more hardly is the various and vagabond
heart of such an indifferent sinner, to be found by any
search. If he enquire for his heart, at that Chamber
where he remembers it was yesterday, in lascivious and
lustful purposes, he shall hear that it went from thence

to some riotous Feasting, from thence to some Blasphemous Gaming, after, to some Malicious Consultation of entangling one, and supplanting another; and he shall never trace it so close, as to drive it home, that is, to the consideration of itself, and that God that made it; nay, scarce to make it consist in any one particular sin. . . .

This *is the full setting of the heart to do evil*, when a man fills himself with the liberty of passing into any sin, in an indifferencie; and then findes no reason why he should leave that way, either by the love, or by the fear of God. If he prosper by his sin, then he findes *no reason*; if he do not prosper by it, yet he findes *a wrong reason*. If unseasonable flouds drown his Harvest, and frustrate all his labours, and his hopes; he never findes, that his oppressing, and grinding of the Poor, was any cause of those waters, but he looks only how the Winde sate, and how the ground lay; and he concludes, that if *Noah*, and *Job*, and *Daniel* had been there their labour must have perished, and been drown'd, as well as his. If a vehement Fever take hold of him, he remembers where he sweat, and when he took cold; where he walked too fast, where his Casement stood open, and where he was too bold upon Fruit, or meat of hard digestion; but he never remembers the sinful and naked Wantonnesses, the profuse and wastful Dilapidations of his own body, that have made him thus obnoxious and open to all dangerous Distempers. Thunder from heaven burns his Barns, and he says, What luck was this? if it had fallen but ten foot short or over, my barns had been safe: whereas his former blasphemings of the Name of God, drew down

Ezek. 14. 14.

that Thunder upon that house, as it was his; and that Lightning could no more fall short or over, then the Angel which was sent to *Sodom* could have burnt another Citie, and have spar'd that; or then the plagues of *Moses* and of *Aaron* could have fallen upon *Goshen*, and have spar'd *Egypt*. His Gomers abound with Manna, he overflows with all for necessities, and with all delicacies, in this life; and yet he finds worms in his Manna, a putrefaction, and a mouldring away, of this abundant state; but he sees not that that is, because his Manna was gathered upon the Sabbath, that there were profanations of the Name and Ordinances of God, mingled in his means of growing rich.

106. *Light Sins.*

THERE are some sins so rooted, so riveted in men, so incorporated, so consubstantiated in the soule, by habituall custome, as that those sins have contracted the nature of Ancient possessions. As men call Manners by their names, so sins have taken names from men, and from places; *Simon Magus* gave the name to a sin, and so did *Gehazi*, and *Sodom* did so: There are sins that run in Names, in Families, in Blood; Hereditary sins, entailed sins; and men do almost prove their Gentry by those sins, and are scarce beleeved to be rightly borne, if they have not those sins; These are great possessions, and men do much more easily part with Christ, then with these sins. But then there are lesse sins, light sins, vanities; and yet even these come to possesse us, and separate us from Christ. How many men neglect this ordinary meanes of their Salvation,

the comming to these Exercises, not because their undoing
lyes on it, or their discountenancing; but meerely out
of levity, of vanity, of nothing; they know not what
to do else, and yet do not this. You heare of one man
that was drowned in a vessell of Wine; but how many
thousands in ordinary water? And he was no more
drowned in that precious liquor, then they in that
common water. A gad of steele does no more choake
a man, then a feather, then a haire; Men perish with
whispering sins, nay with silent sins, sins that never tell
the conscience they are sins, as often as with crying
sins: And in hell there shall meet as many men, that
never thought what was sin, as that spent all their
thoughts in the compassing of sin; as many, who in
a slack inconsideration, never cast a thought upon that
place, as that by searing their conscience, overcame the
sense and feare of the place. Great sins are great
possessions; but levities and vanities possesse us too;
and men had rather part with Christ, then with any
possessions.

107. The Sin of Reason.

PSAL. 55. 19. *Because They have no changes, therefore
They fear not God.* In a Prison, where men wither'd
in a close and perpetual imprisonment; In a Galley, where
men were chain'd to a laborious and perpetual slavery; In
places, where any change that could come, would put them
in a better state, then they were before, this might seem
a fitter text, then in a Court, where every man having set
his foot, or plac'd his hopes upon the present happy
state, and blessed Government, every man is rather to
be presum'd to love God, because there are no changes,

then to take occasion of murmuring at the constancie of Gods goodness towards us. But because the first murmuring at their present condition, the first Innovation that ever was, was in Heaven; The Angels kept not their first Estate: Though as Princes are Gods, so their well-govern'd Courts, are Copies, are representations of Heaven; yet the Copy cannot be better then the Original: And therefore, as Heaven it self had, so all Courts will ever have, some persons, that are under the Increpation of this text, That, *Because they have no changes, therefore they fear not God:* At least, if I shall meet with no conscience, that finds in himself a guiltiness of this sin, if I shall give him no occasion of repentance, yet I shall give him occasion of praysing, and magnifying that gracious God, which hath preserv'd him from such sins, as other men have fallen into, though he have not: For, I shall let him see first, The dangerous slipperiness, the concurrence, the co-incidence of sins; that a habit and custom of sin, slips easily into that dangerous degree

Divisio. of Obduration, that men come to sin upon Reason; they find a *Quia*, a Cause, a Reason why they should sin: and then, in a second place, he shall see, what perverse and frivolous reasons they assign for their sins, when they are come to that; even that which should avert them, they make the cause of them, *Because they have no changes.* And then, lastly, by this perverse mistaking, they come to that infatuation, that dementation, as that they loose the principles of all knowledge, and all wisedom: *The fear of God is the beginning of wisdom;* and, *Because they have no changes, they fear not God.*

Part I.   First then, We enter into our first Part, the slipperiness of habitual sin, with that note of *S. Gregorie*, *Peccatum cum voce, est culpa cum actione; peccatum cum clamore, est culpa cum libertate;* Sinful thoughts produc'd into actions, are speaking sins; sinful actions continued into habits, are crying sins. There is a sin before these; a speechless sin, a whispering sin, which no body hears, but our own conscience; which is, when a sinful thought or purpose is born in our hearts, first we rock it, by tossing, and tumbling it in our fancies, and imaginations, and by entertaining it with delight and consent, & with remembring, with how much pleasure we did the like sin before, and how much we should have, if we could bring this to pass; And as we rock it, so we swathe it, we cover it, with some pretences, some excuses, some hopes of covercling it; and this is that, which we call *Morosam delectationem*, a delight to stand in the air and prospect of a sin, and a loathness to let it go out of our sight. Of this sin *S. Gregory* sayes nothing in this place, but onely of actual sins, which he calls *speaking*; and of habitual, which he calls *crying sins*. And this is as far, as the Schools, or the Casuists do ordinarily trace sin; To find out *peccata Infantia*, speechless sins, in the heart; *peccata vocantia*, speaking sins, in our actions; And *peccata clamantia*, crying and importunate sins, which will not suffer God to take his rest, no nor to fulfil his own Oath, and protestation: He hath said, *As I live, I would not the death of a sinner;* and they extort a death from him. But besides these, Here is a farther degree, beyond speaking sins, and crying sins; beyond actual sins and habitual sins; here are *peccata cum ratione*, and *cum disputatione;* we will reason, we will debate, we will

dispute it out with God, and we will conclude against
all his Arguments, that there is a *Quia*, a Reason, why we
should proceed and go forward in our sin : *Et pudet
non esse impudentes*, as S. *Augustine* heightens this sinful
disposition ; Men grow asham'd of all holy shamefac'd-
ness, and tenderness towards sin ; they grow asham'd
to be put off, or frighted from their sinful pleasure, with
the ordinary terror of Gods imaginary judgements ;
asham'd to be no wiser than S. *Paul* would have them,

1 Cor. 1.21. to be mov'd, or taken hold of, *by the foolishness of preaching;*
or to be no stronger of themselves then so, that we should

Matth. 8. trust to anothers taking of our infirmities, and bearing
of our sicknesses ; Or to be no richer, or no more provi-
dent then so, To sell all, and give it away, and make

Luc. 12. a treasure in Heaven, and all this for fear of Theeves,
and Rust, and Canker, and Moths here. That which is
not allowable in Courts of Justice, in criminal Causes,
to hear Evidence against the King, we will admit
against God ; we will hear Evidence against God ; we
will hear what mans reason can say in favor of the
Delinquent, why he should be condemned ; why God
should punish the soul eternally, for the momentany
pleasures of the body : Nay, we suborn witnesses
against God, and we make Philosophy and Reason
speak against Religion, and against God ; though
indeed, *Omne verum, omni vero consentiens ;* whatsoever is true in Philosophy, is true in Divinity too ;
howsoever we distort it, and wrest it to the contrary.
We hear Witnesses, and we suborn Witnesses against
God, and we do more ; we proceed by Recriminations,
and a cross Bill, with a *Quia Deus*, because God

The Sin of Reason. 175

does as he does, we may do as we do; Because God
does not punish Sinners, we need not forbear sins;
whilst we sin strongly, by oppressing others, that
are weaker, or craftily by circumventing others that
are simple. This is but *Leoninum*, and *Vulpinum*,
that tincture of the Lyon, and of the Fox, that
brutal nature that is in us. But when we come to
sin, upon reason, and upon discourse, upon Meditation,
and upon plot, This is *Humanum*, to become the Man of
Sin, to surrender that, which is the Form, and Essence
of man, Reason, and understanding, to the service of
sin. When we come to sin wisely and learnedly, to sin
logically, by a *Quia*, and an *Ergo*, that, Because God does
thus, we may do as we do, we shall come to sin through
all the Arts, and all our knowledge, To sin Grammatically,
to tie sins together in construction, in a Syntaxis, in
a chaine, and dependance, and coherence upon one
another: And to sin Historically, to sin over sins of
other men again, to sin by precedent, and to practice
that which we had read: and we come to sin Rhetori-
cally, perswasively, powerfully; and as we have found
examples for our sins in History, so we become examples
to others, by our sins, to lead and encourage them, in
theirs; when we come to employ upon sin, that which
is the essence of man, Reason, and discourse, we will
also employ upon it, those which are the properties
of man onely, which are, To speak, and to laugh; we
will come to speak, and talk, and to boast of our sins,
and at last, to laugh and jest at our sins; and as we have
made sin a Recreation, so we will make a jest of our
condemnation. And this is the dangerous slipperiness

of sin, to slide by Thoughts and Actions, and Habits, to contemptuous obduration.

108. *Delight in Evil.*

FIRST then, what is this *setting of the heart upon evil* ; and then, what is this *fulness*, that leaves no room for a Cure ? When a man receives figures and images of sin, into his Fancie and Imagination, and leads them on to his understanding and Discourse, to his Will, to his Consent, to his Heart, by a delightful dwelling upon the meditation of that sin ; yet this is not a *setting of the heart upon doing evil.* To be surpris'd by a Tentation, to be overthrown by it, to be held down by it for a time, is not it. It is not when the devil looks in at the window to the heart, by presenting occasions of tentations, to the eye ; nor when he comes in at the door, to our heart, at the ear, either in lascivious discourses, or Satyrical and Libellous defamations of other men : It is not, when the devil is put to his Circuit, to *seek whom he may devour,* and how he may corrupt the King by his Council, That is, the Soul by the Senses : But it is, when by a habitual custom in sin, the sin arises meerly and immediately from my self : It is, when the heart hath usurp'd upon the devil, and upon the world too, and is able and apt to sin of it self, if there were no devil, and if there were no outward objects of tentation : when our own heart is become *spontanea insania, & voluntarius dæmon,* Such a wilful Madness, and such a voluntary and natural Devil to it self, as that we should be ambitious, though we were in an Hospital ; and licentious, though we were in a wilderness : and voluptuous, though in

Chrysost.

a famine: so that such a mans heart, is as a land of such Gyants, where the Children are born as great, as the Men of other nations grow to be; for those sins, which in other men have their birth, and their growth, after their birth, they begin at a Concupiscence, and proceed to a Consent, and grow up to Actions, and swell up to Habits; In this man, sin begins at a stature and proportion above all this; he begins at a delight in the sin, and comes instantly to a defence of it, and to an obduration and impenitibleness in it: This is the evil of the heart, by the mis-use of Gods grace, to devest and lose all tenderness and remorse in sin.

109. *Excuses.*

LET no man therefore think to present his complexion to God for an excuse, and say, My choler with which my constitution abounded, and which I could not remedy, enclined me to wrath, and so to bloud; My Melancholy enclined me to sadnesse, and so to Desperation, as though thy sins were medicinall sins, sins to vent humors. Let no man say, I am continent enough all the yeare, but the spring works upon me, and inflames my concupiscencies, as though thy sins were seasonable and anniversary sins. Make not thy Calling the occasion of thy sin, as though thy sin were a Mysterie, and an Occupation; Nor thy place, thy station, thy office the occasion of thy sin, as though thy sin were an Heir-loome, or furniture, or fixed to the freehold of that place: for this one proposition, *God is no accepter of persons*, is so often repeated, that all circumstances of Dispositions, and Callings, and time, and place might be involved in it.

110. *Rebuke of Sin.*

THE rebuke of sin, is like the fishing of *Whales*; the Marke is great enough; one can scarce misse hitting; but if there be not *sea room* and line enough, & a dexterity in letting out that line, he that hath fixed his harping Iron, in the Whale, endangers himselfe, and his boate; God hath made us *fishers of Men*; and when we have struck a *Whale*, touch'd the conscience of any person, which thought himselfe above rebuke, and increpation, it struggles, and strives, and as much as it can, endevours to draw fishers, and boate, the Man and his fortune into contempt, and danger. But if God tye a *sicknesse*, or any other calamity, to the end of the line, that will winde up this Whale againe, to the boate, bring back this rebellious sinner better advised, to the mouth of the Minister, for more counsaile, and to a better souplenesse, and inclinablenesse to conforme himselfe, to that which he shall after receive from him; onely calamity makes way for a rebuke to enter.

111. *Names of Sins.*

1 Part.
Notum feci.

FIRST then in this mystery of Confession, we consider *Davids* reflected act, his preparatory act, preceding his confession to God, and transacted in himselfe, of which the first motion is, the *Notum feci*, I acknowledged in my selfe, I came to a feeling in my selfe, what my sinfull condition was. This is our quickning in our regeneration, and second birth; and til this come, a sinner lies as the Chaos in the beginning of the Creation, before the *Spirit of God had moved upon the face of the waters, Dark*, and *voyd*, and *without forme*; He lies, as we may conceive, out of the Authors of Naturall Story, the slime and mud of the River *Nilus* to lie, before the Sun-beames strike upon it; which after, by the heat of those beames, produces severall shapes, and formes of creatures. So till this first beame of grace, which we consider here, strike upon the soule of a sinner, he lies in the mud and slime, in the dregs and lees, and tartar of his sinne. Hee cannot so much as wish, that that Sunne would shine upon him, he doth not so much as know, that there is such a Sunne, that hath that influence, and impression; But if this first beame of Grace enlighten him to himselfe, reflect him upon himselfe, *notum facit,* (as the Text sayes) if it acquaint him with himselfe, then, as the creatures in the Creation, then, as the new creatures at Nilus, his sins begin to take their formes, and their specifications, and they appeare to him in their particular true shapes, and that which hee hath in a generall name, called Pleasure or Wantonnesse, now cals it selfe in his conscience, a direct Adultery, a direct Incest; and that which he hath called Frugality, and providence for family and posterity, tells him plainly, My name is Oppression, and I am the spirit of covetousnesse. Many times men fall into company, and accompany others to houses of riot and uncleannesse, and doe not so much as know their sinfull companions names; nay they doe not so much as know the names of the sins that they commit, nor those circumstances in those sinnes, which vary the very name and nature of the sin.

N 2

112. *Pride.*

SOLITUDE is not the scene of Pride; The danger of pride is in company, when we meet to looke upon another. But in *Adams* wife, *Eve*, her first act (that is noted) was an act of Pride, a hearkning to that voyce of the Serpent, *Ye shall be as Gods*. As soone as there were two, there was pride. How many may we have knowne, (if we have had any conversation in the world) that have been content all the weeke, at home alone, with their worky day faces, as well as with their worky day clothes, and yet on Sundayes, when they come to Church, and appeare in company, will mend both, their faces as well as their clothes. Not solitude, but company is the scene of pride; And therefore I know not what to call that practice of the Nunnes in Spaine, who though they never see man, yet will paint. So early, so primary a sin is Pride, as that it grew instantly from her, whom God intended for a *Helper*, because he saw *that it was not good for man to be alone*. God sees that it is not good for man to be without health, without wealth, without power, and jurisdiction, and magistracy, and we grow proud of our helpers, proud of our health and strength, proud of our wealth and riches, proud of our office and authority over others.

So early, so primary a sin is pride, as that, out of every mercy, and blessing, which God affords us, (and, *His mercies are new every morning*) we gather Pride; wee are not the more thankfull for them, and yet we are the prouder of them. Nay, we gather Pride, not onely out of those things, which mend and improve us, (Gods

Gen. 3. 5.

Gen. 2. 18.

blessings and mercies) but out of those actions of our own, that destroy and ruine us, we gather pride; sins overthrow us, demolish us, destroy and ruine us, and yet we are proud of our sinnes. How many men have we heard boast of their sinnes; and, (as S. *Augustine* confesses of himselfe) belie themselves, and boast of more sinnes then ever they committed? Out of every thing, out of nothing sin grows. Therefore was this commandment in our text, *Sequere, Follow*, come after, well placed first, for we are come to see even children strive for place and precedency, and mothers are ready to goe to the Heralds to know how Cradles shall be ranked, which Cradle shall have the highest place; Nay, even in the wombe, there was contention for precedency; *Iacob* tooke hold of his brother *Esaus* heele, and would have been borne before him.

Gen. 25. 26.

And as our pride begins in our Cradle, it continues in our graves and Monuments. It was a good while in the primitive Church, before any were buried in the Church; The best contented themselves with the Churchyards. After, a holy ambition, (may we call it so) a holy Pride brought them *ad Limina*, to the Churchthreshold, to the Church-doore, because some great Martyrs were buried in the Porches, and devout men desired to lie neare them, as one Prophet did to lie neare another, (*Lay my bones besides his bones.*) But now, persons whom the Devill kept from Church all their lives, Separatists, Libertines, that never came to any Church, And persons, whom the Devill brought to Church all their lives, (for, such as come meerly out of the obligation of the Law, and to redeem that vexation,

Superbia in monumentis.

1 King. 13. 31.

or out of custome, or company, or curiosity, or a perverse and sinister affection to the particular Preacher, though they come to Gods house, come upon the Devils invitation) Such as one Devill, that is, worldly respect, brought to Church in their lives, another Devill, that is, Pride and vain-glory, brings to Church after their deaths, in an affectation of high places, and sumptuous Monuments in the Church. And such as have given nothing at all to any pious uses, or have determined their almes and their dole which they have given, in that one day of their funerall, and no farther, have given large annuities, perpetuities, for new painting their tombes, and for new flags, and scutcheons, every certaine number of yeares.

O the earlinesse! O the latenesse! how early a Spring, and no Autumne! how fast a growth, and no declination, of this branch of this sin Pride, against which, this first word of ours, *Sequere, Follow*, come after, is opposed! this love of place, and precedency, it rocks us in our Cradles, it lies down with us in our graves.

113. *Covetousness.*

*H*AST *thou found honey? Eat so much as is sufficient for thee, lest thou be filled therewith, and vomit it.—* Prov. xxv. 16. . . .

Ne satieris.   Hee doth not say yet, lest thou bee satisfied; there is no great feare, nay there is no hope of that, that he will be satisfied. We know the receipt, the capacity of the ventricle, the stomach of man, how much it can hold; and wee know the receipt of all the receptacles of blood, how much blood the body can have; so wee doe of all the other conduits and cisterns of the body; But this infinite Hive of honey, this insatiable whirlpoole of the covetous mind, no Anatomy, no dissection hath discovered to us. When I looke into the larders, and cellars, and vaults, into the vessels of our body for drink, for blood, for urine, they are pottles, and gallons; when I looke into the furnaces of our spirits, the ventricles of the heart and of the braine, they are but thimbles; for spirituall things, the things of the next world, we have no roome; for temporall things, the things of this world, we have no bounds. How then shall this over-eater bee filled with his honey? So filled, as that he can receive nothing else. More of the same honey hee can; Another Mannor, and another Church, is but another bit of meat, with another sauce to him; Another Office, and another way of Extortion, is but another garment, and another lace to him. But he is too full to receive any thing else; Christ comes to this Bethlem, (Bethlem which is *Domus panis*) this house of abundance, and there is no roome for Christ in this Inne; there are no crums for Christ under this table; There comes *Boanerges*, (*Boanerges*, that is, *filius Tonitrui*, the sonne of Thunder) and he thunders out the *Væ's*, the Comminations, the Judgements of God upon such as hee; but if the Thunder spoile not his drink, he sees no harme in Thunder; As long as a Sermon is not a Sentence in the Starre-chamber, that a Sermon cannot fine and imprison him, hee hath no room for any good effect of a Sermon. The Holy Ghost, the Spirit of Comfort comes to him, and offers him the consolation of the Gospel; but hee will die in his old religion, which is to sacrifice to his owne Nets, by which his

portion is plenteous ; he had rather have the God of
the Old Testament, that payes in this world with milke
and honey, then the God of the New Testament, that
cals him into his Vineyard in this World, and payes him
no wages till the next : one *Iupiter* is worth all the three
Elohims, or the three *Iehovahs* (if we may speake so) to
him. *Iupiter* that can come in a showre of gold, out-
waighs *Iehova*, that comes but in a showre of water, but
in a sprinkling of water in Baptisme, and sels that water
so deare, as that he will have showres of teares for it,
nay showres of blood for it, when any Persecutor hath
a mind to call for it. The voyce of God whom he hath
contemned, and wounded, The voyce of the Preacher
whom he hath derided, and impoverished, The voyce
of the poore, of the Widow, of the Orphans, of the
prisoner, whom he hath oppressed, knocke at his doore,
and would enter, but there is no roome for them, he is
so full. This is the great danger indeed that accompanies
this fulnesse, but the danger that affects him more is
that which is more literally in the text, *Evomet*, he shall
be so filled as that he shall *vomit* ; even that fulnesse,
those temporall things which he had, he shall cast up.

114. *Blasphemy.*

BLASPHEMY, as it is a contumelious speech, dero-
gating from any man, that good that is in him, or
attributing to any man, that ill that is not in him, may
be fastned upon any man. For the most part it is
understood a sin against God, and that directly ; and
here, by the manner of Christ expressing himselfe, it is
made the greatest sin ; *All sin*, even *blasphemy*. And yet,

a drunkard that cannot name God, will spue out a blasphemy against God: A child that cannot spell God, will stammer out a blasphemy against God: If we smart, we blaspheme God, and we blaspheme him if we be tickled; If I lose at play, I blaspheme, and if my fellow lose, he blasphemes, so that God is alwayes sure to be a loser. An Usurer can shew me his bags, and an Extortioner his houses, the fruits, the revenues of his sinne; but where will the blasphemer shew mee his blasphemy, or what hee hath got by it? The licentious man hath had his love in his armes, and the envious man hath had his enemy in the dust, but wherein hath the blasphemer hurt God?

In the Schoole we put it for the consummation of the torment of the damned, that at the Resurrection, they shall have bodies, and so be able, even verbally, to blaspheme God; herein we exceed the Devill already, that we can speake blasphemously. There is a rebellious part of the body, that *Adam* covered with figge leaves, that hath damned many a wretched soule; but yet, I thinke, not more then the tongue; And therefore the whole torment that *Dives* suffered in hell, is expressed in that part, *Father Abraham, have mercy upon me, and send Lazarus, that he may dip the tip of his finger in water, and coole my tongue.* The Jews that crucified God, will not sound the name of God, and we for whom he was Crucified, belch him out in our surfets, and foame him out in our fury: An Impertinent sin, without occasion before, and an unprofitable sin, without recompence after, and an incorrigible sin too; for, almost what Father dares chide his son for blasphemy, that may not

Aquin.22x q.13.ar.4.

Luke16.24.

tell him, Sir I learnt it of you ? or what Master his
servant, that cannot lay the same recrimination upon
him ?

115. *The Burden of Sin.*

FOR mine iniquities are gone over my head, as a heavy
Burden, they are too heavy for me.—Ps. xxxviii. 4. . . .
A second inconvenience intimated in this Metaphore,

Fatigat. a *burden*, is the *fatigat*, a burden *wearies* us, tires us : and
so does our sinne, and our best beloved sinne. It hath
wearied us, and yet we cannot devest it. We would
leave that sin, and yet there is *one talent* more to be added,
one childe more to be provided for, *one office*, or *one title*
more to be compassed, *one tentation* more to be satisfied.
Though we grumble, not out of remorse of *conscience*,
but out of a bodily wearinesse of the sinne, yet wee
proceed in it. How often men goe to *Westminster*, how
often to the *Exchange*, called by unjust suits, or called
by corrupt bargaines to those places, when their ease,
or their health perswades them to stay at home ? How
many go to forbidden beds, then when they had rather
stay at home, if they were not afraid of an unkind interpretation ? *We have wearied our selves in the ways of*
wickednesse ; Plus miles in uno torneamento, quàm sanctus
Monachus in decem annis, says our *Holkot*, upon that
place, a soldier suffers more in one expedition, then
a Monk does, in ten years, says he ; and perchance he
says true, and yet no commendation to his Monke neither ;
for that soldier may doe even the cause of God, more
good, in that one expedition, then that Monke in ten
years : But it is true as *Holkot* intended it, (though
perchance his example doe not much strengthen it)

vicious men are put to more pains, and to doe more things against their own mindes, then the Saints of God are in the ways of holinesse. *We have wearied our selves in the ways of wickednesse*, says he, that is, in doing as other wicked men have done, in ways which have been beaten out to us, by the frequent practise of other men ; but he addes more, *We have gone thorough Deserts, where there lay no way* ; that is, through sins, in which, wee had no example, no precedent, the inventions of our hearts. The covetous man lies still, and attends his *quarter days*, and studies the endorsements of his bonds, and he wonders that the ambitious man can endure the shufflings and thrustings of Courts, and can measure his happinesse by the smile of a greater man : And, he that does so, wonders as much, that this covetous man can date his happinesse by an *Almanack*, and such revolutions, and though he have quick returns of receipt, yet scarce affords himself bread to live till that day come, and though all his joy be in his bonds, yet denies himself a candles end to look upon them. *Hilly ways* are wearisome ways, and tire the ambitious man ; Carnall pleasures are *dirty ways*, and tire the licentious man ; Desires of gain, are *thorny ways*, and tire the covetous man ; Æmulations of higher men, are *dark* and *blinde ways*, and tire the envious man ; Every way, that is out of the way, wearies us ; But, *lassati sumus ; sed lassis non datur requies* ; *we* Lam. 5. 5. *labour, and have no rest*, when we have done ; we are wearied with our sins, and have no satisfaction in them ; we goe to bed to night, weary of our sinfull labours, and we will rise freshly to morrow, to the same sinfull labours again ; And when a sinner does so little remember *yesterday*, how little does he consider to *morrow* ?   He that forgets what he hath *done*, foresees not what he shall suffer : so sin is a burden ; it crookens us, it wearies us ; And those are the two first inconveniences.

116. *The Sinner.*

IT is thy pleasure O God, and thy pleasure shall be infallibly accomplished, that every wicked person should be his owne Executioner. He is *Spontaneus Dæmon*, as S. *Chrysostome* speaks, an In-mate, an in-nate Devill ; a bosome devill, a selfe-Devill ; That as he could be a tempter to himselfe, though there were no Devill, so he could be an Executioner to himselfe, though there were no Satan, and a Hell to himselfe, though there were no other Torment.   Sometimes he staies not the Assises, but prevents the hand of Justice ; he destroies himselfe before his time.   But when he staies, he is evermore condemned at the Assises.   Let him sleepe out as much of the morning as securely as he can ; embellish, and adorne himselfe as gloriously as he can ; dine as largely and as delicately as he can ; weare out as much of the afternoone, in conversation, in Comedies, in pleasure, as hee can ; sup with as much distension, and inducement of drousinesse as he can, that he may scape all remorse, by falling asleepe quickly, and fall asleepe with as much discourse, and musicke, and advantage as he can, he hath a conscience that will survive, and overwatch all the company ; he hath a sorrow that shall joyne issue with him when he is alone, and both God, and the devill, who doe not meet willingly, shall meet in his case, and be in league, and be on the sorrowes side, against him.   The anger of God, and the malice of the devill, shall concurre with his sorrow, to his farther vexation. No one wicked person, by any diversion or cunning, shall avoid this sorrow, for it is in the midst, and in the end of all his forced contentments; *Even in laughing, the heart is* Prov. 14. *sorrowful, and the end of that mirth is heavinesse.* 13.

117. *The Sorrows of the Wicked.*

AND if we consider farther, the manifold Topiques, and places, from which the sorrowes of the wicked arise, That every inch of their ground is overgrown with that venomous weed, that every place, and every part of time, and every person buddes out a particular occasion of sorrow to him, that he can come into no chamber, but he remembers, In such a place as this, I sinned thus, That he cannot heare a Clock strike, but he remembers, At this hour I sinned thus, That he cannot converse with few persons, but he remembers, With such a person I sinned thus, And if he dare goe no farther then to himselfe, he can look scarcely upon any limb of his body, but in that he sees some infirmity, or some deformity, that he imputes to some sin, and must say, By this sin, this is thus: When he can open the Bible in no place, but if he meet a judgement, he must say, *Vindicta mihi,* This vengeance belongs to me, and if he meet a mercy, he must say, *Quid mihi?* What have I to doe to take this mercy into my mouth? In this deluge of occasions of sorrow, I must not say with God to *Abraham,* Look up to heaven, and number the Starres, (for this man cannot look up to heaven) but I must say, Continue thy dejected look, and look downe to the earth, thy earth,

and number the graines of dust there, and the sorrowes
of the wicked are more then they.

118. *The Sins of Memory.*

A HOUSE is not clean, though all the Dust be swept
together, if it lie still in a corner, within Dores;
A Conscience is not clean, by having recollected all her
sinnes in the *Memory*, for they may fester there, and
Gangreen even to *Desperation*, till she have emptied them
in the bottomlesse Sea of the bloud of Christ Jesus: and
the mercy of his Father, by *this* way of *Confession*. But
a house is not clean neither, though the Dust be thrown
out, if there hang *Cobwebs* about the Walls, in how dark
corners soever. A Conscience is not clean, though the
sins, brought to our memory by this Examination, be
cast upon Gods mercy, and the merits of his Sonne, by
Confession, if there remaine in me, but a *Cobweb*, a little,
but a sinfull delight in the *Memory* of those sins, which
I had formerly committed. How many men sinne over
the sinnes of their youth again, in their age, by a sinfull
Delight in remembring those sinnes, and a sinfull *Desire*,
that their Bodies were not past them? How many men
sin over some sins, but *imaginarily*, (and yet *Damnably*)
a hundred times, which they *never sinned actually* at
all, by filling their *Imaginations*, with such thoughts
as these, How would I be revenged of such an Enemy,
if I were in such a place of Authority? How easily
could I overthrow such a wastfull young Man, and compasse his Land, if I had but Money, to feed his humours?
Those sinnes which we have never been able to doe
actually, to the harme of others, we doe as hurtfully to

our owne Souls, by a sinfull *Desire* of them, and a sinfull *Delight* in them.

119. *The Eye of God.*

GOD *cannot be mocked*, saith the Apostle, nor God cannot be *blinded*. He seeth all the way, and at *thy last gaspe*, he will make thee see too, through the multiplying Glasse, the Spectacle of *Desperation*. Canst thou hope that that God, that seeth this darke Earth through all the vaults and arches of the severall spheares of Heaven, that seeth thy body through all thy stone walls, and seeth thy soul through that which is darker then all those, thy corrupt flesh, canst thou hope that that God can be blinded with drawing a curtain between thy sinne and him ? when he is all eye, canst thou hope to put out that eye, with putting out a candle ? when he hath planted legions of Angels about thee, canst thou hope that thou hast taken away all *Intelligence*, if thou have corrupted, or silenced, or sent away a servant ? O bestow as much labour, as thou hast done, to finde corners for sin, to finde out those sinnes, in those corners where thou hast hid them. As Princes give pardons by their own hands, but send Judges to execute Justice, come to him for mercy in the acknowledgement of thy sinnes, and stay not till his Justice come to thee, *when he makes inquisition for blood* ; and doe not think, that if thou feel now at this present, a little tendernesse in thy heart, a little melting in thy bowels, a little dew in thine eyes, that if thou beest come to know, that thou art a sinner, thou dost therefore presently know thy sinnes. Thou wouldst have so much tendernes, so much compassion, if thou knewest that he that sits next thee, were in this danger of Gods heavy indignation; thou wouldst commiserate thy neighbours wretched condition so much. But proceed with thy self further, bring this dawning and breake of day to a full light, and this little sparke to a perfect acknowledgement of thy sinnes. Go home, with this spark of Gods Spirit in you, and there looke upon your *Rentalls*, and know your oppressions, and extorsions; looke upon your *shop-bookes*, and know your deceits and falsifications; looke upon your *ward-robes*, and know your excesses; looke upon your *childrens faces*, and know your fornications. Till then, till you come to this scrutiny, this survey, this sifting of the Conscience, if we should cry *peace, peace,* yet there were no peace.

120. *The World Drowned in Sin.*

WHEN the Holy Ghost hath brought us into the Ark from whence we may see all the world without, sprawling and gasping in the flood, (the flood of sinfull courses in the world, and of the anger of God) when we can see this violent flood, (the anger of God) break in at windowes, and there devoure the licentious man in his sinfull embracements, and make his bed of wanton-nesse his death-bed; when we can see this flood (the anger of God) swell as fast as the ambitious man swels, and pursue him through all his titles, and at last suddenly, and violently wash him away in his owne blood, not alwayes in a vulgar, but sometimes in an ignominious death; when we shall see this flood (the flood of the anger of God) over-flow the valley of the

voluptuous mans gardens, and orchards, and follow him
into his Arbours, and Mounts, and Terasses, and carry
him from thence into a bottomlesse Sea, which no
Plummet can sound, (no heavy sadnesse relieve him) no
anchor take hold of, (no repentance stay his tempested
and weather-beaten conscience) when wee finde our
selves in this Ark, where we have first taken in the fresh
water of Baptisme, and then the Bread, and Wine, and
Flesh, of the Body and Blood of Christ Jesus, Then are
we reproved, forbidden all scruple, then are we convinced,
That as *the twelve Apostles shall sit upon twelve seats,
and judge the twelve Tribes at the last day*; So doth the
Holy Ghost make us Judges of all the world now, and
inables us to pronounce that sentence, That all but they,
who have sincerely accepted the Christian Religion, are
still *sub peccato*, under sin, and without remedy.

121. *The Hand of God.*

THE hand of God shall grow heavy upon a silent
sinner, in his body, in his health; and if he conceive a comfort, that for all his sicknesse, he is rich, and
therefore cannot fayle of helpe and attendance, there
comes another worme, and devours that, faithlesnesse
in persons trusted by him, oppressions in persons that
have trusted him, facility in undertaking for others,
corrupt Judges, heavy adversaries, tempests and Pirats
at Sea, unseasonable or ill Markets at land, costly and
expensive ambitions at Court, one worme or other shall
devoure his riches, that he eased himselfe upon. If he
take up another Comfort, that though health and wealth
decay, though he be poore and weake, yet he hath learning,

and philosophy, and morall constancy, and he can content himselfe with himselfe, he can make his study a Court, and a few Books shall supply to him the society and the conversation of many friends, there is another worme to devoure this too, the hand of divine Justice shall grow heavy upon him, in a sense of an unprofitable retirednesse, in a disconsolate melancholy, and at last, in a stupidity, tending to desperation.

122. *The Sick Soul.*

HE shall suspect his Religion, suspect his Repentance, suspect the Comforts of the Minister, suspect the efficacy of the Sacrament, suspect the mercy of God himselfe. Every fit of an Ague is an Earth-quake that swallows him, every fainting of the knee, is a step to Hell; every lying down at night is a funerall; & every quaking is a rising to judgment; every bell that distinguishes times, is a passing-bell, and every passing-bell, his own; every singing in the ear, is an Angels Trumpet; at every dimnesse of the candle, he heares that voice, *Fool, this night they will fetch away thy soul*; and in every judgement denounced against sin, he hears an *I to maledicte* upon himselfe, *Goe thou accursed into hell fire.*

123. *Sleep.*

Ephes. 4. 24.

THE Sun must not set upon my anger; much lesse will I let the Sun set upon the anger of God towards me, or sleep in an unrepented sin. Every nights sleep is a *Nunc dimittis*; then the Lord lets his servant depart in peace. Thy lying down is a valediction, a parting, a taking leave, (shall I say so?) a shaking hands with God; and,

when thou shakest hands with God, let those hands be
clean. Enter into thy grave, thy metaphoricall, thy
quotidian grave, thy bed, as thou entredst into the Church
at first, by Water, by Baptisme; Re-baptise thy self
every night, in *Iobs Snow water.* . . . Sleep with cleane
hands, either kept cleane all day, by integrity; or
washed cleane, at night, by repentance; and whensoever
thou wakest, though all *Iobs* messengers thunder about
thee, and all *Iobs* friends multiply mis-interpretations
against thee, yet *Iobs* protestation shall be thy protestation, what end soever God have in this proceeding,
It is not for any injustice in my hands, and the other
part of his protestation too, *Also my prayer is pure.*

124. *The Gate of Death.*

AS he that travails weary, and late towards a great
City, is glad when he comes to a place of execution, becaus he knows that is neer the town; so when
thou comest to the gate of death, glad of that, for it
is but one step from that to thy *Jerusalem.* Christ hath
brought us in some neerness to Salvation, as he is *vere
Salvator mundi,* in that we *know, that this is indeed the* Jo. 4. 42.
Christ, the Saviour of the world: and he hath brought
it neerer than that, as he is *Salvator corporis sui,* in that Eph. 5. 23.
we know, *That Christ is the head of the Church, and the
Saviour of that body:* And neerer than that, as he is Esay. 43. 3.
Salvator tuus sanctus, In that we know, *He is the Lord
our God, the holy One of Israel, our Saviour:* But neerest
of all, in the *Ecce Salvator tuus venit,* Behold thy Salvation Esa. 62. 11.
commeth. It is not only promised in the Prophets, nor

only writ in the Gospel, nor only seal'd in the Sacraments, nor only prepared in the visitations of the holy Ghost, but, *Ecce*, behold it, now, when thou canst behold nothing else : The sun is setting to thee, and that for ever ; thy houses and furnitures, thy gardens and orchards, thy titles and offices, thy wife and children are departing from thee, and that for ever ; a cloud of faintnesse is come over thine eyes, and a cloud of sorrow over all theirs ; when his hand that loves thee best hangs tremblingly over thee to close thine eyes, *Ecce Salvator tuus venit*, behold then a new light, thy Saviours hand shall open thine eyes, and in his light thou shalt see light ; and thus shalt see, that though in the eyes of men thou lye upon that bed, as a Statue on a Tomb, yet in the eyes of God, thou standest as a *Colossus*, one foot in one, another in another land ; one foot in the grave, but the other in heaven ; one hand in the womb of the earth, and the other in *Abrahams* bosome : And then *vere prope*, Salvation is truly neer thee, and neerer than when thou believedst, which is our last word.

125. *Our Prison.*

WE are all conceived in close Prison ; in our Mothers wombes, we are close Prisoners all ; when we are borne, we are borne but to the liberty of the house ; Prisoners still, though within larger walls ; and then all our life is but a going out to the place of Execution, to death. Now was there ever any man seen to sleep in the Cart, between New-gate, and Tyborne ? between the Prison, and the place of Execution, does any man sleep ? And we sleep all the way ; from the womb to the grave we are never throughly awake ; but passe on with such dreames, and imaginations as these, I may live as well, as another, and why should I dye, rather then another ? but awake, and tell me, sayes this Text, *Quis homo?* who is that other that thou talkest of ? *What man is he that liveth, and shall not see death?*

126. *All must Die.*

DOTH not man die even in his birth ? The breaking of prison is death, and what is our birth, but a breaking of prison ? Assoon as we were clothed by God, our very apparell was an Embleme of death. In the skins of dead beasts, he covered the skins of dying men. Assoon as God set us on work, our very occupation was an Embleme of death ; It was to digge the earth ; not to digge pitfals for other men, but graves for our selves. Hath any man here forgot to day, that yesterday is dead ? And the Bell tolls for to day, and will ring out anon ; and for as much of every one of us, as appertaines to this day. *Quotidiè morimur, & tamen nos esse æternos putamus,* sayes S. *Hierome* ; We die every day, and we die all the day long ; and because we are not absolutely dead, we call that an eternity, an eternity of dying : And is there comfort in that state ? why, that is the state of hell it self, Eternall dying, and not dead.

But for this there is enough said, by the Morall man ; (that we may respite divine proofes, for divine points anon, for our severall Resurrections) for this death is meerly naturall, and it is enough that the morall man sayes, *Mors lex, tributum, officium mortalium.* First it is *lex,* you Seneca.

were born under that law, upon that condition to die :
so it is a rebellious thing not to be content to die, it
opposes the Law.   Then it is *Tributum*, an imposition
which nature the Queen of this world layes upon us,
and which she will take, when and where she list ; here
a yong man, there an old man, here a happy, there a
miserable man ; And so it is a seditious thing not to be
content to die, it opposes the prerogative.   And lastly,
it is *Officium*, men are to have their turnes, to take their
time, and then to give way by death to successors ; and
so it is *Incivile*, *inofficiosum*, not to be content to die, it
opposes the frame and form of government.   It comes
equally to us all, and makes us all equall when it comes.
The ashes of an Oak in the Chimney, are no Epitaph of
that Oak, to tell me how high or how large that was ;
It tels me not what flocks it sheltered while it stood,
nor what men it hurt when it fell.   The dust of great
persons graves is speechlesse too, it sayes nothing, it
distinguishes nothing : As soon the dust of a wretch
whom thou wouldest not, as of a Prince whom thou
couldest not look upon, will trouble thine eyes, if the
winde blow it thither ; and when a whirle-winde hath
blowne the dust of the Church-yard into the Church, and
the man sweeps out the dust of the Church into the
Church-yard, who will undertake to sift those dusts
again, and to pronounce, This is the Patrician, this is
the noble flowre, and this the yeomanly, this the Plebeian
bran. . . .

Novissi-
mus hostis.
Death is the last, and in that respect the worst enemy.
In an enemy, that appeares at first, when we are or may
be provided against him, there is some of that, which

we call Honour : but in the enemie that reserves himselfe
unto the last, and attends our weake estate, there is
more danger. Keepe it, where I intend it, in that which
is my spheare, the Conscience : If mine enemie meet
me betimes in my youth, in an object of tentation, (so
Josephs enemie met him in *Putifars* Wife) yet if I doe
not adhere to this enemy, dwell upon a delightfull
meditation of that sin, if I doe not fuell, and foment
that sin, assist and encourage that sin, by high diet,
wanton discourse, other provocation, I shall have reason
on my side, and I shall have grace on my side, and I shall
have the History of a thousand that have perished by
that sin, on my side ; Even Spittles will give me souldiers
to fight for me, by their miserable example against that
sin ; nay perchance sometimes the vertue of that woman,
whom I sollicite, will assist me. But when I lye under
the hands of that enemie, that hath reserved himselfe
to the last, to my last bed, then when I shall be able
to stir no limbe in any other measure then a Feaver or
a Palsie shall shake them, when everlasting darknesse
shall have an inchoation in the present dimnesse of mine
eyes, and the everlasting gnashing in the present chattering of my teeth, and the everlasting worme in the present
gnawing of the Agonies of my body, and anguishes of
my minde, when the last enemie shall watch my remedi-
lesse body, and my disconsolate soule there, there, where
not the Physitian, in his way, perchance not the Priest
in his, shall be able to give any assistance, And when he
hath sported himselfe with my misery upon that stage,
my death-bed, shall shift the Scene, and throw me from
that bed, into the grave, and there triumph over me,

God knowes, how many generations, till the Redeemer, my Redeemer, the Redeemer of all me, body, as well as soule, come againe ; As death is *Novissimus hostis*, the enemy which watches me, at my last weaknesse, and shall hold me, when I shall be no more, till that Angel come, *Who shall say, and sweare that time shall be no more*, in that consideration, in that apprehension, he is the powerfullest, the fearefulest enemy ; and yet even there this enemy *Abolebitur*, he shall be destroyed.

127. *Death Inevitable.*

A'DAM might have liv'd, if he would, but *I cannot.* God hath placed an *Ecce*, a marke of my death, upon every thing living, that I can set mine eye upon ; every thing is a remembrancer, every thing is a Judge upon me, and pronounces, I *must* dye. The whole frame of *Heb.* 9. 27. the world is mortall, *Heaven and Earth passe away* : and upon us all, there is an irrecoverable Decree past, *statutum est*, It *is appointed to all men, that they shall once dye.* But when ? quickly ; If thou looke up into the aire, *Job* 7. 7. *remember that thy life is but a winde*, If thou see a cloud in the aire, aske St. *James* his question, what is your *Iam.* 4. 14. life ? and give St. *James* his answer, *It is a vapour that appeareth and vanisheth away.* If thou behold a *Tree*, then *Job* gives thee a comparison of thy selfe ; A *Tree* is an *embleme* of thy selfe ; nay a Tree is the *originall*, thou art but the *copy*, thou art not so good as it : for, *Iob* 14. 7 *There is hope of a tree* (as you reade there) *if the roote wax old*, if *the* stock be dead, if it be cut down, yet by *the sent of the waters*, it will *bud*, but *man is sick*, and *dyeth, and where is he* ? he shall not wake againe, till heaven be no more. Looke upon the *water*, and we are as that, and as that spilt upon the ground : Looke to the *earth*, and we are not like that, but we are earth it self : At our Tables we feed upon the dead, and in that Temple we tread upon the dead : and when we meet in a Church, God hath made many *echoes*, many testimonies of our death, in the walls, and in the windowes, and he onely knowes, whether he will not make another testimony of our mortality, of the youngest amongst us, before we part, and make the very *place of our buriall*, our *deathbed*.

128. *The Expectation of Death*.

NOW the general condemnation, which is upon all mankind, that they must dye, this alone scarce frights any man, scarce averts any man from his purposes. He that should first put to Sea in a tempest, he might easily think, it were in the nature of the Sea to be rough always. He that sees every Church-yard swell with the waves and billows of graves, can think it no extraordinary thing to dye ; when he knows he set out in a storm, and he was born into the world upon that condition, to go out of it again.

129. *The Death-bed*.

ET *in finem*, he loved them to the end. It is much that he should love them *in fine*, at their end ; that he should look graciously at last ; that when their sunne sets, their eyes faint, his sunne of grace should arise, and his East should be brought to their West ; that then, in the shadow of death, the Lord of life should quicken

and inanimate their hearts ; that when their last bell
tolls, and calls them to their first and last judgement,
which to this purpose is all one ; for the passing bell
and the Angels trump sound all but one note : *Surgite
qui dormitis in pulvere, Arise ye that sleep in the dust,*
which is the voice of the Angels ; and, *Surgite qui
vigilatis in plumis, Arise ye that cannot sleep in feathers,*
for the pangs of death, which is the voice of the bell,
is in effect but one voice : for God at the generall judgement, shall never reverse any particular judgement,
formerly given : that God should then come to thy bed
side *Ad sibilandum populum suum,* as the Prophet Ezechiel
saith, to hisse softly for his childe, to speak comfortably
in his eare, to whisper gently to his departing soul, and
to drown and overcome with this soft musick of his all
the clangour of the Angels trumpets, all the horrour of
the ringing bell, all the cries, and vociferations of a
distressed, and distracted, and scattering family ; yea
all the accusations of his own conscience, and all the
triumphant acclamations of the devil himself : that
God should love a man thus *in fine,* at his end, and return
to him then, though he had suffered him to go astray
before, is a great testimonie of an inexpressible love.
Butt this love is not *in fine, in the end* ; but *in finem, to
the end.*

130. *The Death of Ecstasy.*

Prov.
21. 18. *D*EATH *and life are in the power of the tongue,* sayes
Solomon, in another sense ; and in this sense too, If
my tongue, suggested by my heart, and by my heart
rooted in faith, can say, *Non moriar, non moriar* ; If

I can say, (and my conscience doe not tell me, that I belye mine owne state) if I can say, That the blood of my Saviour runs in my veines, That the breath of his Spirit quickens all my purposes, that all my deaths have their Resurrection, all my sins their remorses, all my rebellions their reconciliations, I will harken no more after this question, as it is intended *de morte naturali*, of a naturall death, I know I must die that death, what care I ? nor *de morte spirituali*, the death of sin, I know I doe, and shall die so ; why despaire I ? but I will finde out another death, *mortem raptus*, a death of rapture, and of extasie, that death which S. *Paul* died more then once, The death which S. *Gregory* speaks of, *Divina contemplatio quoddam sepulchrum animæ*, The contemplation of God, and heaven, is a kinde of buriall, and Sepulchre, and rest of the soule ; and in this death of rapture, and extasie, in this death of the Contemplation of my interest in my Saviour, I shall finde my self, and all my sins enterred, and entombed in his wounds, and like a Lily in Paradise, out of red earth, I shall see my soule rise out of his blade, in a candor, and in an innocence, contracted there, acceptable in the sight of his Father.

2 Cor. 12.

Acts 9.

Greg.

131. *The Dead with Us.*

LITTLE know we, how little a way a soule hath to goe to heaven, when it departs from the body ; Whether it must passe locally, through Moone, and Sun, and Firmament, (and if all that must be done, all that may be done, in lesse time then I have proposed the doubt in) or whether that soule finde new light in the same roome, and be not carried into any other, but that the glory of heaven be diffused over all, I know not, I dispute not, I inquire not. Without disputing, or inquiring, I know, that when Christ sayes, *That God is not the God of the dead*, he saies that to assure me, that those whom I call dead, are alive. And when the Apostle

Heb. 11.16. tels me, *That God is not ashamed to be called the God of the dead*, he tels me that to assure me, That Gods servants lose nothing by dying.

Menander. Thraces. He was but a Heathen that said, If God love a man, *Iuvenis tollitur*, He takes him young out of this world ; And they were but Heathens, that observed that custome, To put on mourning when their sons were born, and to feast and triumph when they dyed. But thus much we may learne from these Heathens, That if the dead, and we, be not upon one floore, nor under one story, yet we are under one roofe. We think not a friend lost, because he is gone into another roome, nor because he is gone into another Land ; And into another world, no man is gone ; for that Heaven, which God created, and this world, is all one world. If I had fixt a Son in Court, or married a daughter into a plentifull Fortune, I were satisfied for that son and that daughter. Shall I not be so, when the King of Heaven hath taken that son to himselfe, and maried himselfe to that daughter, for ever ? I spend none of my Faith, I exercise none of my Hope, in this, that I shall have my dead raised to life againe.

This is the faith that sustaines me, when I lose by the death of others, or when I suffer by living in misery my selfe, That the dead, and we, are now all in one Church, and at the resurrection, shall be all in one Quire.

132. *Mourning.*

HERE, in this world, we who stay, lack those who are gone out of it : we know they shall never come to us ; and when we shall go to them, whether we shall know them or no, we dispute. They who think that it conduces to the perfection of happinesse in heaven, that we should know one another, think piously if they think we shall. For, as for the maintenance of publique peace, States, and Churches, may think diversly in points of Religion, that are not fundamentall, and yet both be true and Orthodoxall Churches ; so for the exaltation of private devotion in points that are not fundamentall, divers men may think diversly, and both be equally good Christians. Whether we shall know them there, or no, is problematicall and equall ; that we shall not till then, is dogmaticall and certain : Therefore we weep. I know there are Philosophers that will not let us weep, nor lament the death of any : And I know that in the Scriptures there are rules, and that there are instructions convayed in that example, that *David* left mourning as soon as the childe was dead ; And I know that there are Authors of a middle nature, above the Philosophers, and below the Scriptures, the Apocryphall books, and I know it is said there, Comfort thy selfe, for thou shalt do him no good that is dead, *Et te ipsum pessimabis* (as the vulgat Ecclus. 38. reads it) thou shalt make thy self worse and worse, in 6. the worst degree. But yet all this is but of inordinate lamentation ; for in the same place, the same Wise man sayes, My Son, let thy tears fall down over the dead ; weep bitterly and make great moane, as he is worthy.

When our Saviour Christ had uttered his *consummatum est*, all was finished, and their rage could do him no more harm, when he had uttered his *In manus tuas*, he had delivered and God had received his soul, yet how did the whole frame of nature mourn in Eclipses, and tremble in earth-quakes, and dissolve and shed in pieces in the opening of the Temple, *Quia mortuus*, because he was dead.

Truly, to see the hand of a great and mighty Monarch, that hand that hath governed the civill sword, the sword of Justice at home, and drawn and sheathed the forraigne sword, the sword of war abroad, to see that hand lie dead, and not be able to nip or fillip away one of his own wormes (and then *Quis homo*, what man, though he be one of those men, of whom God hath said, *Ye are gods*, yet *Quis homo, what man is there that lives, and shall not see death ?*) To see the brain of a great and religious Counsellor (and God blesse all from making, all from calling any great that is not religious) to see that brain that produced means to becalme gusts at Councell tables, stormes in Parliaments, tempests in popular commotions, to see that brain produce nothing but swarmes of wormes and no Proclamation to disperse them ; To see a reverend Prelate that hath resisted Heretiques & Schismatiques all his life, fall like one of them by death, & perchance be called one of them when he is dead. To re-collect all, to see great men made no men, to be sure that they shall never come to us, not to be sure, that we shall know them when we come to them, to see the Lieutenants and Images of God, Kings, the sinews of the State, religious Counsellors, the spirit of the Church, zealous Prelates, And then to see vulgar, ignorant, wicked, and facinorous men thrown all by one hand of death, into one Cart, into one common Tideboate, one Hospitall, one Almeshouse, one Prison, the grave, in whose dust no man can say, This is the King, this is the Slave, this is the Bishop, this is the Heretique, this is the Counsellor, this is the Foole, even this miserable equality of so unequall persons, by so foule a hand, is the subject of this lamentation, even *Quia mortuus*, because *Lazarus* was dead, *Iesus wept*.

133. *A Quiet Grave.*

HOW low soever God be pleased to cast you, Though it be to the earth, yet he does not so much cast you downe, in doing that, as bring you home. Death is not a banishing of you out of this world; but it is a visitation of your kindred that lie in the earth; neither are any nearer of kin to you, then the earth it selfe, and the wormes of the earth. You heap earth upon your soules, and encumber them with more and more flesh, by a superfluous and luxuriant diet; You adde earth to earth in new purchases, and measure not by Acres, but by Manors, nor by Manors, but by Shires; And there is a little Quillet, a little Close, worth all these, A quiet Grave. And therefore, when thou readest, That God makes thy bed in thy sicknesse, rejoyce in this, not onely that he makes that bed, where thou dost lie, but that bed where thou shalt lie; That that God, that made the whole earth, is now making thy bed in the earth, a quiet grave, where thou shalt sleep in peace, till the Angels Trumpet wake thee at the Resurrection, to that Judgement where thy

peace shall be made before thou commest, and writ,
and sealed, in the blood of the Lamb.

134. *Eternal Damnation.*

WHEN we shall have given to those words, by which
hell is expressed in the Scriptures, the heaviest
significations, that either the nature of those words can
admit, or as they are types and representations of hell,
as *fire*, and *brimstone*, & *weeping*, and *gnashing*, and
darknesse, and *the worme*, and as they are laid together
Esay 30.33. in the Prophet, *Tophet*, (that is, hell) *is deepe and large*,
(there is the capacity & content, roome enough) *It is
a pile of fire and much wood*, (there is the durablenesse of
it) *and the breath of the Lord to kindle it, like a streame of
Brimstone*, (there is the vehemence of it :) when all is
done, the hell of hels, the torment of torments is the
everlasting absence of God, and the everlasting impossibility of returning to his presence ; *Horrendum est*, sayes
Heb. 10.31. the Apostle, *It is a fearefull thing to fall into the hands
of the living God.* Yet there was a case, in which *David*
found an ease, to fall into the hands of God, to scape the
hands of men : *Horrendum est*, when Gods hand is bent
to strike, *it is a fearefull thing, to fall into the hands of
the living God* ; but to fall out of the hands of the living
God, is a horror beyond our expression, beyond our
imagination.

That God should let my soule fall out of his hand, into
a bottomlesse pit, and roll an unremoveable stone upon
it, and leave it to that which it finds there, (and it shall
finde that there, which it never imagined, till it came
thither) and never thinke more of that soule, never have

more to doe with it. That of that providence of God,
that studies the life of every weed, and worme, and ant,
and spider, and toad, and viper, there should never,
never any beame flow out upon me ; that that God, who
looked upon me, when I was nothing, and called me when
I was not, as though I had been, out of the womb and
depth of darknesse, will not looke upon me now, when,
though a miserable, and a banished, and a damned
creature, yet I am his creature still, and contribute
something to his glory, even in my damnation ; that that
God, who hath often looked upon me in my foulest
uncleannesse, and when I had shut out the eye of the
day, the Sunne, and the eye of the night, the Taper, and
the eyes of all the world, with curtaines and windowes
and doores, did yet see me, and see me in mercy, by
making me see that he saw me, and sometimes brought
me to a present remorse, and (for that time) to a forbearing
of that sinne, should so turne himselfe from me, to his
glorious Saints and Angels, as that no Saint nor Angel,
nor Christ Jesus himselfe, should ever pray him to looke
towards me, never remember him, that such a soule
there is ; that that God, who hath so often said to my
soule, *Quare morieris ?* Why wilt thou die ? and so
often sworne to my soule, *Vivit Dominus*, As the Lord
liveth, I would not have thee dye, but live, will nether
let me dye, nor let me live, but dye an everlasting life,
and live an everlasting death ; that that God, who, when
he could not get into me, by standing, and knocking, by
his ordinary meanes of entring, by his Word, his mercies,
hath applied his judgements, and hath shaked the house,
this body, with agues and palsies, and set this house on

fire, with fevers and calentures, and frighted the Master of the house, my soule, with horrors, and heavy apprehensions, and so made an entrance into me; That that God should frustrate all his owne purposes and practises upon me, and leave me, and cast me away, as though I had cost him nothing, that this God at last, should let this soule goe away, as a smoake, as a vapour, as a bubble, and that then this soule cannot be a smoake, a vapour, nor a bubble, but must lie in darknesse, as long as the Lord of light is light it selfe, and never sparke of that light reach to my soule; What Tophet is not Paradise, what Brimstone is not Amber, what gnashing is not a comfort, what gnawing of the worme is not a tickling, what torment is not a marriage bed to this damnation, to be secluded eternally, eternally, eternally from the sight of God? Especially to us, for as the perpetuall losse of that is most heavy, with which we have been best acquainted, and to which wee have been most accustomed; so shall this damnation, which consists in the losse of the sight and presence of God, be heavier to us then others, because God hath so graciously, and so evidently, and so diversly appeared to us, in his pillar of fire, in the light of prosperity, and in the pillar of the Cloud, in hiding himselfe for a while from us; we that have seene him in all the parts of this Commission, in his Word, in his Sacraments, and in good example, and not beleeved, shall be further removed from his sight, in the next world, then they to whom he never appeared in this. But *Vincenti &* *credenti*, to him that beleeves aright, and overcomes all tentations to a wrong beliefe, God shall give the accomplishment of fulnesse, and fulnesse of joy, and joy rooted in glory, and glory established in eternity, and this eternity is God ; To him that beleeves and overcomes, God shall give himselfe in an everlasting presence and fruition, *Amen.*

135. *Death of the Good and the Bad Man.*

TRULY, if the Death of the wicked ended in Death, yet to scape that manner of death were worthy a Religious life. To see the house fall, and yet be afraid to goe out of it ; To leave an injur'd world, and meet an incensed God ; To see oppression and wrong in all thy professions, and to foresee ruine and wastefulnesse in all thy Posterity ; and Lands gotten by one sin in the Father, molder away by another in the Sonne ; To see true figures of horror, and ly, and fancy worse ; To begin to see thy sins but then, and finde every sin (at first sight) in the proportion of a Gyant, able to crush thee into despair ; to see the Blood of Christ, imputed, not to thee, but to thy Sinnes ; to see Christ crucified, and not crucifyed for thee, but crucified by thee ; To heare this blood speake, not better things, then the blood of *Abel,* but lowder for vengeance then the blood of *Abel* did ; This is his picture that hath been Nothing, that hath done nothing, that hath proposed no *Stephen,* No Law to regulate, No example to certifie his Conscience : But to him that hath done this, Death is but a sleepe. . . .

Now of this dying Man, that dies in Christ, that dies the Death of the Righteous, that embraces Death as a Sleepe, must wee give you a Picture too.

There is not a minute left to do it ; not a minutes sand ; Is there a minutes patience ? Bee pleased to

remember that those Pictures which are deliver'd in
a minute, from a print upon a paper, had many dayes,
weeks, Moneths time for the graving of those Pictures
in the Copper ; So this Picture of that dying Man, that
dies in Christ, that dies the death of the Righteous, that
embraces Death as a Sleepe, was graving all his life ; All
his publique actions were the lights, and all his private
the shadowes of this Picture. And when this Picture
comes to the Presse, this Man to the streights and agonies
of Death, thus he lies, thus he looks, this he is. His
understanding and his will is all one faculty ; He under-
stands Gods purpose upon him, and he would not have
God's purpose turned any other way ; hee sees God will
dissolve him, and he would faine be dissolved, to be with
Christ ; His understanding and his will is all one faculty ;
His memory and his fore-sight are fixt, and concentred
upon one object, upon goodnesse ; Hee remembers
that hee hath proceeded in the sinceritie of a good
Conscience in all the wayes of his calling, and he foresees
that his good name shall have the Testimony, and his
Posterity the support of the good men of this world ;
His sickness shall be but a fomentation to supple and
open his Body for the issuing of his Soule ; and his Soule
shall goe forth, not as one that gave over his house, but
as one that travelled to see and learne better Architecture,
and meant to returne and re-edifie that house, according
to those better Rules : And as those thoughts which
possesse us most awake, meete us again when we are
asleepe ; So his holy-thoughts, having been alwaies
conversant upon the directing of his family, the education
of his Children, the discharge of his place, the safety of

the State, the happinesse of the King all his life ; when he is faln a sleepe in Death, all his Dreames in that blessed Sleepe, all his devotions in heaven shall be upon the same Subjects, and he shal solicite him that sits upon the Throne, & the Lamb, God for Christ Jesus sake, to blesse all these with his particular blessings : for so God giveth Ps. 127. 2. his beloved sleep, so as that they enjoy the next world and assist this.

136. *The Northern Passage.*

NO man kills his enemy therefore, that his enemy might have a better life in heaven ; that is not his end in killing him : It is Gods end ; Therefore he brings us to death, that by that gate he might lead us into life everlasting ; And he hath not discovered, but made that Northerne passage, to passe by the frozen Sea of calamity, and tribulation, to Paradise, to the heavenly Jerusalem.

137. *The Resurrection.*

THE dead heare not Thunder, nor feele they an *In clamore.* Earth-quake. If the Canon batter that Church walls, in which they lye buryed, it wakes not them, nor does it shake or affect them, if that dust, which they are, be thrown out, but yet there is a voyce, which the dead shall heare ; *The dead shall heare the voyce of the Son of* Iohn 5 25. *God,* (sayes the Son of God himself) *and they that heare shall live* ; And that is the voyce of our Text. It is here called a clamour, a vociferation, a shout, and varied by our Translators, and Expositors, according to the origination of the word, to be *clamor hortatorius,* and *suasorius,* and *jussorius,* A voyce that carries with it a penetration, (all shall heare it) and a perswasion, (all shall beleeve it, and be glad of it) and a power, a command, (all shall obey it.) Since that voyce at the Creation, *Fiat*, Let there be a world, was never heard such a voyce as this, *Surgite mortui*, Arise ye dead. That was spoken to that that was meerely nothing, and this to them, who in themselves shall have no cooperation, no concurrence to the hearing or answering this voyce.

138. *The Awakening.*

CŒMITERIA are *Dormitoria*, Churchyards are our beds. And in those beds, (and in all other beds of death) (for, the dead have their beds in the Sea too, and sleepe even in the restlesse motion thereof) the voyce of the Archangel, and the Trumpet of God shall awake them.

139. *The Resurrection of the Body.*

THERE are so many evidences of the immortality of the soule, even to a naturall mans *reason*, that it required not an Article of the Creed, to fix this notion of the Immortality of the soule. But the Resurrection of the *Body* is discernible by no other light, but that of *Faith*, nor could be fixed by any lesse assurance then an *Article* of the *Creed*. Where be all the splinters of that Bone, which a shot hath shivered and scattered in the Ayre? Where be all the Atoms of that flesh, which a *Corrasive* hath eat away, or a *Consumption* hath breath'd, and exhal'd away from our arms, and other Limbs? In what wrinkle, in what furrow, in what bowel of the earth, ly all the graines of the ashes of a body burnt a thousand years since? In what corner, in what ventricle of the sea, lies all the jelly of a Body drowned in the *generall flood* ? What cohærence, what sympathy, what dependence maintaines any relation, any corres- spondence, between that arm that was lost in Europe, and that legge that was lost in Afrique or Asia, scores of yeers between ? One humour of our dead body produces worms, and those worms suck and exhaust all other humour, and then all dies, and all dries, and molders into dust, and that dust is blowen into the River, & that puddled water tumbled into the sea, and that ebs and flows in infinite revolutions, and still, still God knows in what *Cabinet* every *seed-Pearle* lies, in what part of the world every graine of every mans dust lies ; and, *sibilat populum suum*, (as his Prophet speaks in *Zech.*10. 8. another case) he whispers, he hisses, he beckens for the bodies of his Saints, and in the twinckling of an eye, that body that was scattered over all the elements, is sate down at the right hand of God, in a glorious resurrection.

140. *The Last Day.*

THE grave it self shall be open againe ; and *Aperti* *Mat.*27.52. cœli, The heavens shall be open, and I shall see the *Act.* 7. 56. Sonne of man, the Sonne of God, and not see him at that distance, that *Stephen* saw him there, but see him, and sit down with him. I shall rise from the dead, from the darke station, from the prostration, from the proster- nation of death, and never misse the sunne, which shall then be put out, for I shall see the Sonne of God, the Sunne of glory, and shine my self, as that sunne shines. I shall rise from the grave, and never misse this City, which shall be no where, for I shall see the City of God,

the new *Jerusalem*. I shall looke up, and never wonder
when it will be day, for, the Angell will tell me that
*Apoc.*10. 6. *time shall be no more*, and I shall see, and see cheerefully
that last day, the day of judgement, which shall have no
Dan. 7. 9. *night*, never end, and be united to the *Antient of dayes*,
to God himselfe, who had *no morning*, never began.

141. *The Day of Judgement.*

NOW, in respect of the time after this judgement,
(which is Eternity) the time between this and it
cannot be a minute ; and therefore think thy self at that
Tribunall, that judgement now : Where thou shalt
not onely heare all thy sinfull workes, and words, and
thoughts repeated, which thou thy selfe hadst utterly
forgot, but thou shalt heare thy good works, thine almes,
thy comming to Church, thy hearing of Sermons given
in evidence against thee, because they had hypocrisie
mingled in them ; yea thou shalt finde even thy repentance to condemne thee, because thou madest that but
a doore to a relapse. There thou shalt see, to thine
inexpressible terror, some others cast downe into hell,
for thy sins ; for those sins which they would not have
done, but upon thy provocation. There thou shalt
see some that occasioned thy sins, and accompanied
thee in them, and sinned them in a greater measure
then thou didst, taken up into heaven, because in the
way, they remembred the end, and thou shalt sink under
a lesse waight, because thou never lookedst towards him
Bernard.   that would have eased thee of it. *Quis non cogitans
hæc in desperationis rotetur abyssum?* Who can once
thinke of this and not be tumbled into desperation ?

142. *Joy.*

IF you looke upon this world in a Map, you find two
Hemisphears, two half worlds. If you crush heaven
into a Map, you may find two Hemisphears too, two half
heavens ; Halfe will be Joy, and halfe will be Glory ;
for in these two, the joy of heaven, and the glory of heaven,
is all heaven often represented unto us. And as of those
two Hemisphears of the world, the first hath been knowne
long before, but the other, (that of America, which is
the richer in treasure) God reserved for later Discoveries ;
So though he reserve that Hemisphear of heaven, which
is the Glory thereof, to the Resurrection, yet the other
Hemisphear, the Joy of heaven, God opens to our Discovery, and delivers for our habitation even whilst we
dwell in this world. As God hath cast upon the unre-
pentant sinner two deaths, a temporall, and a spirituall
death, so hath he breathed into us two lives ; for so,
as the word for death is doubled, *Morte morieris, Thou* Gen. 2. 17.
shalt die the death, so is the word for life expressed in
the plurall, *Chaiim, vitarum, God breathed into his
nostrils the breath of lives,* of divers lives. Though our
naturall life were no life, but rather a continuall dying,
yet we have two lives besides that, an eternall life reserved
for heaven, but yet a heavenly life too, a spirituall life,
even in this world ; And as God doth thus inflict two
deaths, and infuse two lives, so doth he also passe two
Judgements upon man, or rather repeats the same
Judgement twice. For, that which Christ shall say to
thy soule then at the last Judgement, *Enter into thy* Matt.25.23.
Masters joy, Hee sayes to thy conscience now, *Enter into*

thy Masters joy. The everlastingnesse of the joy is the blessednesse of the next life, but the entring, the inchoation is afforded here. . . .

Howling is the noyse of hell, singing the voyce of heaven ; Sadnesse the damp of Hell, Rejoycing the serenity of Heaven. And he that hath not this joy here, lacks one of the best pieces of his evidence for the joyes of heaven ; and hath neglected or refused that Earnest, by which God uses to binde his bargaine, that true joy in this world shall flow into the joy of Heaven, as a River flowes into the Sea ; This joy shall not be put out in death, and a new joy kindled in me in Heaven ; But as my soule, as soone as it is out of my body, is in Heaven, and does not stay for the possession of Heaven, nor for the fruition of the sight of God, till it be ascended through ayre, and fire, and Moone, and Sun, and Planets, and Firmament, to that place which we conceive to be Heaven, but without the thousandth part of a minutes stop, as soone as it issues, is in a glorious light, which is Heaven, (for all the way to Heaven is Heaven ; And as those Angels, which came from Heaven hither, bring Heaven with them, and are in Heaven here, So that soule that goes to Heaven, meets Heaven here ; and as those Angels doe not devest Heaven by comming, so these soules invest Heaven, in their going.) As my soule shall not goe towards Heaven, but goe by Heaven to Heaven, to the Heaven of Heavens, So the true joy of a good soule in this world is the very joy of Heaven ; and we goe thither, not that being without joy, we might have joy infused

Iohn 16.24. into us, but that as Christ sayes, *Our joy might be full,*

22. perfected, sealed with an everlastingnesse ; for, as he

promises, *That no man shall take our joy from us*, so neither
shall Death it selfe take it away, nor so much as interrupt
it, or discontinue it, But as in the face of Death, when he
layes hold upon me, and in the face of the Devill, when
he attempts me, I shall see the face of God, (for, every
thing shall be a glasse, to reflect God upon me) so in
the agonies of Death, in the anguish of that dissolution,
in the sorrowes of that valediction, in the irreversiblenesse
of that transmigration, I shall have a joy, which shall
no more evaporate, then my soule shall evaporate,
A joy, that shall passe up, and put on a more glorious
garment above, and be joy superinvested in glory. *Amen.*

143. *The Joy of Heaven.*

HUMILIATION is the beginning of sanctification ;
and as without this, without holinesse, no man
shall see God, though he pore whole nights upon the
Bible ; so without that, without humility, no man shall
heare God speake to his soule, though hee heare three
two-houres Sermons every day. But if God bring thee
to that humiliation of soule and body here, hee will
emprove, and advance thy sanctification *abundantiùs,*
more abundantly, and when he hath brought it to the
best perfection, that this life is capable of, he will
provide another *abundantiùs,* another maner of abundance
in the life to come ; which is the last beating of the
pulse of this text, the last panting of the breath thereof,
our anhelation, and panting after the joyes, and glory,
and eternity of the kingdome of Heaven ; of which,
though, for the most part, I use to dismisse you, with
saying something, yet it is alwaies little that I can say

thereof ; at this time, but this, that if all the joyes of all
the Martyrs, from *Abel* to him that groanes now in the
Inquisition, were condensed into one body of joy, (and
certainly the joyes that the Martyrs felt at their deaths,
would make up a far greater body, then their sorrowes
would doe,) (for though it bee said of our great Martyr,
Apoc. 1. 5. or great Witnesse, (as S. *Iohn* calls Christ Jesus) to whom,
all other Martyrs are but sub-martyrs, witnesses that
Lam. 3. 12. testifie his testimony, *Non dolor sicut dolor ejus*, there was
Heb. 12. 2. never sorrow like unto his sorrow, it is also true, *Non
gaudium sicut gaudium ejus*, There was never joy like
unto that joy which was set before him, when he endured
the crosse ;) If I had all this joy of all these Martyrs,
(which would, no doubt, be such a joy, as would worke
a liquefaction, a melting of my bowels) yet I shall have
it *abundantiùs*, a joy more abundant, then even this
superlative joy, in the world to come. What a dimme
vespers of a glorious festivall, what a poore halfe-holyday,
is *Methusalems* nine hundred yeares, to eternity ? what
a poore account hath that man made, that saies, this land
hath beene in my name, and in my Ancestors from the
Conquest ? what a yesterday is that ? not six hundred
yeares. If I could beleeve the transmigration of soules,
and thinke that my soule had beene successively in some
creature or other, since the Creation, what a yesterday
is that ? not six thousand yeares. What a yesterday
for the past, what a to morrow for the future, is any terme,
that can be comprehended in Cyphar or Counters ?
But as, how abundant a life soever any man hath in this
world for temporall abundances, I have life more abundantly then hee, if I have the spirituall life of grace, so

what measure soever I have of this spirituall life of grace, in this world, I shall have that more abundantly in Heaven, for there, my terme shall bee a terme for three lives; for those three, that as long as the Father, and the Son, and the holy Ghost live, I shall not dye.

144. *Little Stars.*

IN that glistering circle in the firmament, which we call the *Galaxie*, the milkie-way, there is not one starre of any of the six great magnitudes, which Astronomers proceed upon, belonging to that circle : it is a glorious circle, and possesseth a great part of heaven, and yet is all of so little starres, as have no name, no knowledge taken of them : So certainly there are many Saints in heaven, that shine as starres, and yet are not of those great magnitudes, to have been *Patriarchs*, or *Prophets*, or *Apostles*, or *Martyrs*, or *Doctours*, or *Virgins* ; but good & blessed souls, that have religiously performed the duties of inferior callings, and no more.

145. *Heirs of Heaven.*

HEIRES of heaven, which is not a Gavel-kinde, every son, every man alike; but it is an universall primo-geniture, every man full, so full, as that every man hath all, in such measure, as that there is nothing in heaven, which any man in heaven wants. Heires of the joyes of heaven; Joy in a continuall dilatation of thy heart, to receive augmentation of that which is infinite, in the accumulation of essentiall and accidentall joy. Joy in a continuall melting of indissoluble bowels, in joyfull,

and yet compassionate beholding thy Saviour ; Rejoycing
at thy being there, and almost lamenting (in a kinde
of affection, which we can call by no name) that thou
couldst not come thither, but by those wounds, which
are still wounds, though wounds glorified. Heires of
the joy, and heires of the glory of heaven ; where if
thou look down, and see Kings fighting for Crownes,
thou canst look off as easily, as from boyes at stool-ball
for points here ; And from Kings triumphing after
victories, as easily, as a Philosopher from a Pageant of
children here. Where thou shalt not be subject to any
other title of Dominion in others, but *Iesus of Nazareth
King of the Iews*, nor ambitious of any other title in
thy selfe, but that which thou possessest, *To be the childe
of God.* Heires of joy, heires of glory, and heires of the
eternity of heaven ; Where, in the possession of this joy,
and this glory, The Angels which were there almost
6000. yeares before thee, and so prescribe, and those
soules which shall come at Christs last comming, and so
enter but then, shall not survive thee, but they, and thou,
and all, shall live as long as he that gives you all that life,
as God himselfe.

146. *Seeing God.*

ALL the world is but *Speculum*, a glasse, in which we
see God ; The Church it self, and that which the
Ordinance of the Church begets in us, faith it self, is
but *ænigma*, a dark representation of God to us, till
we come to that state, *To see God face to face, and to know,
as also we are knowen.*

*Cælum,
Sphæra.*　　Now, as for the sight of God here, our Theatre was the

world, our *Medium* and glasse was the creature, and our
light was reason, And then for our knowledge of God
here, our Academy was the Church, our *Medium* the
Ordinances of the Church, and our Light the light of
faith, so we consider the same Termes, first, for the sight
of God, and then for the knowledge of God in the next
life. First, the Sphear, the place where we shall see him,
is heaven ; He that asks me what heaven is, meanes not
to heare me, but to silence me ; He knows I cannot tell
him ; When I meet him there, I shall be able to tell him,
and then he will be as able to tell me ; yet then we shall
be but able to tell one another, This, this that we enjoy
is heaven, but the tongues of Angels, the tongues of
glorified Saints, shall not be able to expresse what that
heaven is ; for, even in heaven our faculties shall be
finite. Heaven is not a place that was created ; for, all
place that was created, shall be dissolved. God did not
plant a Paradise for himself, and remove to that, as he
planted a Paradise for *Adam*, and removed him to that ;
But God is still where he was before the world was made.
And in that place, where there are more Suns then there
are Stars in the Firmament, (for all the Saints are Suns)
And more light in another Sun, The Sun of righteousnesse, the Son of Glory, the Sun of God, then in all
them, in that illustration, that emanation, that effusion
of beams of glory, which began not to shine 6000. yeares
ago, but 6000. millions of millions ago, had been 6000.
millions of millions before that, in those eternall, in those
uncreated heavens, shall we see God. . . .

The light of glory is such a light, as that our School- *Lux Gloriæ.*
men dare not say confidently, That every beam of it,

is not all of it. When some of them say, That some soules
see some things in God, and others, others, because all
have not the same measure of the light of glory, the rest
cry down that opinion, and say, that as the Essence of
God is indivisible, and he that sees any of it, sees all of
it, so is the light of glory communicated intirely to every
blessed soul. God made light first, and three dayes
after, that light became a Sun, a more glorious Light :
God gave me the light of Nature, when I quickned in
my mothers wombe by receiving a reasonable soule ; and
God gave me the light of faith, when I quickned in my
second mothers womb, the Church, by receiving my
baptisme ; but in my third day, when my mortality
shall put on immortality, he shall give me the light of
glory, by which I shall see himself. To this light of
glory, the light of honour is but a glow-worm ; and
majesty it self but a twilight ; The Cherubims and
Seraphims are but Candles ; and that Gospel it self,
which the Apostle calls the glorious Gospel, but a Star
of the least magnitude. And if I cannot tell, what to
call this light, by which I shall see it, what shall I call
that which I shall see by it, The Essence of God himself ?

147. *The Sight of God.*

Deum.

NO *man ever saw God and liv'd* ; and yet, I shall not
live till I see God ; and when I have seen him
I shall never dye. What have I ever seen in this world,
that hath been truly the same thing that it seemed to
me ? I have seen marble buildings, and a chip, a crust,
a plaster, a face of marble hath pilld off, and I see brick-
bowels within. I have seen beauty, and a strong breath

from another, tels me, that that complexion is from
without, not from a sound constitution within. I have
seen the state of Princes, and all that is but ceremony ;
and, I would be loath to put a *Master of ceremonies* to
define *ceremony*, and tell me what it is, and to include
so various a thing as ceremony, in so constant a thing,
as a Definition. I see a great Officer, and I see a man of
mine own profession, of great revenues, and I see not the
interest of the money, that was paid for it, I see not the
pensions, nor the Annuities, that are charged upon that
Office, or that Church. As he that fears God, fears
nothing else, so, he that sees God, sees every thing else :
when we shall see God, *Sicuti est*, as he is, we shall see *1 John* 3. 2.
all things *Sicuti sunt*, as they are ; for that's their Essence,
as they conduce to his glory. We shall be no more
deluded with outward appearances : for, when this
sight, which we intend here comes, there will be no
delusory thing to be seen. All that we have made as
though we saw, in this world, will be vanished, and I
shall see nothing but God, and what is in him ; and him
I shall see *In carne, in the flesh*, which is another degree
of Exaltation in mine Exinanition.

    I shall see him, *In carne suâ, in his flesh :* And this was *In carne.*
one branch in *Saint Augustines* great wish, That he might
have seen Rome in her state, That he might have heard
S. Paul preach, That he might have seen Christ in the
flesh : *Saint Augustine* hath seen Christ in the flesh one
thousand two hundred yeaers ; in Christs glorifyed
flesh ; but, it is with the eyes of his understanding,
and in his soul. Our flesh, even in the Resurrection,
cannot be a spectacle, a perspective glasse to our soul.

We shall see the Humanity of Christ with our bodily
eyes, then glorifyed ; but, that flesh, though glorifyed,
cannot make us see God better, nor clearer, then the soul
alone hath done, all the time, from our death, to our
resurrection. But as an indulgent Father, or as a tender
mother, when they go to see the King in any Solemnity,
or any other thing of observation, and curiosity, delights
to carry their child, which is flesh of their flesh, and bone
of their bone, with them, and though the child cannot
comprehend it as well as they, they are as glad that the
child sees it, as that they see it themselves ; such a glad-
nesse shall my soul have, that this flesh, (which she will
no longer call her prison, nor her tempter, but her friend,
her companion, her wife) that this flesh, that is, I, in
the re-union, and redintegration of both parts, shall see
God ; for then ; one principall clause in her rejoycing,
and acclamation, shall be, that this flesh is her flesh ;
In carne meâ, in my flesh I shall see God.

Mea.   It was the flesh of every wanton object here, that would
allure it in the petulancy of mine eye. It was the flesh
of every Satyricall Libeller, and defamer, and calumniator
of other men, that would call upon it, and tickle mine ear
with aspersions and slanders of persons in authority.
And in the grave, it is the flesh of the worm ; the possession is transfer'd to him. But, in heaven, it is *Caro mea,*
My flesh, my souls flesh, my Saviours flesh. As my meat
is assimilated to my flesh, and made one flesh with it ;
2 *Pet.* 1. 4. as my soul is assimilated to my God, and *made partaker*
1 *Cor.* 6. 17. *of the divine nature,* and *Idem Spiritus,* the same Spirit
with it ; so, there my flesh shall be assimilated to the
flesh of my Saviour, and made the same flesh with him

too. *Verbum caro factum, ut caro resurgeret* ; Therefore Athanas.
the Word was made flesh, therefore God was made man,
that that union might exalt the flesh of man to the right
hand of God. That's spoken of the flesh of Christ ; and
then to facilitate the passage for us, *Reformat ad immorta-* Cyril.
litatem suam participes sui ; those who are worthy
receivers of his flesh here, are the same flesh with him ;
And, *God shall quicken your mortall bodies, by his Spirit* Rom. 8. 11.
that dwelleth in you. But this is not in consummation,
in full accomplishment, till this resurrection, when it
shall be *Caro mea*, my flesh, so, as that nothing can draw
it from the allegiance of my God ; and *Caro mea, My
flesh*, so, as that nothing can devest me of it. Here a
bullet will aske a man, where's your arme ; and a Wolf
wil ask a woman, where's your breast. A sentence in
the Star-chamber will aske him, where's your ear, and
a months close prison will aske him, where's your flesh ?
A fever will aske him, where's your Red, and a morphew
will aske him, where's your white ? But when after
all this, when *after my skinne worms shall destroy my body,
I shall see God*, I shall see him in my flesh, which shall
be mine as inseparably, (in the *effect*, though not in the
manner) as the *Hypostaticall union* of God, and man, in
Christ, makes our nature and the Godhead one person
in him. My flesh shall no more be none of mine, then
Christ shall not be man, as well as God.

148. *The State of Glory.*

IF *Origen* could lodge such a conceit, that in heaven
at last all things should ebbe back into God, as all
things flowed from him at first ; and so there should

be no other essence but God, all should be God, even the devil himself : how much more may we conceive an uxexpressible association (that is too farre off) an assimilation (that is not neare enough) an identification (the School would venture to say so) with God in that state of glorie ! Whereas the sunne by shining upon the moon, makes the moon a planet, a starre as well as itself, which otherwise would be but the thickest, and darkest part of that sphere : so those beams of glorie which shall issue from my God, and fall upon me, shall make me (otherwise a clod of earth, and worse, a dark soul, a spirit of darknesse) an angel of light, a starre of glorie, a some-thing that I cannot name now, not imagine now, nor to morrow, nor next yeare ; but even in that particular, I shall be like God : that as he that asked a day to give a definition of God, the next day asked a week, and then a moneth, and then a yeare ; so undeterminable would my imaginations be, if I should go about to think now, what I shall be there : I shall be so like God, as that the devil himself shall not know me from God, so farre as to finde any more place to fasten a temptation upon me, then upon God ; not to conceive any more hope of my falling from that kingdome, then of Gods being driven out of it ; for though I shall not be immortall as God, yet I shall be as immortall God. And there is my image of God ; of God considered altogether, and in his unitie, in the state of grace.

I shall have also then the image of all the three persons of the Trinitie. *Power* is the Fathers ; and a greater power, then he exercises here, I shall have there : here he overcomes enemies, but yet here he hath enemies ;

there, there are none : here they cannot prevail ; there they shall not be. So *Wisdome* is the image of the Sonne ; and there I shall have better wisdome : the spirituall wisdome it self is here : for, here our best wisdom is, but to go towards our end ; there it is to rest in our end : here it is to seek to be glorified by God ; there it is that God may be everlastingly glorified by me. The image of the Holy Ghost is *Goodnesse*. Here our goodnesse is mixt with some ill ; faith mixt with scruples, & good works mixt with a love of praise, and hope of better mixt with fear of worse : there I shall have sincere goodnesse, goodnesse impermixt, intemerate, and indeterminate goodnesse ; so good a place, as no ill accident shall annoy it ; so good companie as no impertinent, no importune person shall disorder it ; so full a goodnesse, as no evil of sinne, no evil of punishment for former sins can enter ; so good a God, as shall no more keep us in fear of his anger, nor in need of his mercie ; but shall fill us first, and establish us in that fulnesse in the same instant, and give us a satietie that we can wish no more, and an infallibilitie that we can lose none of that, and both at once. Whereas the *Cabalists* expresse our nearnesse to God, in that state, in that note, that the name of man and the name of God, Adam, and Jehovah, in their numerall letters are equall : so I would have leave to expresse that inexpressible state, so farre as to say, that if there can be other worlds imagined besides this that is under our moon, and if there could be other Gods imagined of those worlds, besides this God to whose image we are made, in *Nature*, in *Grace*, in *Glorie* ; I had rather be one of these Saints in this heaven, than of those

gods in those other worlds. I shall be like the angels
in a glorified soul, and the angels shall not be like me in
a glorified bodie.

149. *Justice*.

AS it is said of old *Cosmographers*, that when they had
said all that they knew of a *Countrey*, and yet much
more was to be said, they said that the rest of those
countries were possesst with *Giants*, or *Witches*, or *Spirits*,
or *Wilde beasts*, so that they could pierce no farther into
that Countrey, so when wee have travell'd as farre as
wee can, with safetie, that is, as farre as *Ancient*, or
Moderne Expositors lead us, in the *discoverie* of these
new Heavens, and *new Earth*, yet wee must say at last,
that it is a *Countrey* inhabited with *Angells*, and *Arch-
angells*, with *Cherubins*, and *Seraphins*, and that wee
can looke no farther into it, with these eyes. Where
it is *locally*, wee enquire not ; We rest in this, that it
is the habitation prepar'd for the blessed *Saints* of *God* ;
Heavens where the *Moone* is more glorious than our
Sunne, and the *Sunne* as glorious as *Hee* that made it ;
For it is he himselfe, the *Sonne* of *God*, the *Sunne* of
glorie. *A new Earth*, where all their *waters* are *milke*,
and all their *milke*, *honey* ; where all their *grasse* is *corne*,
and all their corne, *Manna* ; where all their *glebe*, all
their *clods* of earth are *gold*, and all their *gold* of innumer-
able *carats* ; Where all their *minutes* are *ages*, and all
their *ages*, *Eternity* ; Where every thing, is every minute,
in the highest exaltation, as good as it can be, and yet
super-exalted, & infinitely multiplied, by every minutes
addition ; every minute, *infinitely* better, then ever

it was before. Of these *new heavens*, & this *new earth*
we must say at last, that wee can say nothing; For, *the
eye of Man hath not seene, nor eare heard, nor heart conceiv'd, the State of this place*. We limit, and determine
our consideration with that *Horizon*, with which the
Holy Ghost hath limited us, that it is that *new Heavens*,
and *new Earth, wherein dwelleth Righteousnesse.*

Here then the *Holy Ghost* intends the same *new* Righteous-
Heavens, and *new Earth*, which he doe's in the *Apocalyps*, nesse.
and describes there, by another name, the *new Jerusalem*. 21. 1.
But here, the *Holy Ghost* doe's not proceed, as there, to
enamour us of the place, by a promise of improvement
of those things, which we *have*, and *love* here; but by
a promise of that, which here wee have not at all. There,
and elsewhere, the *holy Ghost* applies himselfe, to the
naturall affections of men. To those that are affected
with *riches*, he saies, that *that new City shall be all of* Verg. 18.
gold, and in the *foundations, all manner of precious stones*;
To those that are affected with *beauty*, hee promises an
everlasting association, with that beautifull Couple, that
faire Paire, which spend their time, in that contemplation, and that protestation, *Ecce tu pulchra dilecta mea*; Cant. 1. 15,
Ecce, tu pulcher; Behold, thou art fair, my Beloved, says 16.
he; and then, she replies, *Behold, thou art fair too*;
noting the mutuall complacencie betweene *Christ* and
his *Church* there. To those which delight in *Musicke*,
hee promises continuall *singing*, and every minute, a *new
song*: To those, whose thoughts are exerciz'd upon
Honour, and *Titles, Civill*, or *Ecclesiasticall*, hee promises
Priesthood, and if that be not honour enough, a *Royall
Priesthood*; And to those, who looke after *military*

honor, *Triumph* after their *victory*, in the *Militant Church* ;
And to those, that are carried with sumptuous, and
magnifique *feasts*, a *Mariage supper* of the *Lambe*, where,
not onely all the rarities of the whole world, but the
whole world it selfe shall be serv'd in ; The whole world
shall bee brought to that *fire*, and serv'd at that *Table*.
But here, the *holy Ghost* proceeds not that way ; by
improvement of things, which wee *have*, and *love* here ;
riches, or *beauty*, or *musicke* or *honour*, or *feasts* ; but by
an everlasting possession of that, which wee hunger,
and thirst, and pant after, here, and cannot compasse,
that is, *Justice* or *Righteousnesse* ; for both these, our
present word denotes, and both those wee want here,
and shall have both, for ever, in these new *Heavens*, and
new Earth.

What would a worne and macerated *suter*, opprest by
the bribery of the rich, or by the might of a potent
Adversary, *give*, or *doe*, or *suffer*, that he might have
Justice ? What would a dejected Spirit, a disconsolate
soule, opprest with the weight of heavy, and habituall
sinne, that stands naked in a frosty Winter of desperation,
and cannot compasse one *fig leafe*, one colour, one excuse
for any circumstance of any sinne, give for the *garment
of Righteousnesse* ? here there is none that doe's right,
none that executes *Justice* ; or, not for *Justice* sake.
Hee that doe's *Justice*, doe's it not at first ; and *Christ*
Luk. 18. 2. doe's not thanke that *Judge*, that did *Justice*, upon the
womans importunity.   *Justice* is no *Justice*, that is
done for fear of an *Appeale*, or a *Commission*.   There may
bee found, that may doe *Justice* at first ; At their first
entrance into a place, to make good impressions, to

establish good opinions, they may doe some *Acts* of *Justice*; But after, either an Uxoriousnesse towards the wife, or a *Solicitude* for children, or a *facility* towards servants, or a *vastnesse* of expense, quenches, and over-com's the love of *Justice* in them; *Non habitat,* In most it is not : but it *dwels* not in any. In our *new Heavens,* and and *new Earth, dwelleth justice.* And that's my comfort ; that when I come thither, I shall have *Justice* at *God's* hands.

150. *Knowledge in Heaven.*

SOME things the Angels do know by the dignity of their Nature, by their Creation, which we know not ; as we know many things which inferior Crea-tures do not ; and such things all the Angels, good and bad know. Some things they know by the Grace of their confirmation, by which they have more given them, then they had by Nature in their Creation ; and those things only the Angels that stood, but all they, do know. Some things they know by Revelation, when God is pleased to manifest them unto them ; and so some of the Angels know that, which the rest, though confirm'd, doe not know. By Creation, they know as his Subjects ; by Confirmation, they know as his Servants ; by revelation, they know as his Councel. Now, *Erimus sicut Angeli,* says Christ, *There we shall be as the Angels* : The knowledge which I have by Nature, shall have no Clouds ; here it hath : That which I have by Grace, shall have no reluctation, no resistance ; here it hath : That which I have by *Revelation,* shall have no suspition, no jealousie ; here it hath : sometimes it is hard to distinguish between a respiration from God, and a suggestion from the Devil. There our curiosity shall have this noble satisfaction, we shall know how the Angels know, by knowing as they know. We shall not pass from Author, to Author, as in a Grammar School, nor from Art to Art, as in an University ; but, as that General which Knighted his whole Army, God shall Create us all Doctors in a minute. That great Library, those infinite Volumes of the Books of Creatures, shall be taken away, quite away, no more Nature ; those reverend Manuscripts, written with Gods own hand, the Scriptures themselves, shall be taken away, quite away ; no more preaching, no more reading of Scriptures, and that great School-Mistress, Experience, and Observation shall be remov'd, no new thing to be done, and in an instant, I shall know more, then they all could reveal unto me. I shall know, not only as I know already, that a Bee-hive, that an Ant-hill is the same Book in *Decimo sexto*, as a Kingdom is in *Folio*, That a Flower that lives but a day, is an abridgment of that King, that lives out his threescore and ten yeers ; but I shall know too, that all these Ants, and Bees, and Flowers, and Kings, and Kingdoms, howsoever they may be Examples, and Comparisons to one another, yet they are all as nothing, altogether nothing, less than nothing, infinitely less than nothing, to that which shall then be the subject of my knowledge, for, *it is the knowledge of the glory of God.*

Eternity. 235

151. *Eternity.*

HOW barren a thing is Arithmetique ? (and yet
Arithmetique will tell you, how many single graines
of sand, will fill this hollow Vault to the Firmament)
How empty a thing is Rhetorique ? (and yet Rhetorique
will make absent and remote things present to your
understanding) How weak a thing is Poetry ? (and yet
Poetry is a counterfait Creation, and makes things that
are not, as though they were) How infirme, how impotent
are all assistances, if they be put to expresse this Eternity ?

152. *Eternity.*

IF I had *Methusalems yeers*, and his yeers multiplyed
by the minutes of his yeers, (which were a faire terme)
if I could speak till the Angels Trumpets blew, and you
had the patience of Martyrs, and could be content to
heare me, till you heard the *Surgite Mortui*, till you were
called to meet *the Lord Jesus in the clouds*, all that time
would not make up one minute, all those words would
not make up one syllable, towards this *Eternity*, the
period of this blessednesse.

153. *Eternity.*

A STATE but of one Day, because no Night shall
over-take, or determine it, but such a Day, as is not
of a thousand yeares, which is the longest measure in the
Scriptures, but of a thousand millions of millions of
generations : *Qui nec præceditur hesterno, nec excluditur* August.
crastino, A day that hath no *pridie,* nor *postridie,* yesterday
doth not usher it in, nor to morrow shall not drive it
out. *Methusalem,* with all his hundreds of yeares, was

but a Mushrome of a nights growth, to this day, And all the foure Monarchies, with all their thousands of yeares, And all the powerfull Kings, and all the beautifull Queenes of this world, were but as a bed of flowers, some gathered at six, some at seaven, some at eight, All in one Morning, in respect of this Day. In all the two thousand yeares of Nature, before the Law given by *Moses,* And the two thousand yeares of Law, before the Gospel given by Christ, And the two thousand of Grace, which are running now, (of which last houre we have heard three quarters strike, more then fifteen hundred of this last two thousand spent) In all this six thousand, and in all those, which God may be pleased to adde, *In domo patris,* In this House of his Fathers, there was never heard quarter clock to strike, never seen minute glasse to turne.

154. *Joy in Heaven.*

IT is time to end ; but as long as the glasse hath a gaspe, as long as I have one, I would breathe in this ayre, in this perfume, in this breath of heaven, the contemplation of this Joy. *Blessed is that man, qui scit jubilationem,* says *David, that knowes the joyfull sound :* For, *Nullo modo beatus, nisi scias unde gaudeas* ; For though we be bound to rejoyce alwayes, it is not a blessed joy, if we do not know upon what it be grounded : or if it be not upon everlasting blessednesse. *Comedite amici,* says Christ, *bibite & inebriamini. Eat and drink, and be filled.* Joy in this life, *Vbi in sudore vescimur,* where grief is mingled with joy, is called meat, says Saint *Bernard,* and Christ cals his friends to eat in the first

*Psal.*89.15.

August.

Cant. 5. 1.

Bernard.

word. *Potus in futuro*, says he, Joy in the next life, where
it passes down without any difficulty, without any opposition, is called drink ; and Christ calls his friends to drink :
but the overflowing, the *Ebrietas animæ*, that is reserved
to the last time, when our bodies as well as our souls,
shall enter into the participation of it : Where, when wee
shall love every one, as well as our selves, and so have
that Joy of our owne salvation multiplied by that number,
wee shall have that Joy so many times over, as there
shall bee soules saved, because wee love them as our
selves, how infinitely shall this Joy be enlarged in loving
God, so far above our selves, and all them. Wee have
but this to add. *Heaven* is called by many pretious names ; *Matt. 9. 15.*
Life. Simply and absolutely there is no life but that. *Luc. 12. 32.*
And *Kingdome* ; Simply, absolutely there is no Kingdom, *Esay 66.23.*
that is not subordinate to that. And *Sabbatum ex
Sabbato*, A Sabbath flowing into a Sabbath, a perpetuall
Sabbath : but the Name that should enamour us most,
is that, that it is *Satietas gaudiorum* ; fulnesse of Joy. *Psal.16.11.*
Fulnesse that needeth no addition ; Fulnesse, that
admitteth no leake. And then though in the Schoole
we place Blessednesse, *In visione*, in the sight of God, yet
the first thing that this sight of God shall produce in
us (for that shall produce the Reformation of the Image
of God, in us, and it shall produce our glorifying of God)
but the first thing that the seeing of God shall produce
in us, is Joy. The measure of our seeing of God is the
measure of Joy. See him here in his Blessings, and you
shall joy in those blessings here ; and when you come to
see him *Sicuti est*, in his Essence, then you shall have
this Joy in Essence, and in fulnesse ; of which, God of

his goodnesse give us such an earnest here, as may binde to us that inheritance hereafter, which his Sonne our Saviour Christ Jesus hath purchased for us, with the inestimable price of his incorruptible blood. *Amen.*

155. *Donne's Last Sermon.*

IN all our *periods* and *transitions* in this life, are so many passages from *death* to *death* ; our very *birth* and entrance into this life, is *exitus à morte*, an *issue from death*, for in our mothers *wombe* wee are *dead so*, as that wee doe *not know* wee *live*, not so much as wee do in our *sleepe*, neither is there any *grave* so close, or so *putrid* a *prison*, as the *wombe* would be unto us, if we stayed in it *beyond* our time, or dyed there *before* our time. In the *grave* the *wormes* doe not kill us, we *breed* and *feed*, and then *kill* those wormes, which we our selves produc'd. In the wombe the dead *child* kills the *Mother* that conceived it, & is a murtherer, nay a *parricide*, even after it is dead. And if wee bee not dead so in the *wombe*, so as that being dead wee kill her that gave us our first life, our life of *vegetation*, yet wee are dead so, as *Davids Idols* are dead. In the *wombe* we have *eyes and see not, eares and heare not* ; There in the wombe wee are fitted for *workes of darkenes*, all the while deprived of light : And there in the *wombe* wee are taught *cruelty*, by being *fed with blood*, and may be *damned*, though we be *never borne*. . . .

Psal. 115. vers. 6.

Wee have a winding sheete in our Mothers wombe, which growes with us from our conception, and wee come into the world, wound up in that *winding sheet*, for wee come to *seeke a grave* ; And as prisoners discharg'd of actions may lye for fees ; so when the *wombe* hath discharg'd us, yet we are bound to it by *cordes of flesh* by such a *string*, as that wee cannot goe thence, nor stay there ; wee celebrate our owne funeralls with cryes, even at our birth ; as though our *threescore and ten years life* were spent in our mothers labour, and our circle made up in the first point thereof ; we begge our *Baptisme*, with another *Sacrament*, with *teares* ; And we come into a world that lasts many ages, but we last not. . . .

This whole *world* is but an *universall churchyard*, but our *common grave*, and the life & motion that the greatest persons have in it, is but as the shaking of buried bodies in their grave, by an *earth-quake*. That which we call life, is but *Hebdomada mortium*, a *weeke of death*, seaven dayes, seaven periods of our life spent in dying, *a dying seaven times over*, and there is an end. *Our birth dyes* in *infancy*, and our *infancy* dyes in *youth*, and *youth* and the rest dye in *age*, and *age* also dyes, and *determines all*. Nor doe all these, youth out of infancy, or age out of youth arise so, as a *Phœnix* out of the *ashes* of another *Phœnix* formerly *dead*, but as a *waspe* or a *serpent* out of *caryon*, or as a *Snake* out of *dung*. Our *youth* is *worse* then our *infancy*, and our *age* worse then our *youth*. Our *youth* is *hungry and thirsty*, after those *sinnes*, which our *infancy knew not* ; And our *age* is *sory* and *angry*, that it *cannot pursue* those *sinnes* which our *youth did* ; & besides, al the way, so many deaths, that is, so many deadly calamities accompany every condition, and every period of this life, as that death it selfe would bee an ease to them that suffer them : Upon this sense doth *Job* wish that *God had not given him* an *issue* from the *first death*, from the

10. 18. *wombe, Wherefore hast thou brought me* forth *out of the wombe ? O that I had given up the Ghost,* and no eye seene me ? I should have beene as though I had not beene. . . .

But for us that dye now and sleepe in the state of the dead, we must al passe this *posthume* death, this *death* after *death,* nay this death after buriall, this *dissolution* after *dissolution,* this *death* of *corruption* and *putrefaction,* of *vermiculation* and *incineration,* of *dissolution* and *dispersion* in and *from* the *grave,* when these bodies that have been the *children* of *royall parents,* & the *parents of royall children,* must say with *Job, Corruption thou art my father,* and *to the Worme thou art my mother & my sister. Miserable riddle,* when the *same worme* must bee *my mother,* and *my sister,* and *my selfe. Miserable incest,* when I must be *maried* to my *mother* and my *sister,* and bee both *father* and *mother* to my own *mother* and *sister, beget & beare* that *worme* which is all that *miserable penury ;* when my *mouth* shall be *filled* with *dust,* and the Vers.24.20. *worme* shall *feed,* and *feed sweetely* upon me, when the *ambitious* man shall have *no satisfaction, if* the *poorest alive* tread upon him, nor the *poorest* receive any *contentment* in being made *equall* to *Princes,* for they *shall bee* Job 23. 24. *equall* but *in dust.* One dyeth at his full strength, being wholly at ease, & in quiet, and another dyes in the *bitternes of his soul,* and never *eates* with *pleasure,* but they lye downe *alike* in *the dust,* and the *worme covers* Vers.14.11. *them ;* In *Job* and in *Esay, it covers them and is spred under them,* the worme is spred *under thee,* and the worme *covers thee,* There's the *Mats* and the *Carpets* that *lye under,* and there's the *State* and the *Canapye,* that *hangs over* the greatest of the sons of men ; Even those bodies that were *the temples of the holy Ghost*, come to this *dilapidation*, to ruine, to rubbidge, to dust, even the *Israel of the Lord*, and *Jacob* himself hath no other specification, no other denomination, but that, *vermis Jacob*, Thou *worme of Jacob*. Truely the consideration of this *posthume death*, this death after buriall, that after *God*, (with whom are the *issues of death*) hath delivered me from the *death* of the *wombe*, by bringing mee into the *world*, and from the manifold *deaths* of the *world*, by laying me in the *grave*, I must dye againe in an *Incineration* of this *flesh*, and in a dispersion of that dust. That all that *Monarch*, who spred over many nations alive, must in his dust lye in a corner of that *sheete of lead*, and there, but so long as that lead will laste, and that privat and *retir'd man*, that thought himselfe his owne for ever, and never came forth, must in his dust of the grave be published, and, (such are the *revolutions* of the *graves*) bee mingled with the dust of every high way, and of every dunghill, and swallowed in every puddle and pond; This is the most inglorious and contemptible *vilification*, the most deadly and peremptory *nullification* of man, that we can consider.

NOTES

No. **1.** *The Preacher.* I, p. 338. Sermon XXXIV. '*Preached upon Whitsunday.*'

l. 5. 'red earth'. Cf. The *Litanie*, i.

> From this red earth, O Father, purge away
> All vicious tinctures.

(Poems, ed. Grierson, i, p. 338.)
Donne was extremely fond of this pun on the Hebrew word *Adam* or red earth—a pun, Coleridge remarks, which was common in Donne's age, but unworthy of him (*Coleridge*, p. 148).

p. 2, l. 7. 'a little parke in the midst of a forest'. In a prayer printed at the end of his *Essays in Divinity*, Donne writes, 'I am a man and no worm, and within the pale of Thy Church and not in the wild forest' (Gosse, *Life*, ii, p. 103).

l. 11. 'Sancerraes'. Sancerre in France was a stronghold of Protestantism during the religious wars. In 1573 it was besieged by the Catholics for nine months, and its defenders suffered extreme privations. In his *Elegie*, viii, l. 10, Donne refers to 'Sancerra's starved men' (*Poems*, i, p. 91, and note ii, p. 74).

2. *When I consider.* I, p. 223. Sermon XXII. '*Preached at S. Pauls, upon Easter-day,* 1627' (March 25).

3. *I am Not all Here.* II, p. 116. Sermon XIV. '*Preached at Lincolns Inne.*' Donne was Reader at Lincoln's Inn from October 1616 to February 1622.

4. *Imperfect Prayers.* I, p. 820. Sermon LXXX. '*Preached at the funerals of Sir* William Cokayne *Knight, Alderman of* London, *December* 12. 1626.' See note on No. 47.

5. *Powers and Principalities.* I, pp. 452–3. Sermon XLV. '*Preached upon All-Saints Day.*'

6. *Infecting God.* I, pp. 589–90. Sermon LVIII. '*Preached upon the* Penitentiall Psalmes.'

7. *Forgiveness of Sins.* I, p. 311. Sermon XXXI. '*Preached at S.* Pauls, *upon Whitsunday.* 1629' (May 24).

8. *Forgive my Sins.* II, p. 224. Sermon XXVI. '*Preached to the King, at White-Hall, the first Sunday in Lent.*' Probably 1627 (E. M. Spearing, *A Chronological Arrangement of Donne's Sermons*, Mod. Lang. Review, October 1913).

9. *Let Me Wither.* I, pp. 665–6. Sermon LXVI. 'The second of my Prebend Sermons upon my five Psalmes. *Preached at S. Pauls, Ianuary* 29. 1625' (1626). 'This Second Prebend Sermon, which is a long poem of victory over death, is one of the most magnificent pieces of religious writing in English literature' (*Gosse*, ii, p. 239). For Donne's Prebend Sermons, see note on No. 20. For other passages from this sermon, see Nos. 20, 41, 80, 142.

10. *Donne and the Worm.* II, p. 7. Sermon I. 'A Sermon Preached *At the Earl of* Bridgewaters *house in London at the mariage of his daughter, the* Lady Mary, *to the eldest sonne of the* L. Herbert *of Castle-iland,* Novemb. 19. 1627.'

This Earl of Bridgewater was John, first Earl, 1579–1649, son of Donne's former patron Sir Thomas Egerton, Lord Ellesmere. Donne's wife, Mary More, was a niece of the second Lady Egerton. It was this Lord Bridgewater's children who acted in *Comus* in 1634. His daughter Mary married Richard, son of Edward, Lord Herbert of Cherbury (*D. N. B.*).

11. *Preaching Consolation.* I, p. 745. Sermon LXXIII. '*Preached to the King in my Ordinary wayting at* White-hall, 18. *Aprill* 1626.'

In Donne's *Divine Poems* there is one addressed '*To M*ʳ Tilman *after he had taken orders*' in which several phrases occur similar to phrases in this extract:

Chang'd onely Gods old image by Creation,
To Christs new stampe, at this thy Coronation.
(ll. 17, 18.)

Maries prerogative was to beare Christ, so
'Tis preachers to convey him, for they doe
As angels out of clouds, from Pulpits speake; (ll. 41–3.)
(*Poems*, i, pp. 351–2.)

12. *The Beauty of the Soul.* II, p. 367. Sermon XL. '*Preached at Saint* Pauls.'

13. *Spiritual Liberality.* I, pp. 762–3. Sermon LXXV. '*Preached to the King at* White-hall, *April* 15. 1628' (Easter Sunday).

l. 21. 'that Meteor'. Donne used meteor in the sense of a body in mid-air, between heaven and earth. Thus he writes in a letter to Sir H. Goodyer, 'Our nature is Meteorique, we respect (because we partake so) both earth and heaven' (*Letters*, 1651, p. 46).

p. 15, l. 12. 'To bow downe those Heavens'. Cf. Donne's verse-epistle *To M*ʳ Tilman *after he had taken orders,*

How brave are those, who with their Engine, can
Bring man to heaven, and heaven againe to man?
(*Poems*, i, p. 352.)

14. *Eagle's Wings.* I, pp. 435–6. Sermon XLIV. '*Preached at S.* Dunstanes *upon Trinity-Sunday.* 1627.'

p. 16, l. 12. 'He flings open the gates of Heaven'. Cf. *To Mr Tilman,* ll. 39–40:

> To open life, to give kingdoms to more
> Than Kings give dignities ; to keepe heavens doore ?
>
> (*Poems,* i, p. 352.)

15. *The Hour-Glass.* III, p. 61. Sermon V. 'A Lent-Sermon Preached to the King, At White-hall, *February* 12. 1629' (1630).

l. 14. 'stare', i. e. a starling.

16. *Preaching.* I, pp. 692–3. Sermon LXVIII. 'The fourth of my Prebend Sermons upon my five Psalmes : *Preached at S.* Pauls, 28. Ianuary, 1626' (1627).

17. *Applause.* II, p. 371. Sermon XL. *Ante,* No. 12.

p. 20, l. 6. 'murmurings'. 'The sermons of this time seem to us now to be overloaded—too long—artificial, and sometimes in bad taste....That they were listened to with great attention, and often produced very great effect upon the audience, we know. Frequently the preacher was interrupted by expressions of dissent or by loud applause' (*Jessopp,* pp. 137–8).

In an elegy '*In memory of Doctor* Donne', by R. B. (Richard Brathwaite ?) the author states that the old-fashioned 'doctrine-men' did not like or approve of Donne's preaching, and 'humm'd against him' (*Poems,* i, p. 386).

18. *The Bellman.* III, p. 205. Sermon XV. 'A Sermon Preached at *White-hall. February* 29. 1627' (1628).

p. 21, l. 6. 'that good Custome in these Cities', i. e. the 'Waits', or wind-instrumentalists maintained by the city, who perambulated the streets, often in the morning.

19. *Favourite Scriptures.* II, pp. 159 (correctly 151)–152. Sermon XIX. '*Preached at Lincolns Inne.*'

p. 22, l. 11. 'such forms, as I have been most accustomed to'. Donne almost never refers to himself as an author in his sermons. He once, however, says, '*Adams* sin, 6000 years agoe, is my sin ; and their sin, that shall sinne by occasion of any wanton *writings* of mine, will be my sin, though they come after'. (II, p. 171.)

20. *The Psalms.* I, p. 663. Sermon LXVI. See *ante,* No. 9. The Sermon was on Psalm lxiii. 7.

p. 24, l. 3. 'third obligation'. Donne, as Dean, was one of the prebendaries of St. Paul's. 'The Psalter was divided up among the thirty prebendaries, each of whom was supposed to recite his five psalms daily, and to make them his special subject of meditation. Donne took his place in the Chapter as prebendary of Chiswick, and his five psalms were the 62nd to the 66th inclusive ' (*Jessopp*, p. 141). See note on No. 46.

21. *Sanctified Passions.* III, pp. 257–8. Sermon XVIII. ' A Sermon Preached to Queen *Anne*, at *Denmarke-house.* December. 14, 1617.'

22. *Style and Language.* I, pp. 556–7. Sermon LV. ' *Preached upon the* Penitentiall Psalmes.'

23. *Style of the Holy Ghost.* I, p. 812. Sermon LXXIX. ' *Preached at* S. Pauls.'

24. *Compliments.* I, p. 176. Sermon XVIII. ' *Preached at S. Pauls, in the Evening, upon Easter-day.* 1623 ' (April 13).
l. 2. ' Complement' in the sense of the more modern ' compliment '. First instance in the *N. E. D.*, 1578.
Donne in his Fourth Satire writes,

so did hee
With his long complementall thankes vexe me.
(<i>Poems</i>, i, p. 164.)</div>

This use (not noted in the *N. E. D.*) is probably the first appearance of the word in this sense, if the Satire was written in 1597.

25. *Lying at Aix.* II, p. 183. Sermon XXI. ' *Preached at Lincolns Inne.*'
l. 1. ' Aquisgrane '. The Roman name for Aix-la-Chapelle was Aquisgranum. This visit to Aix was no doubt in 1612, when Donne accompanied Sir Robert and Lady Drury to France, and afterwards to Spa.

26. *Farewell on Going to Germany.* III, p. 280. Sermon XIX. ' A Sermon of Valediction at my going into *Germany*, at *Lincolns-Inne, April.* 18. 1619.' Donne was appointed to go as King's Chaplain with Viscount Doncaster on his mission to the German Princes. In Donne's *Divine Poems* there is *A Hymne to Christ, at the Authors last going into Germany* (*Poems*, i, p. 352). In his *Bibliography of John Donne*, Mr. Geoffrey Keynes mentions a volume *Sapientia Clamitans*, by William Milbourne Priest (1638), which includes (pp. 251–319) a different, and probably earlier, text of this farewell sermon. I have not been able to examine this book, as the copy said to be in the British Museum could not be found there.

27. *The Vicar of St. Dunstan's.* II, pp. 424–5. Sermon XLV. ' *Preached at Saint* Dunstans *Aprill* 11. 1624. *The first Sermon in that Church, as Vicar thereof.*' In March 1624 Donne was presented to the living of St. Dunstan's by Richard Sackville, Earl of Dorset. This first sermon, Dr. Jessopp says, was ' a kind of manifesto setting

Notes. 247

forth the preacher's view of the reciprocal duties of the pastor and his flock' (*Jessopp*, p. 164).

28. *Funeral Sermon on Magdalen Herbert, Lady Danvers.* 'A Sermon of Commemoration of the Lady *Dǎuers*, late Wife of S*ʳ. Iohn Dǎuers.* Preach'd at *Chilsey*, where she was lately buried. By *Iohn Donne* D. of S*ᵗ. Pauls, Lond.* 1. *Iuly* 1627' (London, 1627), pp. 1–4, 126–70. This sermon was not reprinted in the folios, but is included in Alford's edition (vi, p. 244) and was printed in Pickering's edition of *Devotions by John Donne, D.D.* (1840), pp. 158–97.

Lady Danvers was, by her first husband, Richard Herbert, of Montgomery Castle, the mother, among other children, of Lord Herbert of Cherbury, and George Herbert. In 1608 she married 'Sir John Danvers, an intelligent and wealthy young man not quite half her age' (*Gosse*, ii, p. 228). For her friendship with Donne, see *ibid.*, i, p. 162 f., *Poems*, ii., pp. xxiv f., and Walton's 'Life of George Herbert'. For Donne's poems to Mrs. Herbert, see *Poems*, i, pp. 61, 92, 216, 317.

Lady Danvers lived at Danvers House, Chelsea, where Donne took refuge during the plague of 1625 (see No. 35). Lady Danvers died in the first days of June 1627, and was buried in Chelsea Church on June 8. Donne had undertaken to preach her funeral sermon, but it was postponed to July 1 (*Gosse*, ii, p. 247). Walton in his *Life of Mr. George Herbert*, says 'I saw and heard this Mr. *John Donne* (who was then Dean of St. *Pauls*) weep, and preach her Funeral Sermon, in the Parish-Church of *Chelsey* near *London*, where she now rests in her quiet Grave' (Walton's *Lives*, 1670, 'The Life of Mr. George Herbert', p. 19). Donne's 'affection to her was such, that he turn'd Poet in his old Age, and then made her *Epitaph*; wishing, all his Body were turn'd into Tongues, that he might declare her just praises to posterity' (*ibid.*, p. 16).

29. *Death of Elizabeth and Accession of James I.* III, p. 351. Sermon XXIV. 'A Sermon Preached at *Pauls* Cross to the Lords of the Council, and other Honorable Persons, 24. *Mart.* 1616 [1617]. It being the Anniversary of the Kings coming to the Crown, and his Majesty being then gone into *Scotland*.'

'When James I started on his memorable "Progress" to Scotland on the 15th March 1617, he appears to have ordered that Donne should preach at Paul's Cross on the 24th of March, the anniversary of his coming to the Crown' (*Jessopp*, p. 122). This was Donne's first appearance in the famous open-air pulpit, which stood at the north-east corner of old St. Paul's. 'Paul's Cross was the pulpit not only of the Cathedral; it might almost be said, as preaching became more popular, and began more and more to rule the public mind, to have become that of the Church of England. . . . Excepting the King and his retinue, who had a covered gallery, the congregation, even the Mayor and the Aldermen, stood in the open air' (H. H. Milman, *Annals of S. Paul's Cathedral*, 1869, pp. 163–4). For Donne's Sermon on this occasion, see *Jessopp*, pp. 122–3; *Gosse*, ii, pp. 114–16. On March 29, 1617, John Chamberlain wrote to Sir Dudley Carleton, 'I had almost forgotten, that on Monday, the 27th [24th] of this month, being the king's day, the archbishop of Canterbury, the lord keeper [Bacon], lord privy seal, the Earl of Arundel, the Earl of Southampton, the Lord Hay, the comptroller, Secretary Winwood, the master of the Rolls, with divers other great men, were at Paul's Cross, and heard Donne, who made there a dainty sermon upon the 11th verse of the 22d of Proverbs, and was exceedingly well liked generally, the rather for that he did Queen Elizabeth great right, and held himself close to the text, without flattering the time too much' (*C. & T. Jas. I*, ii, p. 4). On May 10 Chamberlain writes, 'I know not how to procure a copy of Dr. Donne's sermon if it come not in print, but I will inquire after it' (*ibid.*, p. 10).

p. 48, l. 8. 'recognitions'. Misprinted 'recognitious' in the folio. A few other obvious misprints have been silently corrected.

30. *The Gunpowder Plot.* II, pp. 402–3. Sermon XLIII. '*A Sermon upon the fift of* Novemb. 1622, *being the Anniversary celebration of our Deliverance from the* Powder Treason. Intended for *Pauls Crosse,* but by reason of the weather, Preached in *the Church.*'

On December 1, 1622, Donne wrote to Sir Thomas Roe, James I's Ambassador to the Ottoman Porte, and after mentioning his sermon at St. Paul's Cross on September 14, 1622 (which was printed by royal command in 1622) he adds: 'Some weeks after that I preached another at the same place, upon the Gunpowder Day; therein I was left more to mine own liberty, and therefore I would I could also send your Lordship a copy of that, but that one, which also by commandment I did write after the preaching, is as yet in his Majesty's hand, and I know not whether he will in it, as he did in the other, after his reading thereof, command it to be printed; and whilst it is in that suspense, I know your Lordship would call it indiscretion to send out any copy thereof; neither truly am I able to commit that fault, for I have no copy' (*Gosse*, ii, pp. 174–5).

31. *Preached to the Honourable Company of the Virginian Plantation,* 1622. '*A* Sermon upon the VIII Verse of the I. Chapter of the Acts of the Apostles. *Preach'd* to the Honourable Company of the Virginian Plantation. 13°. *Novemb.* 1622. By Iohn Donne *Deane of St Pauls,* London 1622' (London, 1622), pp. 11–13, 18–22, 42–6. This sermon is not in the folios; it was re-issued in *Four Sermons* 1625, and *Five Sermons* 1626, and reprinted by Alford, vi, pp. 223–41. In 1622 the Earl of Southampton was chosen treasurer of the Virginia Company, and Nicholas Ferrar, afterwards of Little Gidding, deputy treasurer. 'It must have been at their invitation that Donne was invited to preach before the Company, and to impress upon the *adventurers*, who included among them a large number of bishops, clergy, and devout laity, an appeal from the missionary point of view' (*Jessopp*, p. 149). 'This sermon may with truth, be called the first *missionary sermon* ever preached in England since Britain had become a Christian land' (*ibid.*, p. 148). See, however, next.

32. *The Mission of England.* III, p. 195. Sermon XIV. 'A Second Sermon Preached at *White-hall. April* 2. 1621.'

l. 6. '*Islands* . . . Islands,' misprinted '*Island* . . . Island' in the folio.

33. *James I.* II, p. 406. Sermon XLIII. See *ante*, No. 30, Donne's 'Gunpowder Plot' Sermon. Now that James I was negotiating for the Spanish Marriage, and had released from prison a large number of Roman Catholics, there were many rumours that the King intended to make a change of religion (*C. & T. Jas. I*, i, pp. 300, 326, 356).

34. *Death of James I.* II, p. 303. Sermon XXXIII. 'Preached at *Denmark house*, some few days before the body of King *James*, was removed from thence, *to his buriall*, Apr. 26. 1625.' James I died at Theobalds on March 27. His body was embalmed and taken on April 4 to Denmark House, where it lay in state until the funeral on May 7 (*C. & T. Charles I*, i, pp. 3, 22). On April 3 Donne delivered his first sermon before Charles I at Saint James's (see No. 75).

35. *The Plague*, 1625. III, pp. 293–6 (Qqq 1–2 v). Sermon XXI. 'A Sermon Preached at St. *Dunstans January* 15. 1625[1626]. The First Sermon after Our Dispersion, by the Sickness.' During the great plague of 1625, when London was almost deserted, Donne withdrew to Sir John Danvers's house in Chelsea, where he spent his time writing out and revising his sermons. (*Gosse*, ii, pp. 222, 225.)

36. *Difficult Times.* II, p. 158 (correctly 150). Sermon XVIII. 'Preached at Lincolns Inne.' Donne resigned his divinity readership at Lincoln's Inn on February 11, 1622. This undated sermon was probably preached shortly before his resignation, during the negotiations for the Spanish Match.

p. 62, l. 30. 'hull it out'. To 'hull' is an obsolete nautical term, meaning 'to float or be driven by the force of the wind or current on the hull alone ; to drift to the wind with sails furled ; to lie a-hull' (*N. E. D.*). Cf. *Richard III*, iv. iv. 439, and *Henry VIII*, ii. iv. 197 'thus hulling in The wild Sea of my Conscience'.

37. *Polemical Preaching.* I, pp. 778–9. Sermon LXXVII. '*Preached at S.* Pauls, *May* 21. 1626.' In 1622, during his negotiations with Spain, James I had forbidden polemical preaching, and Donne had, by royal command, delivered a Sermon at Paul's Cross on September 15, to explain to the populace the King's *Instructions to Preachers* (*Gosse*, ii, p. 160). 'He gave no great satisfaction'; Chamberlain writes, 'or, as some say, spoke as if himself were not so well satisfied' (*C. & T. Jas. I*, ii, p. 333). Now that England was at war with Spain and fighting to help the German Protestants, what Donne calls 'the beating of our Drums in the Pulpit' was again allowed.

38. *The World Decays.* I, p. 357. Sermon XXXVI. '*Preached upon Whitsunday.*' Donne, as Dean, was required to preach the Whitsunday Sermon at St. Paul's. For the letter of St. Cyprian, see *Ramsay*, p. 86. Cf. Donne's *First Anniversary*, ll. 201-4:

> So did the world from the first houre decay,
> That evening was beginning of the day,
> And now the Springs and Sommers which we see,
> Like sonnes of women after fiftie bee.

> (*Poems*, i, p. 237.)

39. *Imperfection.* I, pp. 823-4. Sermon LXXX. See *ante*, No. 4. The 'new philosophy' is of course the Copernican hypothesis. 'Copernicus' displacement of the earth, and the consequent disturbance of the accepted mediæval cosmology with its concentric arrangement of elements and heavenly bodies, arrests and disturbs Donne's imagination much as the later geology with its revelation of vanished species and first suggestion of a doctrine of evolution absorbed and perturbed Tennyson when he wrote *In Memoriam* and throughout his life' (Grierson, *Poems*, ii, pp. 188-9). In his *First Anniversary* Donne writes:

> And new Philosophy calls all in doubt,
> The Element of fire is quite put out;
> The Sun is lost, and th' earth, and no mans wit
> Can well direct him where to looke for it.

> (*Poems*, i, p. 237.)

40. *Man.* I, pp. 64-5. Sermon VII. '*Preached upon Christmas day.*' Probably 1629 (*Spearing*).

41. *Afflictions.* I, pp. 664-5. The Second Prebend Sermon (LXVI). See *ante*, Nos. 9, 20.

42. *Discontent.* I, p. 45. Sermon V. '*Preached at Pauls, upon Christmas Day.* 1627.'

43. *The World a House.* I, p. 146. Sermon XV. '*Preached at White-hall, March* 8. 1621' (1622). Coleridge, referring to this extract, writes, 'This is one of Donne's least estimable discourses ... yet what a Donne-like passage is this that follows!' (*Coleridge*, p. 132).

44. *Mundus Mare.* I, pp. 735-7. Sermon LXXII. 'At the

Haghe Decemb. 19. 1619. I Preached upon this Text [Mat. iv. 18–20]. Since in my sicknesse at *Abrey-hatche* in Essex, 1630, revising my short notes of that Sermon, I digested them into these two.' LXXII is the second of these two sermons. Donne arrived with Lord Doncaster (see *ante*, No. 26) at The Hague in December 1619. In his will Donne bequeaths to his friend Henry King 'that medal of gold of the synod of Dort which the estates presented me withal at the Hague '. (*Gosse*, ii, p. 360.)

45. *The Indifference of Nature.* II, p. 37. Sermon V. '*Preached at a Christning.*'
l. 4. ' hoise ' is the older form of ' hoist '.

46. *Wealth.* I, p. 659. ' The first of the Prebend of *Cheswicks* five Psalmes; which five are appointed for that Prebend; as there are five other, for every other of our thirty Prebendaries.   Serm. LXV. *Preached at S.* Pauls, *May 8. 1625.*'

47. *A London Merchant.* I, pp. 824–6. See *ante*, Nos. 4, 39. Funeral Sermon of Sir William Cokayne, who was Lord Mayor of London, 1619–20 (*Dict. Nat. Biog.*). He was ' a merchant of great consequence, reputed to be one of the richest men in England. Lady Cokayne's father, Richard Morris, had preceded Donne's father as Master of the Ironmongers' Company.' (*Gosse*, ii, pp. 237–8.)
p. 78, l. 7. ' A publique heart '. *Publique* is here used with the meaning of the later ' public-spirited ', first found in 1677 (*N. E. D.*).
p. 80, l. 17. ' this Quire '. It is plain from this, that (as Mr. Gosse remarks) ' the Aldermen of the City had been lately admitted by the Dean and Chapter to seats in the choir of St. Paul's. . . . From this it appears that until that date the choir had, as in Catholic times, been reserved for the clergy ' (*Gosse*, ii, p. 238).

48. *Sickness.* II, p. 167. Sermon XX. ' *Preached at Lincolns Inne.*'

49. *Public Opinion.* I, p. 589. Sermon LVIII. See *ante*, No. 6.

50. *Joy.* II, p. 467. Sermon L. ' *A Sermon Preached in Saint* Dunstans.'

51. *Women.* I, pp. 242–3. Sermon XXV. '*Preached at S.* Pauls, *upon Easter-day.* 1630 ' (March 28).

52. *Cosmetics.* I, p. 642. Sermon LXIV. ' *Preached upon the* Penitentiall Psalmes.'

53. *The Skin.* II, p. 113. Sermon XIV. See *ante*, No. 3.

54. *Mud Walls.* II, pp. 168–9. Sermon XX. See *ante*, No. 48.

55. *Ignorance.* I, p. 287. Sermon XXIX. ' *Preached at S.* Pauls *upon Whitsunday.* 1628.'

56. *The Imperfection of Knowledge.* I, p. 818. Sermon LXXX. See *ante*, Nos. 4, 39, 4 7.

57. *Change of Mind.* I, p. 483. Sermon XLVIII. '*Preached at S. Pauls in the Evening, Vpon the day of S. Pauls Conversion.* 1628' (January 25, 1629).

58. *Reason and Faith.* II, pp. 324–7. Sermon XXXVI. '*Preached at Saint Pauls upon Christmasse day,* 1621.' In his verse epistle to the Countess of Bedford, Donne writes,

> Reason is our Soules left hand, Faith her right,
> By these wee reach divinity, thats you.
>
> (*Poems*, i, p. 189; see also p. 267.)

l. 1. '*lamps*'. In his *Epithalamions*, xi, Donne writes,

> Now, as in Jullias tombe, one lampe burnt cleare,
> Unchang'd for fifteene hundred yeare,

(*Poems*, i, p. 140; for origin of this legend, see note, *ibid.*, ii, p. 98.)

l. 15. '*vanish it selfe*'. In his *Litanie*, vii, Donne writes,

> Let not my minde be blinder by more light
> Nor Faith, by Reason added, lose her sight.
>
> (*Poems*, i, p. 340.)

p. 102, l. 11. '*blow that coale*'. Cf. *Devotions*, p. 3. '*God*, who as hee is *immortall* himselfe, had put a *coale*, a *beame* of *Immortalitie* into us, which we might have blowen into a *flame*, but blew it out, by our first sinne.'

59. *True Knowledge.* I, p. 165. Sermon XVII. '*Preached at White-hall, March* 4. 1624' (1625).

60. *Terrible Things.* I, pp. 690–2. Sermon LXVIII. See *ante*, No. 16.

61. *The Fate of the Heathen.* I, pp. 261–2. Sermon XXVI. '*Preached upon Easter-day*.' Probably 1623 (*Spearing*).

62. *The Church a Company.* II, p. 469. Sermon L. See No. 50.

63. *God Proceeds Legally.* II, pp. 230–1. Sermon XXVII. '*Preached to the King, at White-Hall, the first of April,* 1627.' Laud, then Bishop of Bath and Wells, was present at this sermon, and seems to have suspected from it that Donne was preparing to support Abbot, the Archbishop of Canterbury, and the Calvinistic party, in the controversy then under discussion, about Montague's attack on them. Laud wrote to Donne at once commanding a copy of the sermon to be sent to the king, greatly to Donne's dismay. But when Charles I had read the sermon and listened to Donne's explanation, he restored him to favour. For Donne's letters about this incident, see *Gosse*, ii, pp. 243–6. Dr. Jessopp, quoting the end of the extract as given in this volume (p. 114, l. 28 f.) says, 'after carefully reading the sermon several times, I can find only one passage that may have hurt the prejudices or irritated the susceptibilities of some of the audience as possibly reflecting upon themselves' (*Jessopp*, p. 188).

l. 7. 'hisse', misprinted 'kisse' in folio.

64. *The Church.* I, pp. 369–70. Sermon XXXVII. '*Preached upon Whitsunday.*'

p. 116, l. 13. 'thou art a little world'. Cf. *Sacred Sonnets*,

> I am a little world made cunningly
> Of Elements. (*Poems*, i, p. 324.)

For this notion, which frequently recurs in Donne, of man as a microcosm, or little world, see *Ramsay*, p. 275.

65. *Reverence in Church.* II, pp. 470–1. Sermon L. See *ante*, Nos. 50, 62.

66. *Going to Church.* I, pp. 35–6. Sermon IV. '*Preached at S. Pauls upon Christmas day.* 1626.'

l. 9. 'mocke us'. Coleridge notes 'What then, was their guilt, who by terror and legal penalties tempted their fellow Christians to this treacherous mockery? Donne should have asked himself that question.' (*Coleridge*, p. 112.)

67. *Prayer.* II, p. 366. Sermon XL. See *ante*, Nos. 12, 17.

68. *Prayer.* I, p. 522. Sermon LII. '*Preached upon the Penitentiall Psalmes.*'

l. 8. 'his Sister'. Donne repeats this in his *Devotions*, p. 255.

69. *The Time of Prayer.* I, pp. 596–7. Sermon LIX. '*Preached upon the Penitentiall Psalmes.*'

p. 123, l. 15. 'the greatest Christian Prince'. The King of France's title was *Roi très chrétien*. Donne was in Paris in 1612 with Sir Robert Drury, but Louis XIII was then only eleven years old. In a letter to Sir Henry Wotton, written in 1612, Donne refers to a previous visit to France during the lifetime of Henry IV (*Gosse*, i, p. 293). The above reference is probably therefore to Henry IV.

p. 124, l. 13. 'Bolls', earlier spelling of 'bowls'.

70. *At Table and Bed.* II, p. 88. Sermon XI. '*Preached at Lincolns Inne, preparing them to build their Chappell.*' In 1617, when the foundation-stone of the new chapel was laid. On Ascension Day, 1623 (May 22), Donne preached at the consecration of the chapel his 'Encaenia' Sermon, which was published in the same year, but has not been reprinted. On May 30 Chamberlain wrote, 'Lincoln's Inn new chapel was consecrated with much solemnity, by the Bishop of London, on Ascension-day, where there was great concourse of noblemen and gentlemen ; whereof two or three were endangered, and taken up dead for the time, with the extreme press and thronging. The Dean of St. Paul's made an excellent sermon, they say, about dedications ' (*C. & T. Jas. I*, ii, p. 402).

l. 5. '*table*'. In an undated letter Donne writes, ' we at our lay altars (which are our tables, or bedside, or stools)'. (*Gosse*, i, p. 223.)

71. *Unconscious Prayer.* I, p. 90. Sermon IX. '*Preached upon Candlemas day.*' Probably either in 1617, or 1623 (*Spearing*).

72. *Sermons.* I, pp. 113–14. Sermon XII. '*Preached upon Candlemas day.*'

73. *New Doctrines.* III, p. 4. Sermon I. 'A Lent-Sermon Preached at White-hall, *February* 20. 1617.' (1618). On February 21 Chamberlain wrote ' Dr. John Donne preached yesterday at Whitehall ; but the king was not there, being weary belike of the former night's watching ' (*C. & T. Jas. I*, ii, p. 67).

l. 4. '*Resistibility*, and *Irresistibility* of grace '. This was a much disputed point between the Calvinist and Arminian parties ; in 1622 James I forbade any one under the degree of a bachelor of divinity to ' presume to preach in any popular auditory the deep points of predestination, election, reprobation, or of the universality, efficacy, resistibility or irresistibility of God's grace ' (Gardiner, *History of England*, 1603–1642, iv, p. 347). For Donne's use of these controversies in his secular verse, see *Poems*, ii, p. 46.

74. *Papist and Puritan.* I, p. 493. Sermon XLIX. '*Preached on the Conversion of S.* Paul. 1629 ' (January 25, 1630).

75. *Theological Dissensions.* 'The First Sermon Preached to King Charles, At Saint Iames : 3° April. 1625. *By* Iohn Donne, *Deane of* Saint *Pauls* London 1625 ', pp. 12–16. This sermon has never been reprinted. On April 5 Sir William Neve, after describing the removal of James I's body to Denmark House, wrote : ' The King kept privately his bed, or chamber, at St. James's until Sunday last, and then dined abroad, in the privy-chamber, being in plain black cloth cloak to the ancle ; and so went after dinner into the chapel, Dr. Donne preaching, Lord Davers carrying the sword before him, his majesty looking very pale, his visage being the true glass of his inward, as well as his accoutrements of external mourning.' (*C. & T. Chas. I*, i, pp. 3–4.) Donne's letters show plainly the extreme agitation caused in him by the royal command to preach before the new king. ' Towards the time of the service,' he writes to Sir Robert Ker at Court, ' I ask your leave that I may hide myself in your out-chamber '; and in another note he refuses an invitation to dinner, saying 'after the sermon, I will steal into my coach home '. (*Gosse*, ii, p. 220.)

p. 132, l. 8. 'Ejulations', old word for wailing, lamentation.

76. *Despair.* II, p. 363. Sermon XXXIX. '*Preached at Saint Pauls.*'

77. *The Sociableness of God.* II, p. 280. Sermon XXXII. '*Preached to the Earl of* Exeter, *and his company, in his Chappell at* Saint *Johns*; 13. *Jun.* 1624.' William Cecil, son of Thomas Cecil, first Earl of Exeter.

78. *God a Circle.* I, pp. 13–14. Sermon II. '*Preached at* Pauls, upon *Christmas Day, in the Evening.* 1624.'
In a verse-epistle to the Countess of Bedford Donne wrote 'In those poor types of God (round circles)' (*Poems*, i, p. 220, and note ii, p. 176). See also *Divine Poems, The Annunciation and Passion* (*ibid.*, i, p. 334), and *Devotions*, p. 16, 'O Eternall, and most gracious *God*, who considered in thy selfe, art a Circle.'

79. *God's Mirror.* I, pp. 226–7. Sermon XXIII. '*Preached at* S. Pauls, *for Easter-day.* 1628' (April 13).

80. *God's Names.* I, p. 670. Sermon LXVI. See *ante*, Nos. 9, 20, 41.

81. *God's Mercies.* I, pp. 12–13. Sermon II. See *ante*, No. 78.
l. 13. 'ragges of time'. Donne in his famous poem beginning 'Busie old foole, unruly Sunne' uses this phrase,

> Love, all alike, no season knowes, nor clyme,
> Nor houres, dayes, moneths, which are the rags of time.
>
> (*Poems*, i, p. 11.)

p. 139, l. 9. 'God made Sun and Moon'. Professor Saintsbury, in quoting this passage, describes it as 'a passage than which I hardly know anything more exquisitely rhythmed in the whole range of English from Ælfric to Pater. . . . The Shakespearian magnificence of the diction, such as the throng of kindred but never tautological phrase in "wintered and frozen", etc., and the absolute perfection of rhythmical—never metrical—movement, could not be better wedded. It has, I have said, never been surpassed. I sometimes doubt whether it has ever been equalled' (*A History of English Prose Rhythm*, 1912, pp. 162–3).

82. *God not Cruel.* II, p. 224. Sermon XXVI. See *ante*, No. 8.

83. *The Voice of God.* I, p. 465. Sermon XLVI. '*Preached at* S. Pauls, *The Sunday after the Conversion of* S. Paul. 1624.' (January 30, 1625).

84. *God's Language.* II, pp. 359–60. Sermon XXXIX. See *ante*, No. 76.
p. 143, l. 21. 'fall into some such sinne'. In 1608 Donne wrote to Sir H. Goodyer, 'when a man is purposed to do a great sin, God

infuses some good thoughts which make him choose a less sin'.
(*Gosse*, i, p. 190.)

85. *God's Anger.* II, p. 170. Sermon XX. See *ante*, Nos. 48, 54.

86. *God's Faults.* I, pp. 726–7. Sermon LXII. Preached at
The Hague. See *ante*, No. 44.

l. 2. 'qualities and affections of man'. Cf. *Devotions*, p. 178, 'God
is presented to us under many human affections, as far as *infirmities*:
God is called *angry*, and *sorry* and *weary*, and *heavy*.'

p. 145, l. 29. 'enormious'; obsolete form of 'enormous'.

87. *God's Judgements.* III, pp. 82–3. Sermon VI. 'A Sermon
Preached at White-hall, April 21. 1616.' Donne was ordained in
January 1615. His earliest dated sermon that has come down to
us was preached before Queen Anne at Greenwich on April 30, 1615
(the Sermon II, No. XXXV, ascribed to February 21, 1611, must be
wrongly dated). This sermon is the next in date which has been
preserved, as was perhaps his first sermon at Court, after his appoint-
ment as Chaplain to the King in the summer of 1615. Izaak
Walton says of his first sermon at Whitehall 'though much were
expected from him, both by His Majesty and others, yet he was so
happy (which few are) as to satisfie and exceed their expectations'
(Walton's *Lives*, 1670, p. 38). Dr. Jessopp writes of this sermon:
'On the 21st April 1616 we find Donne preaching at Whitehall just at
the time when the horrible revelations connected with the murder
of Sir Thomas Overbury were being discussed by every one and were
the subject of common talk. The sermon . . . contains some fine
passages which the congregation can hardly have helped applying to
the dreadful circumstances uppermost in the minds of all' (*Jessopp*,
p. 112). For other passages from this sermon, see also Nos. 105, 108.

l. 19. 'infus'd'. In a verse-epistle of Donne's to Sir Edward
Herbert, written in 1610, he says,

> As Soules (they say) by our first touch, take in
> The poysonous tincture of Originall sinne.

(*Poems*, i, p. 194.)

See also Donne's letter of October 9, 1607 (*Gosse*, i, p. 176).

88. *Terrible Things.* I, pp. 701–2. Sermon LXIX. 'The fifth
of my Prebend Sermons upon my five Psalmes: *Preached at S.
Pauls.*' On January 28, 1627, Donne preached his fourth prebend
sermon (I, LXVIII). The prebend sermons followed one another
at intervals of a few months, so this sermon may be safely assigned
to 1627 (*Spearing*).

l. 17. 'spectacle', old use of the singular for 'spectacles'.

89. *God's Malediction.* II, p. 227. Sermon XXVI. See *ante*,
Nos. 8, 82.

90. *God's Power.* 'A Sermon, Preached to the Kings M^tie at Whitehall, 24 *Febr.* 1625. By Iohn Donne Deane of Saint *Pauls*, London. *And now by his* Maiestes *commandment Published.*' London, 1626, pp. 16–18. This sermon was re-issued in *Five Sermons*, but has not been reprinted since.

91. *Access to God.* I, pp. 500–1. Sermon L. '*Preached upon the Penitentiall* Psalmes.'

92. *The Image of God in Man.* 'The Second Sermon preached before King Charles, Upon the xxvi verse of the first Chapter of Genesis. By Dr. Donne Dean of Pauls' (Cambridge, 1634), pp. 22–3. In *Six Sermons*, No. II; reprinted II, No. XXIX. This is evidently a continuation of II, No. XXVIII, which was preached to the King in April 1629, on the same text (*Spearing*). For the origin of the idea in this extract, see *Ramsay*, p. 229.

93. *Man God's Enemy.* II, p. 372. Sermon XL. See *ante*, Nos. 12, 17, 67.
l. 5. 'as the Mouse is to the Elephant'. See Donne's *Progresse of the Soule*, ll. 381–91 (*Poems*, i, pp. 310–11, and note, II, p. 223).

94. *The Atheist.* I, p. 486. Sermon XLVIII. See *ante*, No. 57.

95. *The Angels.* II, p. 7. Sermon I. See *ante*, No. 10.

96. *The Devil.* I, pp. 65–6. Sermon VII. See *ante*, No. 40. Miss Ramsay has collected many passages from Donne's sermons on the important question of the possible salvation of the Devil. (*Ramsay*, p. 210 f.)

97. *The Creation.* II, p. 280. Sermon XXXII. See *ante*, No. 77.

98. *The Heavens and Earth. Six Sermons.* I, pp. 1–3. 'Two Sermons preached before King Charles, Upon the xxvi verse of the first Chapter of Genesis.' Reprinted, II, No. XXVIII. '*Preached to the King, at the Court in April*, 1629.'

99. *The Creation of a Harmonious World.* III, p. 20. Sermon II. 'A Lent-Sermon Preached at White-hall, February 12. 1618' (1619).
l. 3. 'an Instrument, perfectly in tune'. In his *Obsequies to the Lord Harrington* (1614) Donne begins:

> Faire soule, which wast, not onely, as all soules bee,
> Then when thou wast infused, harmony,
> But did'st continue so; and now dost beare
> A part in Gods great organ, this whole Spheare:
>
> (*Poems*, i, p. 271.)

100. *God and Adam and Eve.* 'A Sermon Upon the xxii verse of the v Chapter of John. By D^r. Donne Dean of *Pauls*' (Cambridge,

1634), pp. 9–10. This Sermon is No. V of the *Six Sermons* ; reprinted, II, No. XII. '*Preached at Lincolns Inne.*'

l. 9. ' Shall we ', ' Shall we not ' in original quarto, and folio.

101. *The World since the Fall.* II, p. 223. Sermon XXVI. See *ante*, Nos. 8, 82, 89.

102. *Silkworms.* II, p. 143. Sermon XVII. '*Preached at Lincolns Inne.*'

103. *Original Sin.* II, pp. 187–8. Sermon XXII. '*Preached at Lincolns Inne.*'

104. *Original Sin.* III, p. 183 (Bb 4). Sermon XIII. 'A Sermon Preached at *White-hall, April* 19. 1618.'

105. *The Heart of the Sinner.* III, pp. 86–7. Sermon VI. Donne's first sermon at Court. See *ante*, No. 87.

106. *Light Sins.* I, p. 164. Sermon XVII. See *ante*, No. 59.
p. 171, l. 8. ' gad ' is an old word for ' spike '.

107. *The Sin of Reason.* III, pp. 89–92. Sermon VII. 'A Sermon Preached at White-hall, *Novemb.* 2. 1617.'
p. 173, l. 15. ' covercling ', Alford's emendation of ' coveraling ' in the folio, from the old word found in Chaucer, ' covercle ', a cover, a lid. But the Bodleian copy of the folio has the correction ' concealing ' in a contemporary hand.

108. *Delight in Evil.* III, pp. 84–5. Sermon VI. See *ante*, Nos. 87, 105.

109. *Excuses.* I, p. 390. Sermon XXXIX. '*Preached upon Trinity-Sunday.*'

110. *Rebuke of Sin.* II, pp. 74–5. Sermon X. '*Preached at the Churching of the Countess of* Bridgewater.' Frances, daughter of Ferdinand Stanley, Earl of Derby. See note on No. 10.

111. *Names of Sins.* I, p. 584. Sermon LVIII. See *ante*, Nos. 6, 49.

112. *Pride.* I, p. 730. Sermon LXXII. Preached at The Hague. See *ante*, Nos. 44, 86.
p. 181, l. 5. ' boast of their sinnes '. Cf. *Devotions*, p. 240. ' There are many sins, which we *glorie* in doing, and would not do, if no body should know them.'

113. *Covetousness.* I, pp. 714–15. Sermon LXX. '*Preached at* White-hall, *April* 8. 1621.'
p. 183, l. 8. ' not thimbles ' in the folio. Corrected to ' but ' by Alford.

114. *Blasphemy.* I, pp. 343–4. Sermon XXXV. *Preached upon Whitsunday.*

115. *The Burden of Sin.* II, pp. 193–4. Sermon XXIII. *'Preached at Lincolns Inne.'*

116. *The Sinner.* I, p. 634. Sermon LXIII. *'Preached upon the* Penitentiall Psalmes.'

117. *The Sorrows of the Wicked.* I, p. 631. Sermon LXIII. See *ante*, No. 116.

118. *The Sins of Memory.* II, pp. 462–3. Sermon XLIX. *'A Sermon Preached at Saint* Dunstan's *upon* New-years-day, 1624.'

119. *The Eye of God.* II, pp. 336–7. Sermon XXXVII. *'Preached at* St. Pauls *on Midsommer day.* 1622.'

120. *The World Drowned in Sin.* I, pp. 365–6. Sermon XXXVII. *'Preached upon Whitsunday.'*

121. *The Hand of God.* I, p. 579. Sermon LVII. *'Preached upon the* Penitentiall Psalmes.'

122. *The Sick Soul.* II, p. 169. Sermon XX. See *ante*, No. 48.

123. *Sleep.* I, p. 129. Sermon XIII. *'Preached in* Lent, *to the* King. April 20. 1630.' This date must be a mistake, as Easter fell on March 28 in 1630 *(Spearing).*

A few sentences, too outspoken for modern reprinting, have been omitted from this extract.

p. 195, l. 2. 'thy metaphoricall, thy quotidian grave'. Cf. *Meditations*, p. 44, 'every nights bed is a *type* of the *grave*'.

l. 5. '*Iobs Snow water*'. See *Job* ix. 30.

124. *The Gate of Death.* III, pp. 294–5. Sermon XX. 'Two Sermons, to the Prince and Princess *Palatine*, the Lady *Elizabeth*, at *Heydelberg* when I was commanded by the King to wait upon my L. of *Doncaster* in his Embassage to *Germany. First Sermon as we went out*, June 16. 1619.' The other sermon has not been preserved. The Ambassador and his party arrived on June 10 at Heidelberg, the capital of the Elector Palatine (afterwards King of Bohemia) who had married the Lady Elizabeth, daughter of James I. Donne's epithalamion beginning ' Haile Bishop Valentine, whose day this is ', was written for the marriage of the Lady Elizabeth. *(Poems*, i, p. 127.)

l. 4. 'glad of that', read 'be glad of that'. P. 294 of the folio ends 'becaus he knows' with 'that' as catchword; p. 295 begins 'be that is' with 'glad' as the first word of the second line. The 'be' has been printed at the beginning of the first line instead of the second. It may be noted that 'glad' is found in Elizabethan English in the old sense 'be glad', 'rejoice', but 'is glad' in l. 2 is against its use in this sense here.

125. *Our Prison.* I, p. 267. Sermon XXVII. *'Preached to the*

LL. upon Easter-day, at the Communion, The King being then dangerously sick at *New-Market.*' In 1619. 'On the 28th March 1619,
being Easter Day, he was called upon to preach before the Lords at
a time of great public anxiety. Queen Anne of Denmark had died
on the first of the month, and James I, after taking his leave of his
Consort, had gone to Newmarket. Here he had himself fallen
seriously ill, and on the day when Donne preached at Whitehall,
he was reported to be "dangerously sick"' (*Jessopp,* p. 124).

126. *All must Die.* I, pp. 147–9. Sermon XV. '*Preached at*
White-hall, *March 8. 1621*' (1622).

p. 198, l. 14. 'The ashes of an Oak'. Coleridge quotes the passage
that follows, adding, 'Very beautiful indeed'. (*Coleridge,* p. 130.)

p. 199, l. 13. 'Spittles', i. e. spitals or hospitals.

l. 16. 'when I lye'. Coleridge quotes this passage also, remarking,
'This is powerful; but is too much in the style of the monkish
preachers : *Papam redolet.* Contrast with this Job's description
of death, and St. Paul's *sleep in the Lord'* (*ibid.,* p. 131).

127. *Death Inevitable.* II, p. 270. Sermon XXX. '*Preached to
the Countesse of* Bedford, *then at* Harrington *house.* January 7. 1620'
(1621). For Donne's friendship with Lucy, Countess of Bedford,
who, as Professor Grierson says, 'occupies the central place among
Donne's noble patrons and friends', see *Poems,* ii, p. 152. A study
of the Countess of Bedford's life, with that of the other ladies who
patronized the Elizabethan poets, would be of considerable interest
for the light it would throw on the social background of the age of
Shakespeare—a subject about which we have really very little
information.

l. 2. '*Ecce*', short for '*Ecce signum*'. P. 201, l. 5, '*echoes*'
is apparently a mistake for '*ecces*'.

l. 19. *sent,* old form of 'scent'.

p. 201, l. 5. 'that Temple', printed 'this Temple' in some copies
of the folio; in others, 'the Temple'.

128. *The Expectation of Death.* III, p. 13. Sermon I. See *ante,*
No. 73.

129. *The Death-bed.* 'A Sermon Upon the xliiii verse of the xxi
Chapter of Matthew. By D^r. Donne Dean of *Pauls*' (Cambridge,
MDCXXXIIII, pp. 5–6). In *Six Sermons,* No. IV. Reprinted, II,
No. XXXV, where it is dated 'February 21. 1611'—plainly an error,
as Donne was ordained in 1615.

130. *The Death of Ecstasy.* I, pp. 273–4. Sermon XXVII. See
ante, No. 125. Professor Grierson quotes this passage, remarking,
'This is the highest level that Donne ever reached in eloquence
inspired by the vision of the joy and not the terror of the Christian
faith'. (*Poems,* ii, p. liv. See also *Ramsay,* p. 260 f.)

131. *The Dead with Us.* I, pp. 219–20. Sermon XXII. See *ante*, No. 2.

p. 204, l. 18. 'into another Land'. In 1629 Donne wrote to Mrs. Cockain, consoling her for the death of her son, ' Since I am well content to send one son to the Church, the other to the Wars, why should I be loth to send one part of either son to heaven and the other to the earth ? ' (*Gosse*, ii, p. 261).

132. *Mourning.* I, pp. 157–8. Sermon XVI. '*Preached at* White-hall, *the first Friday in* Lent. 1622 ' (February 28, 1623).

l. 21. 'Authors of a middle nature '. ' A whimsical instance of the disposition in the mind for every pair of opposites to find an intermediate,—a *mesothesis* for every *thesis* and *antithesis*. Thus Scripture may be opposed to philosophy ; and then the Apocryphal books will be philosophy relatively to Scripture, and Scripture relatively to philosophy.' (*Coleridge*, p. 135.)

133. *A Quiet Grave.* I, p. 463. Sermon XLVI. See *ante*, No. 83. l. 12. 'Quillet '. A beautiful old word, now only in local or antiquarian use, for a small plot or narrow strip of land.

134. *Eternal Damnation.* I, pp. 776–7. Sermon LXXVI. ' *Preached to the Earle of* Carlile, *and his Company, at* Sion.' Probably after 1622, when Donne's friend, Viscount Doncaster, was created Earl of Carlisle (*Spearing*).

This passage, on the ground that Marston also wrote sermons, which have perished, while those of Donne have been preserved, is quoted by Mr. A. H. Bullen, in his introduction to *The Works of John Marston*, 1887, i, pp. lix–lx. I must express my debt to Mr. Bullen, for although two folios of Donne's Sermons had stood for years on my bookshelves, it was not until I read this extract in his *Marston*, that it occurred to me that it might be interesting to read them.

p. 209, l. 28. ' standing, and knocking '. Cf. *Holy Sonnets*, xiv :

> Batter my heart, three person'd God ; for you
> As yet but knocke. (*Poems*, i, p. 328.)

135. *Death of the Good and the Bad Man.* III, pp. 217–18. Sermon XV. See *ante*, No. 18.

136. *The Northern Passage.* I, p. 463. Sermon XLVI. See *ante*, Nos. 83, 133.

137. *The Resurrection.* I, p. 257. Sermon XXVI. See *ante*, No. 61.

138. *The Awakening.* I, p. 263. Sermon XXVI. See *ante*, Nos. 61, 137.

139. The *Resurrection of the Body.* II, p. 3. Sermon I. See *ante*, Nos. 10, 95. In an undated letter, probably written in 1612, in which

Donne wrote begging some favour of Lord Rochester, he says, ' And since good divines have made this argument against deniers of the Resurrection, that it is easier for God to unite the principles and elements of our bodies, howsoever they be scattered, than it was at first to create them out of nothing, I cannot doubt but that any distractions or diversions in the ways of my hopes will be easier to your Lordship to reunite than it was to create them '. (*Gosse*, ii, p. 23.)

140. *The Last Day.* II, p. 343. Sermon XXXVII. See *ante*, No. 119.

141. *The Day of Judgement.* I, p. 371. Sermon XXXVII. See *ante*, No. 120.
l. 14. ' for thy sins '. Cf. *A Hymne to God the Father*, ii,

> Wilt thou forgive that sinne which I have wonne
> Others to sinne ? and, made my sinne their doore ?
>
> (*Poems*, i, p. 369.)

142. *Joy.* I, pp. 672–3. Sermon LXVI. The Second Prebend Sermon. See *ante*, Nos. 9, 20, 41, 80.

143. *The Joy of Heaven.* I, p. 75. Sermon VII. See *ante*, No. 40.

144. *Little Stars.* *Six Sermons*, II, pp. 9, 10. See *ante*, No. 92.

145. *Heirs of Heaven.* I, p. 340. Sermon XXXIV. See *ante*, No. 1.

146. *Seeing God.* I, pp. 230–1. Sermon XXIII. See *ante*, No. 79.
l. 1. *Speculum.* This is an earlier instance of speculum for mirror or reflector than the one given in the *N. E. D.* (1646).

147. *The Sight of God.* II, p. 117. Sermon XIV. See *ante*, Nos. 3, 53.

148. *The State of Glory.* *Six Sermons*, II, pp. 36–8. Reprinted II, p. 261. See *ante*, Nos. 92, 144.

149. *Immortality.* The Chelsea Sermon, pp. 106–18. See *ante*, No. 28. Reprinted in Alford, vi, pp. 265–7.

150. *Knowledge in Heaven.* III, pp. 389–90. Sermon XXV. ' A Sermon Preached at the Spittle Upon *Easter-Munday*, 1622 ' (April 22). The ' Spittle ' was the old priory of St. Mary Spital, Bethnal Green, where there was a pulpit Cross, something like St. Paul's Cross, where sermons on the Resurrection were preached in the afternoons of Easter Monday, Tuesday, and Wednesday.

151. *Eternity.* I, p. 266. Sermon XXVI. See *ante*, No. 61.

152. *Eternity.* II, p. 413. Sermon XLIV. ' *Preached at* St. Pauls *Crosse*, Novemb. 22, 1629.' ' The preaching of this sermon overtaxed Donne's failing strength ; for when Christmas day came

Notes. 263

he was, for the first time, unable to appear in the pulpit of St. Pauls.'
(*Jessopp*, p. 200.)

153. *Eternity.* I, pp. 747–8. Sermon LXXIII. See *ante*, No. 11.

154. *Joy in Heaven.* II, pp. 473–4. Sermon L. See *ante*, Nos. 50, 62, 65.

155. *Donne's Last Sermon.* 'Deaths Duell, or, A Consolation to the Soule, against the dying Life, and liuing Death of the Body. *Deliuered in a Sermon at White Hall, before the* Kings Maiesty, *in the beginning of Lent,* 1630 [1631]. By that late learned and Reuerend Diuine, Iohn Donne, D͞r· in Diuinity, & Deane of S. *Pauls,* London. *Being his last Sermon, and called by his Maiesties housbold* The Doctors owne Funerall Sermon' (London, 1632), pp. 5–6, 9–12, 20. This sermon was reprinted in the third folio, No. XXVI.

p. 239, l. 2. 'flesh'. This is the reading in the folio for '*bestæ*' in the quarto.

p. 240, l. 30. 'state'. 'State' is used here in the old sense of 'canopy'. Cf. *Paradise Lost*, x. 445:

> Ascended his high Throne, which under state
> Of richest texture spred, at th' upper end
> Was plac't in regal lustre.

The devices on the back and front of the cover represent Donne's family seal (a sheaf of snakes) and the seal designed for himself (Christ crucified on an anchor).

To Mr *George Herbert*, with one of my Seals, of the Anchor and Christ.

A Sheafe of Snakes used heretofore to be
My Seal, The Crest of our poore Family.
Adopted in Gods Family, and so
Our old Coat lost, unto new armes I go.
The Crosse (my seal at Baptism) spred below,
Does, by that form, into an Anchor grow.
Crosses grow Anchors ; Bear, as thou shouldst do
Thy Crosse, and that Crosse grows an Anchor too.
But he that makes our Crosses Anchors thus,
Is Christ, who there is crucifi'd for us.
Yet may I, with this, my first Serpents hold,
God gives new blessings, and yet leaves the old ;
The Serpent, may, as wise, my pattern be ;
My poison, as he feeds on dust, that 's me.
And as he rounds the Earth to murder sure,
My death he is, but on the Crosse, my cure.
Crucifie nature then, and then implore
All Grace from him, crucified there before ;
When all is Crosse, and that Crosse Anchor grown,
This Seal 's a Catechism, not a Seal alone.
Under that little Seal great gifts I send,
Wishes, and prayers, pawns, and fruits of a friend.
And may that Saint which rides in our great Seal,
To you, who bear his name, great bounties deal.

From Izaak Walton's *Life of Donne.*

a pught londam 88